Ho! To the Land of Sunshine

Ho! To the Land of Sunshine

A History of the Belen Cutoff

WILLIAM PENNER | SHAWN KELLEY | NICHOLAS PARKER

Table of Contents

Acknowledgments

My association with the Belen Cutoff began in 2004 and grew from a small archaeological survey in Abo Canyon to the varied mitigation efforts that produced this book, eventually comprising nearly nine years of my professional career. Any project of that length and complexity owes it success to many groups and individuals, and I hope this volume helps partially repay everyone's investments of time and energy.

The mitigation effort began in a National Historic Preservation Act Section 106 process led by the United States Army Corps of Engineers (USACE) and joined by 10 other consulting parties. Staff archaeologists John Schelberg and Lance Lundquist provided continuity and expert guidance even as the USACE lost several individuals to retirement during the project. Katherine Slick, New Mexico's former State Historic Preservation Officer, and her staff at the Historic Preservation Division contributed greatly, as did individuals from the Bureau of Land Management. The other eight consulting parties, which included the Advisory Council on Historic Preservation and National Trust for Historic Preservation, made sure the research was meaningful and spoke to the affected communities. Teresa Pasqual, Director of the Historic Preservation Office of Acoma Pueblo, helped illuminate the pueblo's relationships and history with the railroad. Henry Walt, Mike Marshall, and John Brayer worked with the project team on behalf of the Pueblo of Isleta to ensure rock art in Abo Canyon was not damaged during construction.

The core team for the Abo Canyon Second Track Project included Dean Bressler of HDR Inc. (HDR) and Lewis Ruder of the BNSF Railway (BNSF), who have been involved with this project since its inception and deserve special recognition. When something was needed, they were responsive and made it happen—it has been a real privilege to work with them over these past nine years. Robert Boileau, Tom Schmidt, David Miller, Jeff Malloy and Lee Hostler of BNSF were also critical to our success, along with Shannon-Wilson, Transystems, Ames Construction, Matheson Mining Consultants, Dale Harrison, and other specialists who helped preserve Abo Canyon and its resources. Teresa Hurt from Parametrix guided the cultural resource efforts and added to our understanding of the region's prehistory and history.

Several research institutions and colleagues played significant roles in developing this book. The Kansas Historical Society, which maintains the premier collection of material related to the Atchison, Topeka, and Santa Fe Railway (AT&SF), first gave me an idea of how much information there was about Abo Canyon and the Belen Cutoff. Sitting in their facilities and looking at historical photographs of archaeological sites I only knew as ruins was amazing. Visiting the Archives and Special Collections at the New Mexico State University Library was an equal revelation when Dean Wilkey and Rick Hendricks brought out the Lee Myers collection and its many previously unidentified photographs and letters about the Belen Cutoff. The

University of New Mexico's Center for Southwest Research was also an invaluable resource.

Francisco Sisneros generously shared his time and knowledge about the Abo region and his family history. Chances are that if someone is from the area between Belen and Manzano, Francisco not only knows them but probably also knows who their great-grandparents were and where they came from. Margaret McDonald's various studies of historical change in Belen set a standard for scholarship to which we aspired. On the other end of the Cutoff, Randy Dunson provided access to an unparalleled private collection of AT&SF memorabilia, equipment, and historical materials. He also shared the results of his decades-long research efforts and oral histories, his memories of growing up on the Cutoff, and his expertise with running trains and working on the railroad for much of his life. Randy helped me understand how the railroad worked and what railroaders' experiences would have been like.

We were fortunate to have the opportunity to talk with a large number of people about the Belen Cutoff and the changes it brought about. We can't include the entire list here, but everyone brought something meaningful to our work and cared enough to share their histories with us. Several accompanied us on trips through Abo Canyon (and elsewhere) and provided critical contexts for our investigations, including Dorothy Cole; Jack Hewett; Frank Hill; Victor Pineda; Bill Pohl; Juan J. Sanchez; Richard Spencer; Billy Bob Williams; Martina Brazil Franklin and Polly Sisneros; Biddie and Gorden McMath; Albert McNeil, Bill Huckabay, and Jerry Shaw; Al and Joe Padilla; Fidel Padilla and Eliseo R. Sisneros; and Francisco, Martin, and Sylvestre Sisneros. Bill Pohl and Juan J. Sanchez were particularly generous with their time and took us all over the Scholle area, reanimating the social life of the region in the early twentieth century through tours of hidden stills and abandoned homesteads. Fidel Padilla and Eliseo R. Sisneros brought new perspectives on railroaders in Abo Canyon. Spending time with people on the Cutoff was a privilege and an honor.

I owe a great debt to my co-authors Shawn Kelley and Nicholas Parker. Shawn was the primary contact some people had with this project and he represented it well. He started in 2007 by interviewing knowledgeable local residents to identify historic properties. Since then he has talked to many, many individuals about the region's history and their lives, in the process becoming at least as obsessed as I am with this unheralded portion of New Mexico. Nicholas was always ready to collaborate to make our research efforts better. His dedication, professionalism, and insight were crucial to the quality of this volume.

For those I have inadvertently omitted in these acknowledgments, I apologize. There are many people who contributed to making this book a reality and I thank every one of you for your efforts. I hope some of you can find your histories herein and recognize the ways you helped change New Mexico.

William Penner

APACHE IND. Park View Hopewell Tierra Amarilla Tusas Tres Piedras Questa Cerro Red River Aqua de Lobo Arroyo Seco Baldy Dawson Green Mt. Dorsey Palo Blanco Tripod Mt. Gladston

Blanco Largo Angels Pk. Huerfanito Gallina Canjilon Vallecitos Petaca Arroyo hondo Taos Ranches of Taos Mora Peak Rayado Colmor Cimarron Elizabeth town Maxwell City Chico Springer

Coyote Pedernal Peak Elrito Ojo Caliente Rio Chama Abiquiu Lyden Velarde Tramja Truchas Penasco Chacon Guadalupita Ocate Nolan Levi Wagon mound Sauz Pasamonte Beenham Mesteno

Chaca Mesa Cuba Sulphur Espanola Rio Grande Sta. Santa Cruz Chamita Chimayo Cordova Cleveland Mora Lacueva Willis Rociada Sapello Shoemaker Roy Albert Solana

Cabezon Miller Casasalazar Perea Bland Jemes Penablanca Thornton Algodones Bernalillo Sandoval SANTA FE Waldo Lamy Pojuaque Beulah Hot Spr. Guillou Los Alamos Las Vegas Sanchez Watrous Chaperito Mideo Belranch Campana Canadian Ata

Mt. Taylor Seboyeta Old Albuquerque Cubero Albuquerque Pajarito Isleta Cerrillos Madrid San Pedro Alameda Galisteo San Jose San Miguel Villanueva Anton Chico Colonias Chapelle Sena Casaus Gallinas Spring Tucumcari Palomas

Laguna El Rito Armijo Suwanee Garcia Rio Puerco Escobosa Moriarty McIntosh Peralta Los Lunas Tome Tajique Estancia Padernal Mt. Pintada Santa Rosa Puerto de Luna Los Tanos Montoya Bluffs of L.

Belen Jarales Bernardo Lajoya Sta. Lajoya Polvadera Magdalena Mt. Kelly Socorro Eastview Manzano Willard Progresso Blanca Camaleon Pinoswells Marino Duran P.O. Trinchora Sta. Guadalupe Pastura Aragon Leoncita Guadalupe Salado Fort Sumner Langton Flor Glen

Law Hill Pyramid Chupadera Mesa Tecolote Vista Gallinas Torrance

San Antonio Lemitar Coyote Ancho Jacks Pk. Jicarilla Jicarilla Mts. Whiteoaks Richardson Capitan M Boaz Elkins Campbell

Magdalena Mts. Elmendorf San Marcial Clyde Occura Pk. Pope Osouro Nogal Parsons Coalora Capitan Walnut Ft. Stanton Lincoln Hondo Roswell South Springs

Parajo Monticello Fairview Lava Capitol Pk. Crocker Oscura Bonito Angus Ruidoso Picacho Orchard Park Dexter Greenfield Hagerman

Cuchillo Engle Three Rivers Sta. Salinas Pk. Pilot Knob Tularosa Temporal MESCALERO APACHE IND. RES. Pajarito Mt. Felix Rio Felix Hope Dayton Lakewood

Arrey Lake Valley Garfield Rincon Upham Point of Rocks Dog Cannon Escondida Alamogordo Russia Weed Cloudcroft Elk Lower Penasco Artesia Rio Penasco Avalon

Nutt Florida Easley Hockett Dona Ana Lascruces Brice P.O. or Jarilla Jarilla Jc. or Orogrande P.O. Soledad Carlsbad Florence

1 | Introduction

Setting and context: from geography to a new railroad

New Mexico is a vast, complicated place united by aridity and divided by geography. How people responded to this complexity had profound historical consequences, leaving behind a mosaic of success and failure—both often resident in the same story. The Native Americans who occupied New Mexico and the Southwest for the longest periods of time adapted to the dry, shifting climate by changing life strategies, using different parts of the landscape as conditions allowed, thereby generating alternating cycles of use and abandonment. The Spaniards who came north to settle in the 1600s and 1700s followed a similar pattern and soon found their greatest opportunities living along the few small permanent streams and rivers.

Changes accelerated in New Mexico during the nineteenth century as fortunes rose and fell. After the Spanish empire collapsed, it was replaced by Mexico, and then again by the United States. The nomadic cultures of the Comanche and others shifted or lost their territories in response to outside pressures, leaving the plains in an uneasy balance. Hispanos moved swiftly into broader areas and exploited many new opportunities. Goods and outside influence flowed westward along the Santa Fe Trail, reorienting the local axis of power away from Mexico. Military personnel continued the gradually escalating federal engagement with New Mexico as it played its small role in the broader conflict of the Civil War. These soldiers and engineers brought their perspectives on what the territory could become and created some of the early maps that stirred outside interests.

Railroads were one of the key developments and powerful industries of the latter nineteenth century. In particular, the almost messianic drive to create a transcontinental system involved considerable money and effort by corporations and the government. Where these railroads could be reasonably located was dictated in part by the rugged topography of the western United States, as well as by where economic opportunities seemed most promising. Although two routes along the 32nd and 35th parallels through New Mexico were identified by the Pacific Railroad surveys of 1853 to 1855, it was not until the early 1880s that railroads finally arrived. In the span of only three years, nearly 1,000 miles of track had been built (Myrick 1990). As the railroads expanded their scope, there was a parallel growth in settlement across the Southwest resulting from the Homestead Act of 1862 that opened large areas as public

FIG 1.1
Sawing driven pilings for a bridge pier on the Pecos River
Photograph of crew on the Pecos River Bridge construction
sometime in 1906 (Courtesy of New Mexico State University
Library, Archives and Special Collections [NMSU ASC]).

domain. The confluence of these two historical trends—each made possible by various geographers, cartographers, financiers, laborers, speculators, settlers, and boosters—shaped the story of the Belen Cutoff. Construction of the Cutoff in 1908 was an essential component to the completion of a viable heavy-freight transcontinental line by the Atchison, Topeka and Santa Fe Railway (AT&SF) and had profound effects on the development of the eastern plains of New Mexico.

The region of New Mexico that encompasses the Belen Cutoff extends from the high, windswept *Llano Estacado* (Staked Plains) to the valley of the Rio Grande, located several hundred miles to the west. Most of that stretch is little troubled by topography with expansive views of flat or undulating plains in all directions, interrupted only by the long journey south of the Pecos River. This vastness begins to relent just east of the Rio Grande as mountains rise up and form a ragged and formidable north-south barrier. Here, near the center of New Mexico, the ancient Precambrian quartzites of the Manzano and Los Pinos Mountains dip toward each other and are split by the relatively unknown mountain pass at Abo Canyon, which drains the upland area. Farther along, an easy slope continues to the valley bottom along the Rio Grande where the majority

of New Mexicans make their homes.

This geography, in particular the topographic challenge of Abo Canyon, is indirectly responsible for this book. In the first decade of the twentieth century, the AT&SF faced the considerable difficulties of building the Belen Cutoff through the critical 5-mile long stretch of Abo Canyon, which was the only simple, viable route to the Rio Grande Valley in central New Mexico. While less difficult segments of this railroad were improved, second tracks added, and efficiencies gained over the next hundred years, nothing changed in the single track of the canyon. Eventually, at the turn of this century, the BNSF Railway (BNSF), corporate heir to the AT&SF, decided to address the bottleneck.

The cost of engineering a new route was certainly a concern, but other elements proved to be almost as complicated. The necessity of obtaining permits and right-of-way for construction subjected the project to federal review under legislation such as the National Environmental Policy Act and the National Historic Preservation Act. These laws required the United States Army Corps of Engineers and Bureau of Land Management to consider how a second track might affect the natural and cultural environment. In particular, one of the major

FIG 1.2
Advertisement for AT&SF Indian Detours
Brochure from 1936 advertising the Indian Detours offered
by the AT&SF (Courtesy of Shawn Kelley).

questions was how the new line would potentially impact the prehistoric and historic sites and values that remained in Abo Canyon, including the campsites and other features left behind from the original railroad construction.

After a process lasting nearly five years with input from many members of the public, tribal governments, and various historic preservation entities, the federal agencies accepted BNSF's proposal to build a second track through Abo Canyon even though its construction would adversely affect some cultural resources. As a result, the parties involved in the environmental review agreed on a diverse set of ways to mitigate some of these impacts. These efforts included excavations of archaeological sites, conducting many interviews with knowledgeable local residents about their lives and relationships with the railroad and its legacy, developing high-school curricula on regional history, various technical reports, and completion of this book about the Belen Cutoff and how it changed New Mexico.

Telling the story of the Belen Cutoff

When we started our research it quickly became apparent that scholars had largely overlooked the Belen Cutoff, focusing instead on the AT&SF's transcontinental route through Raton Pass and on to California along the 35th parallel. The efforts of AT&SF to spur business along this line and promote a unique brand were part of creating a mythic Southwest. AT&SF's advertising materials, evocative built environments, and romantic association with natural wonders and Native Americans, as exemplified by the Harvey Indian Detours, helped construct part of our collective historical imagination. Whether we know it or not, much of how we thought, and still think, about the Southwest and its people was formed by the iconography and ideology of the early railroad. By comparison, the Belen Cutoff barely registers in most people's minds; it merely shortened an east-west trip across New Mexico by roughly 6 miles, lessened the ruling grade for trains, and carried little passenger traffic—hardly the stuff of legend.

Why then study the Belen Cutoff at all—perhaps others have been correct to pass it by in favor of other topics? There are several compelling reasons of both national and regional importance. For AT&SF, the Belen Cutoff eliminated the steep grades of Raton Pass and enabled the efficient shipping of heavy freight. It opened up a legitimate transcontinental line with the capacity to compete with rivals like the Union Pacific

Belen, New Mexico.

Scholle Store
Burned April 1900

John Becker Store

mill

FIG 1.3
Downtown Belen
Downtown Belen in 1900, showing the Scholle store, the Becker
store, and the Belen Roller Mill (Courtesy of NMSU ASC).

and set the stage for the immense movements of goods and materials that came to define the previous century and this one. For New Mexico, the Belen Cutoff, along with other rail lines, transformed the eastern plains in the first half of the twentieth century. The railroad aided and accelerated the expansion of Hispano families into new areas and created the jobs and conditions that led to so many homesteaders coming into the region. Significantly, New Mexico grew more from 1900 to 1910 than in any other 10-year period; its population increased by 67 percent overall and the area along the Cutoff experienced an astounding 140 percent growth (United States Census Bureau [USCB] 1913a; 1901).

Our primary goal for this book is to tell the story of the Belen Cutoff and provide new perspectives on the transformation of the eastern plains and its people with the arrival of the railroad. This includes discussions of the entire Cutoff, but focuses on the area between Fort Sumner and Belen, two significant railroad towns representing eastern and central New Mexico, respectively. More specifically, we considered the local settlements near Abo Canyon—those closest to BNSF's second track project—including Mountainair, Abo Nuevo, Abo Viejo, and Scholle.

A significant challenge faced when explaining the Belen Cutoff or any history is the availability of information. For example, AT&SF's focus on operating an efficient and competitive train system with thousands of miles of track was reflected in their internal documents, which show the railroad's concerns regarding geography, design, shipping, raw materials, and cost. However, this historical record did not always include the experiences and narratives of average laborers or how AT&SF's decisions affected nearby communities or individuals. Presenting a more complete and balanced history of the region requires additional modes of inquiry, including examination of the material culture left behind, local newspaper accounts, other extant documentary evidence and primary materials, as well as the remembered pasts of the people we interviewed during this project. The relative importance of each source depends on the time period under consideration. For example, newspapers are of limited value when looking at the beginnings of the Eastern Railway of New Mexico (ERNM), another name for the Cutoff, as most towns where newspapers would come to be published did not exist when construction occurred. Likewise, oral histories from local families tend to focus on the twentieth century. Where possible we attempted to examine bills of

FIG 1.4
Canuto Sisneros and friends
Picture taken in 1920 of (from left to right).: Jose Sisneros, Juan Vallejos, Canuto Sisneros, and Eligio Salas (Courtesy of Polly Sisneros).

lading, business ledgers, census materials, land patents, personal and business correspondence, historic photographs, and as-built drawings to help in our research.

Our secondary goal is to do justice to those who contributed their time and knowledge to ensuring that this project would be meaningful to the broadest audience. There are still many people who experienced the changes and trends that so profoundly shaped eastern New Mexico along the Cutoff. Descendants of the original settlers and homesteaders remain in the region and made themselves available to talk about their lives and those of their parents, grandparents, and great-grandparents. We managed to interview roughly 70 of these individuals, which is fortunate because if this project occurred 20 years from now, there would be few people in the area who remembered what life was like in the later nineteenth and early twentieth centuries.

Relationships are strong here and people look out for one another, a tradition maintained from a time when the local community provided almost everything. As we began to meet residents and explain what we hoped to accomplish with our mitigation efforts, they were gracious enough to welcome us into their homes, share their information, and introduce us to other knowledgeable friends and neighbors. The interviews and recounting of family histories tapped into a source of pride about what the people of the region had accomplished. Growing up and making a living in places such as Scholle or Roundtop was not an easy accomplishment. Interviewees wanted to pass along some of what they knew, sometimes because their own children no longer lived in the area and they lacked the opportunities to talk about the region's history. As descendants of the original settlers move away, it is getting harder to track down old photographs, letters, or other materials that give immediacy and vitality to the historical record. Thankfully, interviewees generously provided us with many images and materials from their personal collections, many of which have never been published. The cooperation of these wonderful people has made this book far better and richer than we ever could have accomplished alone. All of us, from the authors to agencies and BNSF Railway, extend our deepest thanks to those who participated and made this volume a reality.

2 | From megafauna to pueblos and pastoralism: east-central New Mexico prior to the railroad

This chapter attempts to summarize the environment of east-central New Mexico from prehistory to the 1800s in order to understand what life was like before the Belen Cutoff. Many things changed in the 12,000 years since humans came to inhabit the region. Mammoths and mastodons died off due to climate change and early humans. In response, people moved to a more diverse subsistence including agriculture from Mesoamerica. The pueblos of the Salinas Province thrived for a few centuries and were abandoned just before the Pueblo Revolt briefly pushed Spaniards out of New Mexico. After the reconquest, Native Americans and Hispanos interacted in conditions that ranged from collaboration to conflict. Hispanos from Rio Grande communities come to reoccupy the former Salinas Province by the early nineteenth century and create land-grant settlements such as Manzano. Jurisdiction over the region changed two times, and eventually Native Americans no longer dominated the llano. By the end of the 1800s, Hispano villagers were continuing their expansion and growth, loggers had come into the mountains, and herds of Texas cattle grazed the plains in great numbers.

Environmental setting and early prehistory

For today's motorists, leaving the Rio Grande Valley and passing through the mountains onto the plains must seem so commonplace as to hardly be mentioned. The apparent ease of this journey and terrain, however, masks the difficulties faced by the previous inhabitants and travellers. Since humans first came to the region nearly 12,000 years ago the region has become more arid and cool. Mastodons, mammoths, bison, camelids, and other megafauna dependent on ample playas and water eventually gave way to animals such as modern species of bison and pronghorn that could thrive in an area with limited or no perennial drainages. Eastern New Mexico was once, however, a much wetter place.

In 1926 near Folsom, New Mexico a cowboy named George McJunkin found an in-situ spear point together with an extinct species of bison. This discovery helped to confirm the presence of humans in the Americas during the Pleistocene and eventually led to other similar finds. Notably, excavations in the 1920s and 1930s at Blackwater Draw near Clovis, New Mexico unearthed distinctive stone tools embedded in skeletons of mammoths and other ancient species. The users of these large spear points and other tools found at Blackwater Draw, and their strategy of hunting megafauna, came to be known as the Clovis culture. Clovis peoples were for many years thought to be the earliest inhabitants of the continent, although recent research has strongly suggested that other groups came beforehand. Clovis hunters were highly mobile and followed big game across a vast area with their success dependent on a relatively wet climate and habitat capable of supporting megafauna.

Around 8,000 years ago New Mexico's weather became dryer and cooler at the onset of the Holocene, eventually limiting available water sources, which contributed to the extinction of megafauna and other large mammals. Over the next seven or eight millennia, during what archaeologists refer to as the Archaic period, humans responded to the new climate by diversifying and coming to rely on a greater variety of animal and plant foods. The introduction of agriculture from Mesoamerica (maize, beans, and squash for example) about 3,000 years ago was of great importance. This new technology came to have as profound an impact on the Southwest as the previous collapse of big game populations.

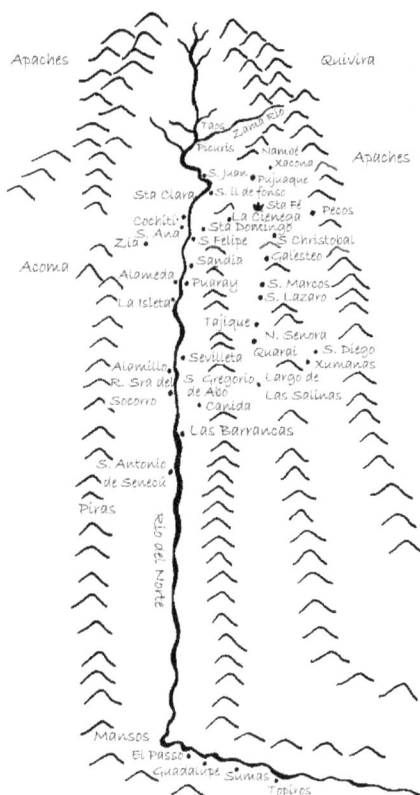

Apaches

Quivira

Apaches

Taos
Picuris
Namué
Xacona
S. Juan
Pujuaque
Sta Clara
S. Il de fonso
Cochiti
La Cienega
Sta Fé
Pecos
Zia
S. Ana
Sta Domingo
S. Felipe
S. Christobal
Sandia
Galesteo
Alameda
Puaray
S. Marcos
La Isleta
S. Lazaro
Tajique
N. Senora
Alamillo
Sevilleta
Quarai
S. Diego
R. Sra del
S. Gregorio
Xumanas
Socorro
de Abo
Largo de
Cañida
Las Salinas
Las Barrancas
S. Antonio
de Seneca
Piras
RIO DEL NORTE
Acoma

Mansos
El Passo
Guadalupe
Sumas
Topiros

FIG 2.1
Central New Mexico pueblos in 1680
Map adapted from Peñalosa's 1680 map of New Mexico
(Wheat 1957).

By the beginning of the last millennia, east-central New Mexico was fairly similar to what we know today—the dry grasslands of the plains grading into the mountains and continuing on to the Rio Grande and its year-round water. Persistent aridity unites this cross-section of the state. The climate varies due to elevation, but it is almost always dry. Lower areas can receive as little 8 inches of rainfall annually and higher locations might get 18 inches. This moisture usually arrives in the summer with brief, heavy thunderstorms that often harm as much as they help, making travel challenging if not impossible. Temperatures exhibit similar extremes and farmers near the mountains can have as few as 90 days to plant, grow, and harvest their crops between the spring and fall frosts.

Thin ribbons of green—cottonwoods and willow—line the rivers and junipers and piñon pines dot the lower slopes of the mountains and foothills. Everywhere else is sparse grass, with occasional shrubs or cacti like snakeweed, yucca, cane cholla, or prickly pear. Hawks and other birds are frequently seen on the plains along with coyotes, prairie dogs, jackrabbits, and pronghorn. Larger mammals like mule deer, bighorn sheep, and mountain lions can be found closer to the mountains.

This environment of relative scarcity was what the Tompiro, Jumano, and others encountered when their populations began to grow in Abo Pass and along the eastern slopes of the Manzanos and Los Pinos Mountains in the fifteenth century. These groups are thought to have grown out of regional cultures that shared traits from both the Anasazi (now commonly referred to as the Ancestral Puebloan) located primarily along the Rio Grande to the west and the Jornada Mogollon who inhabited areas to the south and east. The local occupations from about A.D. 800 to 1500 were notable for their gradual increase in dryland agriculture and transition from pithouse dwellings, to aboveground *jacal* structures (a technology consisting of a wood frame plastered over with adobe). These building traditions eventually shifted again and lead to the larger, multi-room masonry pueblos encountered by Juan de Oñate's colonizing expedition of 1598. Researchers are still debating the exact cultural affiliations of the major local settlements in the area centered on Abo Pass— some feel all were Tompiro and others think the Jumano were also present—but by the early seventeenth century these pueblos were similar enough to collectively become known to the Spanish as the Salinas Province (Levine 1987, Hickerson 1994).

FIG 2.2
Mission pueblos of the Salinas Province

The Salinas Province after Spanish contact

Franciscan friars began efforts to convert the pueblos to Catholicism soon after Oñate entered New Mexico and settled in the northern Rio Grande. By the end of the 1620s, they had established missions at Abo, Pueblo de los Jumanos (Gran Quivira), and Quarai (Figure 2.2). Friars at the three missions relied on local native labor to construct their massive churches and living areas. The Salinas missions were in operation from approximately 1620 to 1678, a period marked by conflicts among the Spanish, pueblo groups, and various Athapaskan tribes, including the Navajo and Apache. Populations were displaced, and many pueblos were abandoned. Conflict and diseases introduced by the Spanish, possible incursions or hostilities from other native groups, and an increasingly dry climate, led to a dramatic decline in the native population in the seventeenth century (Marshall and Marshall 1999). The last two factors would blunt re-expansion into the Salinas region over the next century. Life on the dry uplands of the Salinas Province was no longer tenable by the 1670s and the Tompiro left the area. The remaining pueblos in New Mexico responded to the adverse conditions and revolted in 1680, forcing the Spanish to leave New Mexico and spend the next 12 years in El Paso.

In 1692, Diego de Vargas led a Spanish reconquest of New Mexico. During this period, some Rio Grande pueblos were subject to conflict and subsequently abandoned, occasionally to be reoccupied later. The Spanish colonists in the core settlements along the Rio Grande developed several techniques to minimize and mitigate disagreements and friction with native peoples. One critical effort was the establishment of *Genízaro* ("Christianized" Indian) settlements in several key locations on the Spanish periphery, including the Belen area. The Genízaros had lost much of their native identity through capture or displacement and often intermarried with the Spanish colonists, providing buffers from Apache attacks and also functioning as cultural intermediaries (Jenkins and Schroeder 1974; Brooks 2002).

The Salinas Province in the 1700s remained relatively quiet, albeit marked by intermittent violence and unease that was enough to prevent widespread reoccupation by Euroamericans until the early nineteenth century. Villagers from the Rio Grande used the area, however, for seasonal pasturage of their sheep. Several Native American groups, including the Apache and Navajo, did periodically occupy the region,

A death in the Sisneros family

Since 1823, my compadre, José Maria, myself and our boys had been bringing our cows or sheep and goats and our oxen to graze at the top of the [Abo] cañon (canyon) at that chamizal (pasture) which we called Las Saladas (located just south of present-day Scholle).... My compadre and I were thinking of moving permanently to this land, but only the tragedy that befell my son, Luciano, dissuaded us....

I [had] decided to send Luciano back to Casa Colorada for provisions.... He was riding his horse down the cañon and he was ambushed by Indians.... We could hear him shouting for help. We went to meet him, but already he was surrounded. Brave Luciano told me he would rather be killed than be taken captive. The Indians obliged him and speared my son Luciano to death piercing his body from side to side. These Indians came after me also, but an old Indian stepped in and asked them to spare me since we knew one another from Casa Colorada and had even been friends.

Adapted from Mariano Pino's account (Sisneros n.d.).

following a traditional, mobile strategy of hunting, gathering, and horticulture, sometimes supplemented by raiding.

Initial resettlement of the Salinas Province

New Mexico underwent several major changes in the early nineteenth century, including becoming part of the newly formed Republic of Mexico in 1821. The Spanish population was growing and moving into different places to seek new opportunities as less land was available along the river valleys for farming and ranching. In 1815, the governor of New Mexico petitioned colonists to settle several areas, such as the "ancient pueblo of Manzano" (located 5 miles north of the mission at Quarai) (Foote 1989:3). A number of Hispanic families answered the call and relocated from the Rio Grande Valley to just northeast of Abo Pass where arable lands were available. The Lucero family, who settled around the old mission at Quarai, was among the first to reoccupy the area.

Bartolome Baca was also one of the earlier settlers and provides an example of the potential difficulties. In 1819, he obtained a grant along the eastern slopes of the Manzano Mountains. Bartolome used the land for grazing sheep, cattle, and horses and also developed a system of spring-fed irrigation agriculture. By 1833, however, he abandoned the grant due to the depredations of Navajo raiders (Foote 1989:4). This cycle was not unusual during the Mexican period, when nomadic Indians intensified their raiding of frontier settlements—an increase argued to be a result of the Mexican government's inability to provide supplementary aid to defend colonists.

The Manzano grant was made to Hispanic farmers and ranchers in 1829 (Foote 1989). Settlers in Manzano were frequently in contact with nomadic Indians and had particularly difficult relations with the Navajo. As a result, the town was organized for defense and included a *torreón* (watchtower) on the southwest edge of the plaza (Hurt 1941 [1989]). Despite the friction with native groups, many Indians were incorporated into Manzano society, often first as *peones* (slaves or indentured servants) and later through intermarriage (Hurt 1941 [1989]; Brooks 2002; Francisco Sisneros, personal communication 2008). Economic interests in the grant were diverse. For example, José Chavez y Noriega obtained a mining claim in 1842 for lands near Abo where he also pastured his work animals (Foote 1989:11).

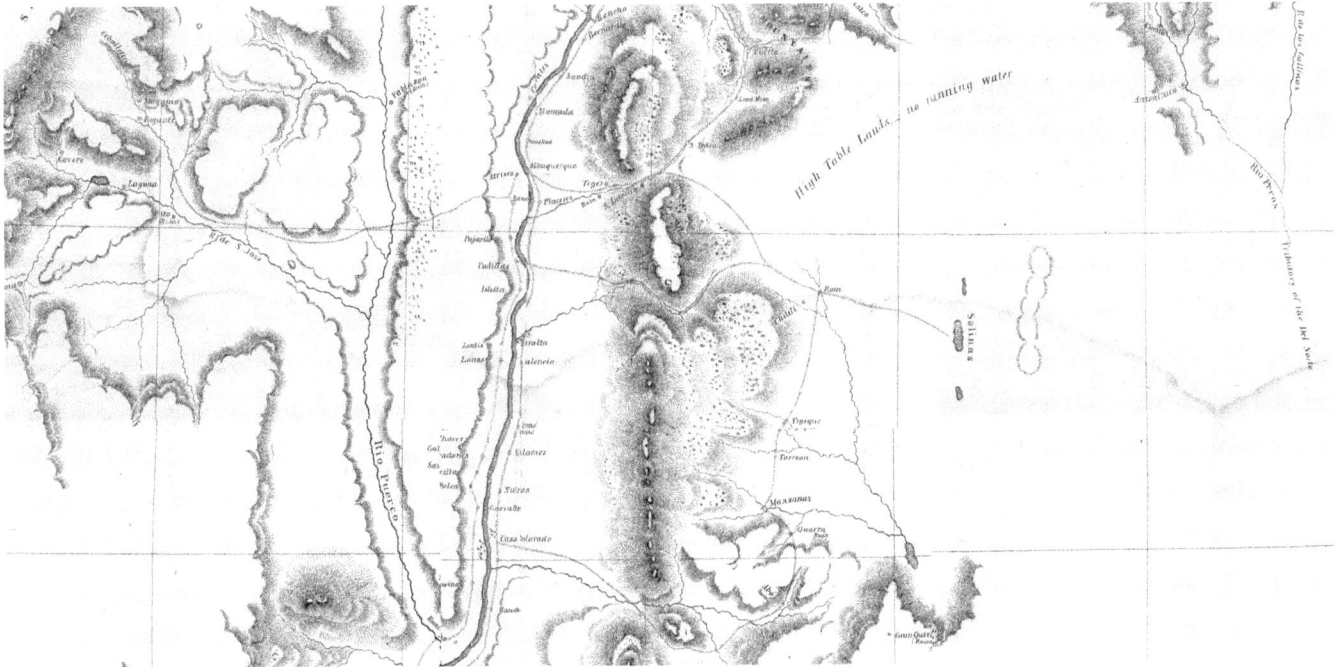

FIG 2.3
Abert's 1846–47 map of central New Mexico
Adapted from Abert (1847 [1962]).

The early Territorial period

Mexico's rule was fairly short-lived and ended in 1846, when the United States took over during the Mexican-American War. The 1848 Treaty of Guadalupe Hidalgo formally made New Mexico a permanent holding of the United States. Mapping New Mexico, and determining who owned what, became one of the most important issues that arose out of the new territorial status. James Abert visited in 1847 and produced the first territorial map, which focused on the major population centers of the northern Rio Grande (Figure 2.3). Tajique, Torreon, and Manzano are noted, and the primary regional road is shown heading through the Abo ruins. Abert did not record anyone living at Abo during his visit, nor did Major James Henry Carleton when he came through six years later in 1853.

The U.S. Congress approved the Manzano Land Grant by 1860, although it did not include many of the people in outlying settlements who previously thought they were living in the grant. The Treaty of Guadalupe Hidalgo recognized existing grants, but the adjudication of titles to private or common lands became politicized, and many communities lost their upland grazing areas due to misunderstandings and deceit (Hall 1991).

In 1861 the Civil War came to central New Mexico when Union military personnel established a camp just above La Salada, a perennial spring close to modern-day Scholle. Soldiers set up the outpost to secure Abo Pass from invading Texas Volunteers intent on making the New Mexico Territory part of the new Confederacy. These soldiers' letters provide a glimpse of the Union Army's efforts in the fall of 1861 and winter of 1862 (Wilson 2001:166–175). Most show a concern for the security of Abo Pass with topics of discussion including Navajo raids, the absence of Texas Volunteers, and troop movements within the territory (Wilson 2001:166–175). Captain Isaiah Moore also produced another map of the area, this one showing several communities formed since Abert's visit—Punta de Agua, Cieneguilla, and Barrancas Coloradas (Wilson 2001:166).

Ciboleros and concentration camps

In many ways the people of Manzano and the other villages on the east side of the mountains lived in a different world than the families along the Rio Grande. The crops they grew and foods they ate were similar, but the axis of power and people they had to accommodate extended far onto the plains and on

Indita de Manuelito	Ballad of Manuelito
Con que sentimientos estas.	With what sentiments you are.
Que en El ojo de Gallina	Who at the Ojo de Gallina
Que mataron debajo de paz.	Was killed during a truce.
No to mataron peleando	They didn't kill you fighting
Ni tampoco a bein a bien.	Nor by honorable means
Que mataron a traicion,	Who was killed treacherously,
Charley el Capitan Gray.	By Charley, the Captain Gray.
Yo soy el Indio Manuel	I am the Indio Manuel
Que el mundo cause ruin.	Who causes ruin to the world.
Yo me vivo depurado	I live a purified life
En El Ojo de Gallina.	At the Spring of Gallina.
Por beber un trago	I drink a large swallow
De whiskey de una cantina.	Of whiskey from a canteen.

Indita de Manuelito
Señor Chavez of Torreón wrote this song in the nineteenth century, and Hurt (1941 [1989]) noted that old men in Manzano still sang it in the 1940s.

into Texas and beyond. Native Americans such as the Apaches were well known to Manzaneños, and an 1850 account from James B. Calhoun noted that "the Jicarilla Apaches remain yet in the neighborhood of Manzano. They visit Manzano whenever they choose, and buy and sell without hindrance" (Hurt 1941 [1989]). In contrast, Manzano had poorer relations with the Navajo, as evidenced by Calhoun's 1851 account.

> *The Navajos continue in small parties, to commit depredations, and have not the slightest idea we can effectively check them. They never regard the loss of a few men and captives. A few days since, the Navajos drove off stock from near Manzano. The Apaches, whose localities have been in that neighborhood for months past, ascertained the fact, pursued the Navajos, recovered and returned the stock and brought in a scalp. Four were wounded and three have died since* (Hurt 1941 [1989]).

Manzaneños also had relations with other Plains Indians such as the Comanche, whose friendship was built through interactions with *ciboleros* (buffalo hunters) from the Hispano villages (ibid.). During the mid-nineteenth century, hunting buffalo was very important to Manzano's subsistence strategy. Men would travel out onto the Llano Estacado for months at a time using wagons pulled by oxen to transport the meat, firearms, and lances to kill the animals. Villagers often met Plains Indians during these hunts and some even learned the Comanche language (ibid.).

Until the Civil War, there were not enough American military forces in New Mexico to substantially change the regional balance of power. Difficulties from raiding Navajo continued until 1863, when Kit Carson was ordered to round them up and move them to Bosque Redondo, south of present-day Fort Sumner. Conditions on the "Long Walk" to the camp were terrible and not much improved on their arrival. Nearly 9,000 people were forced to live in an area totaling less than 40 square miles (Thompson 1972). Crops failed repeatedly over the multiyear experiment. The Navajo and Apache also living on the doomed reservation did not get along, and costs ran to almost a million dollars a year to support all the people (ibid.). Several Navajo escaped the camp, and some made their way to Manzano, where they were taken in as family servants. One such individual working in a Manzano household later married into the

Yo soy el Indio Manuel	I am the Indian Maunel
El hermano de Mariano	The brother of Mariano
Que con'la flecha en el mano	Who with the arrow in my hand
Emplamo de dos o tres	Impales two or three
Sea Indio, sea Cristiano,	Whether Indian, Christian,
Americano, o Frances.	American, or French.
Cherley se reclamo sus bueyes,	Charley recovered his oxen,
Balido de occasion	Taking advantage of the opportunity
E le respondio el Bacon,	And Bacon answered him,
Oh, Charley no me das us bueyes,	"Oh, Charley don't give me your oxen,
?No es esa tu religion?	Isn't that your religion?
No lo permiten tus leyes.	Your laws don't permit it."
Adios, todos mis amigos,	Goodbye, all my friends,
Ya se muere Manuelito.	Manuelito is now dying,
Ya ni pelearon conmigo	You didn't fight with me
La gente de Manzanito.	You people of Manzano.
Para cantar esta indita	In order to sing this ballad
Del Apache Manuelito	Of the Apache Manuelito
Para cantar la bonito	In order to sing the beautiful
Como lo canto el le quito	As he sang it he [died?]
Al primero toque de Diana	At the time of reveille
Un dia en el Rio Bonito.	One day on the Rio Bonito.
Gobernador de Santa Fe,	Governor of Santa Fe,
Tu mi muerte te declaras	My death you declared.
Y mantienes de café	You are sustained by coffee
Porque nunca me alarza.	So that I would never run away
Varios bueyes me robo	You robbed me of several oxen
Para que tu los pagradas.	You will have to pay for them.

family after the death of a wife (Hurt 1941 [1989]; Francisco Sisneros, personal communication 2010). As much as anything, this frequent and close contact with Native Americans distinguished life in Manzano in the early nineteenth century. A ballad written by a poet in Torreón to commemorate the life of Manuelito, an Apache chief considered a friend by Manzaneños, captures the importance of these relationships (Hurt 1941 [1989]).

Compadrasco and the village networks

The village of Barrancas Colorados mentioned previously (also known as Arroyo Colorado) was a small settlement southwest of Manzano just outside the grant boundaries. The Sisneros had lived here since the 1850s, when they came up from Casa Colorada along the Rio Grande. They grew staple crops such as corn and chile along with wheat to trade or sell for cash. In addition, they herded sheep, moving them in the winter to lower-elevation pastures near the ruins of Abo. Men in the family also spent a period as *fleteros* (freighters) moving goods along the Santa Fe Trail (Sisneros 1996). This occupation was not uncommon among the men of the Rio Abajo and ended up making the fortunes of individuals such as Felipe Chaves, a prominent civic leader in Belen in the late nineteenth century.

By 1866, the Sisneros family moved permanently to Abo and left Arroyo Colorado. Abo was similar to all of the nearby small villages in how they maintained relationships with Manzano, one another, and the places from where they had originally come, such as La Joya, Belen, and Casa Colorada. Historian Francisco Sisneros, a descendant of these settlers, calls this structure of mutual aid, dependency, and relationships a triangular system of *compadrasco* (literally meaning god-parenthood but generally considered more broadly). In an interview with Cheryl Foote (1989), Nick Esquibel commented on the centrality of Abo in this arrangement.

They were very hospitable. When the men rode from Belen or La Joya to the Manzano villages, Manzano, Torreón, and so forth, the route went right through Grandpa's (Joaquin Sisneros') ranch. It took a day's trip from those villages to the place; therefore many travelers could use this place as a paraje, which means stopping place. Everybody could stop and there was no

	1860	1870	1890	1900	1910	1930	1940	1950
Cienega	194	N/A	331	182	247	241	219	84
Punta de Agua	237	238	290	100	632	393	414	215
Abo	N/A	N/A	N/A	N/A	309	318	424	335

FIG 2.4
Populations in Cienega, Punta de Agua, and Abo (1860 to 1950)
Adapted from Foote 1989

charge. Grandma and Grandpa had started their inter-relations with the people from La Joya. . . . Grandpa married someone from La Joya.

Although the census data are not perfectly reliable due to changes in enumeration and precinct, it is fairly clear the villages enabled by Manzano grew in size during the nineteenth century (Figure 2.4). Their trajectory of development was changed, however, by not being within the land grant. Because villagers' land had an uncertain status within the public domain, they frequently moved to formalize their ownership by patenting it under the Homestead Act of 1862. This practice became more widespread as large portions of grants were not recognized by the United States (Foote 1989:14; Sisneros 1996).

Homesteading gave secure property rights to the villagers, but it also altered their relationships with lands once considered common resources (Hall 1991). Prime locations such as springs came to be owned by certain groups, for example, the Sisneros family at Abo. One of the ultimate consequences of homesteading would only be realized later in the twentieth century, when the railroad boom and influx of Anglo settlers alienated villagers from the grazing lands they used to rely on.

Texas longhorns and timber

The area along the Belen Cutoff encompasses two distinct geographic areas: the intermountain zone near the Manzano and Los Pinos Mountains and the high plains farther east. Hispanos had successfully occupied the first region for most of the 1800s but only used the Llano Estacado seasonally for hunting buffalo and pasturing sheep. Some of the reluctance to move away from the mountains had to do with villagers' knowledge of adverse agricultural conditions on the plains (it was too dry to consistently allow farming without irrigation, information that would have helped the later homesteaders). The other factor was that Native Americans were already living there, even if only sporadically. Indian peoples stopped or slowed the advance of Hispanos and Anglos onto the plains, but the internment of the Navajo and Apache at Fort Sumner helped remove some of the final barriers to occupy lands of the public domain. With the fort's captive market of almost 9,000 people needing food, and little competition for the short grasses of the llano, Texans flooded into eastern New Mexico with their longhorn cattle. Pioneer stockmen such as Lonny Horn, George Slaughter, Jack Lewis, and George McLean ran

FIG 2.5
B. B. Spencer's sawmill
B. B. Spencer's sawmill near Eastview sometime
around 1898 (Courtesy of Richard Spencer).

their animals near what would become Clovis, forming the primary use of the region up until the railroad arrived in the early twentieth century (McAlavy 1976).

Hispanos also increased their use of the llano even while they still accessed summer pasturage for their animals in the higher, wooded elevations of the nearby mountains. In time, the available timber resources drew new people to the region such as B. B. Spencer, who established the first sawmill in the southern Manzanos in 1887. Here Richard Spencer (2008) recalls what the early days were like:

As far as I know, he was the first Anglo that got here and he started the first mill in the area. The Kaysers, I think, were close behind him or right about that same time. He brought a boiler for the mill through Oklahoma to White Oaks. Supposedly it took eight oxen to pull it and was 30 feet long. He had ten wagons when he came to New Mexico.

The first mill originally was in Barranco Canyon south of Eastview back behind the red cliffs. They actually used the oxen then to pull the trees down to the mill and

that kind of stuff. The first mill there that I know about, he did kind of a unique thing. He dammed up a canyon and created a spring. Then it was kind of a sponge and it collected water, and he had a pipe comin' out of the bottom of that dam that he got water from, and that was where he ran his steam motor. And I would assume because the timber was easy and there was nobody up here, he started low there at the red bluffs, went on up Barranco Canyon, and then went on over to the Eastview area. The Cienegita area there, that's in the Forest Service now, is where he had his big mill, and there was probably 60, 70 men working there. He had a two-story commissary and that was a big mill. And then he had mills up at Chilili and clear on up at Mora, New Mexico.

I guess that was the Cienegita mill that kicked off from the railroad. He probably wasn't the only contractor that had that contract; there were other mills up here. Before the railroad, B. B. was getting into Belen and around this area to sell most of his lumber. After the railroad he was takin' it by wagons. He had a mule yard up there, a wagon yard, in Mountainair. B. B.

FIG 2.6
B. B. Spencer and family at their homestead near Eastview
The Spencer homestead at Eastview sometime in the 1890s, pictured from left to right: unknown, unknown, unknown, Elizabeth Spencer, B. B. Spencer, and Jim Spencer (Courtesy of Richard Spencer).

provided crossties and bridge timbers, as far as I know, those bridge timbers that are down in Abo Canyon came from there.

B. B. had come across the Oklahoma Territory and married a lady there, and she was with him when he came up through New Mexico, through White Oaks and up to Eastview. And then something happened along the trail there, as far as their marriage was concerned. Then he got a mail-order bride. She got here from Ohio and didn't think much of the Wild West, so she went back home. Later on was my grandmother, Sarah Ellen. B. B. married her after he was up here. They needed a school-teacher and he went to Albuquerque. She was goin' through to California from Kansas, and she was a school-teacher, so he talked her into comin' back up to Eastview, which was the area up here where we lived. Two years, three years, whatever it was after that, they got married.

In 1922 he got run over by the railroad, by the train, and killed out west of Mountainair. When he did, they lost the ranch and lost all this country up here, because they owed some money on it. My father was

with him. He was in the hospital for eighteen months, ended up with a stiff leg out of the deal, and my grand-father ended up dead.

B. B. Spencer's most lasting legacy was perhaps his introduction of full-time work in the cash economy into Manzano society. Spencer's employment of so many villagers fit in well with the extant economic system, and he became a proxy *patron* (boss). This role would later be filled by other outsiders such as Tenos Tabet, a Syrian shopkeeper, and I. G. and A. B. McKinley, a father and son who ran multiple sawmills in the Manzanos and had large contracts with AT&SF to supply railroad ties (McKinley 2008; Hurt 1941 [1989]). As we discuss in later chapters, logging was a mixed blessing for the region because it helped villages succeed for a period but left them devastated in the 1930s, when all the easily accessible timber had been cut.

There were a few Anglos who had come to the region prior to B. B. Spencer, including one of its most unusual immigrants, Charles L. Kusz Jr. He was born in New York in 1849 and made his way to Manzano via the Colorado mining districts in 1880 or 1881. Variously a rancher, notary public, post-master, and Valencia County representative for the Bureau of

FIG 2.7
Belen Roller Mills
Belen Roller Mills around 1890
(Courtesy of NMSU ASC).

Immigration, Kusz's most important contribution was his publication of a newspaper called *The Gringo and the Greaser*. His editorials swung back and forth and never seemed to settle on whether Kusz loved the area or hated it (Herzog 1964). All of his opinions were strongly held, however, and are probably the reason unknown assailants killed him in his home after he had put out just two years of the periodical.

By the late 1800s, a number of German immigrants had come to the region and exerted significant influence. Paul Fredrick August Kayser VI in Eastview began a large family that would come to include individuals who helped build the Belen Cutoff. August Kayser, a well-known local section foreman in the mid-twentieth century, was also a member of this clan. Frederick Scholle started a large store in Belen and was one of the first to homestead at the town that would grow up to bear his name. John Becker outdid them all in his accomplishments: successful booster for Belen's location on the ERNM, founder of the Becker-Dalies store, founder of the Belen Roller Mills, and founder of the First National Bank. Becker's story was that of the successful immigrant and businessman, the archetypal booster.

As the nineteenth century drew to a close, all the ingredients for regional change were in place. Large sections of land on the llano were open for expansion. Hispanos in Abo Pass continued forming new villages and communities as they moved into broader areas. Civic leaders in Belen and elsewhere looked to increase business and grow their towns. Homestead laws, the promotion industry, and an obliging territorial government were only waiting for the railroad to help create a new world in east-central New Mexico.

3 | One half mile shorter, but all of it up: constructing the Eastern Railway of New Mexico

Constructing the Belen Cutoff through east-central New Mexico was perhaps the largest mobilization of workers and materials in the region's history. Nearly 2,000 individuals helped to build the roughly 200-mile-long segment of track over several years. AT&SF surveyors started to investigate route possibilities seriously in 1902, construction continued intermittently from 1903 to 1907, and most of AT&SF's transcontinental rail traffic shifted to the line by 1908. This chapter considers the Cutoff and the people who built it, in particular what their experiences and environments were like.

By the mid-nineteenth century, Major James Henry Carleton had already considered a potential rail line cutting through Abo Canyon and linking the eastern plains with the Rio Grande Valley and points west. He made this observation shortly after the Mexican-American War when traveling in New Mexico and taking stock of the United States' new territory. His journals show he did not have a great opinion of New Mexico, and it must have seemed quite distant from the nearest rail line, many hundreds of miles to the east. By creating narratives and maps telling of the region's importance, Carleton (along with others such as Abert) helped explain New Mexico to outside interests. Although he was a reluctant booster, his vision of a new rail line would have major impacts on east-central New Mexico in due time. Creating conditions where these prospects could be realized took a significant investment of monies and military power from the federal government. This process was synergistic with development of the transcontinental railroad, each allowing the other to exert influence for both good and bad. Limiting raiding from nomadic tribes was likely positive for most New Mexican villagers, although this came at a cost to them and their Native American neighbors in

the form of reduced opportunities and the loss of land. By the late nineteenth century, the effort of pacification was mostly over and the great governmental and corporate effort to survey the territories had begun.

Surveying the Cutoff: our eyes look ever toward the virgin wonders of the hills

AT&SF first seriously considered a route through east-central New Mexico in 1879. By this point, they already knew their route south over Raton Pass and on to Las Vegas, but the way forward from there was not clear. Would it be better to trend along the Pecos River out to the plains and then south to Abo Canyon, thereby avoiding difficult terrain near Glorieta Pass, or just follow the Santa Fe Trail into the Rio Grande Valley? Availability of coal and timber were major concerns, but ultimately the strategic decision to go through Glorieta Pass was made because AT&SF could "occupy the settled portion of [New Mexico] against all rivals" (KSHS Santa Fe Splinters [SFS] 20, W. R. Morley to W. B. Strong, January 10, 1879). Building through New Mexico's most developed area also placed AT&SF on the "good side of the population" and gave "people the advantages of

FIG 3.1: **The War Song of the Engineer**

Our gleaming girders overcast
The foaming flood from strand to strand,
We chain the deadly desert fast
And bind it with an iron band.

We rob of earth her priceless hoard;
We rend her bosom with our drills,
And lo! Our eyes look ever toward
The virgin wonders of the hills.
Down there below the tropic stars,
Thoughtful of nations yet to be,
We rend away the land that bars
The mighty commerce of the sea.

Lo! In the city's throbbing heart,
Or in the country's quiet lanes,
We fashion with our magic art
The steel-shod pathway of the trains.

We chain the demon of the storm,
We speak across the boundless air:
Our Gog and Magog take the form
Of endless motion everywhere.

Tho' life is lost on every side,
We fear not death, nor any fear;
But shout across the chasms wide
The war-song of the Engineer.

Poem by Deane S. Thomas appeared in Santa Fe Employes' [sic]
Magazine May 1907 (Courtesy of Kansas State Historical Society [KSHS]).

railroad communication [that went] far to secure their influence and help in legislative matters and local laws and their execution" (*ibid.*; SFS 20, A. A. Robinson to W. B. Strong, April 17, 1879).

AT&SF's initial foray into New Mexico used geography to control access and limit competition as in the passes at Raton and Glorieta. Their original transcontinental line through New Mexico from Raton to Deming (then on to the Pacific in Mexico using joint trackage with the Southern Pacific Railroad) recognized the demand for access to resources such as the mining districts at Silver City, Lake Valley, and Kelly. In 1889, AT&SF revived their interest in the rail possibilities for Abo Canyon and sent locating engineer Philip Smith to look at potential lines. Smith reconfirmed that Abo Canyon was critical for the railroad and also observed a small population increase in east-central New Mexico, noting the area appeared "somewhat improved and the farmer has made his appearance among these mountains" (SFS 25, P. Smith to L. Kingman, May 17, 1888). Momentum was mounting for rail construction in the territory and surveys were being completed for feasible (and nearly infeasible) routes to important timber or mineral resources (Figure 3.2).

The concerns of the AT&SF in the early twentieth century were different from those just a few decades before. Traffic had increased enough on their line that moving heavy freight over the steep grades of Raton and Glorieta was getting difficult and expensive. AT&SF's financial position was much improved after going bankrupt in the 1890s. Other railroads such as the El Paso and Northeastern; Chicago, Rock Island, and Pacific; and Santa Fe Central were already building into east-central New Mexico. These factors and the realization that soon someone else might build through Abo Canyon led AT&SF president E. P. Ripley to initiate work in 1902 on what would become the ERNM, more commonly known as the Belen Cutoff (Figure 3.3).

F. Meredith Jones was AT&SF's chief locating engineer, and his primary objective was to make the route as efficient as possible by keeping grades low and minimizing curvature. To accomplish this, he had multiple survey crews come from Kansas and elsewhere to spread out across east-central New Mexico and look at potential lines. Creating a new railroad was difficult in the best circumstances, and Jones wrote to James Dun, Chief Engineer, that AT&SF's people at headquarters did "not appreciate the amount of travel that is necessary to inspect on the ground all important lines," even given the small

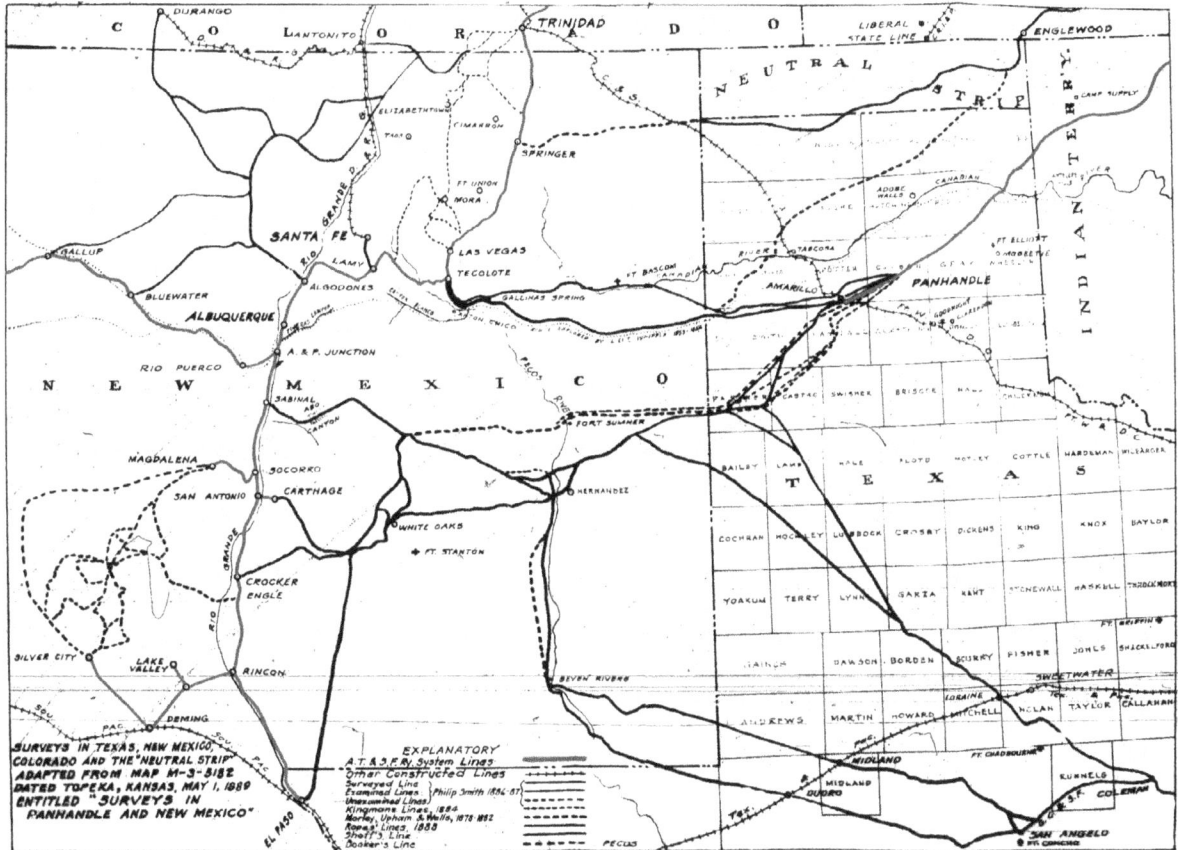

FIG 3.2
Railroad surveys in New Mexico and the Texas Panhandle
Adapted from 1889 map titled *Surveys in Panhandle and New Mexico* (Courtesy of KSHS).

FIG 3.3
The Belen Cutoff
Map adapted from *Santa Fe Lines: Colorado, New Mexico and Panhandle of Texas* (Courtesy of NMSU ASC).

FIG 3.4

Surveyors at work somewhere along the Cutoff

Photograph shows F. Meredith Jones and J. V. Key in
a typical box tent (Courtesy of KSHS).

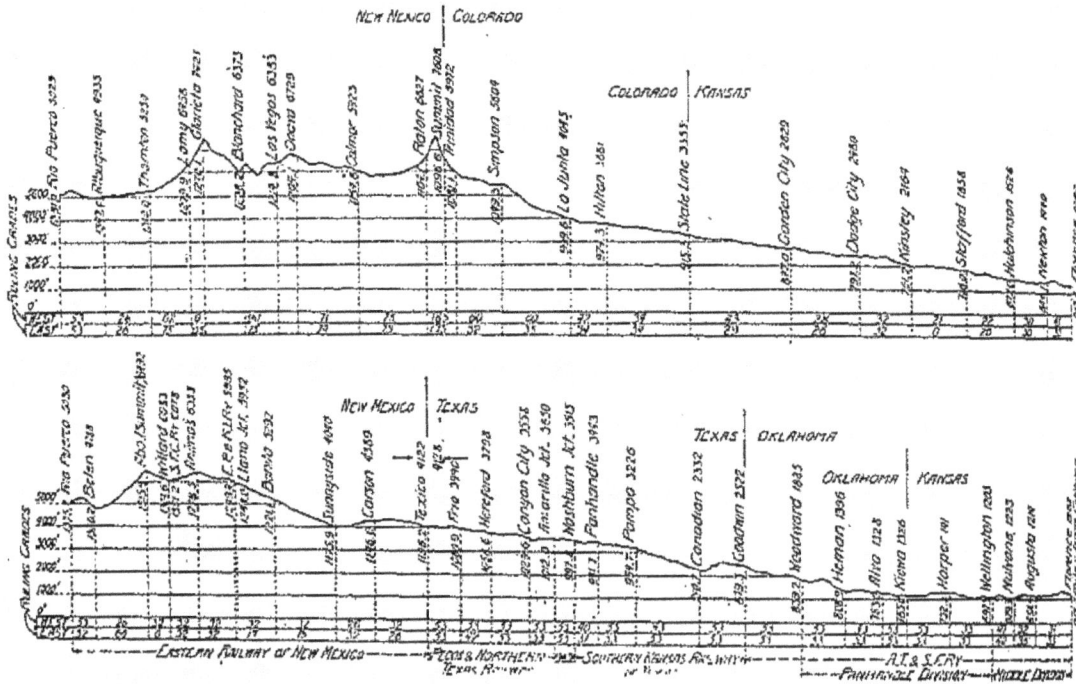

FIG 3.5

Ruling grades on the original AT&SF line and the Belen Cutoff

Chart appeared in *Santa Fe Employes' [sic] Magazine* May 1907
(Courtesy of KSHS).

FIG 3.6
Chief Locating Engineer F. Meredith Jones
Courtesy of KSHS

FIG 3.7
Charles Lantry
Charles Lantry was an owner of the
Lantry-Sharp Construction Company, the
contractors who built the Belen Cutoff
(Courtesy of KSHS).

size of the roughly 270-mile-long Cutoff (SFS 26, July 16, 1902). Towns and people were few, camping was rough, food was mostly canned, and work occurred in adverse conditions. One surveyor, Robert Dyrenforth, complained of the difficulties and dangers in a letter he sent to E. P. Ripley.

We are in a wild country; mountain lions, wild cats, and wolves are abundant. Last night while snipe hunting near camp, we were met and pursued by mountain lions. In my position as flagman, constantly behind the party, alone, it is necessary that I be well armed. . . . It might be well to have at least ten guns with about two hundred rounds of ammunition [as] the next place in which we operate is full of bears and the men feel unsafe without proper weapons with which to defend themselves (SFS 26, June 11, 1902).

Several locations became important early on in planning the ERNM, including Willard, Belen, and, most critically, Abo Canyon. Willard already had train service on the New Mexico (Santa Fe) Central by 1902 and therefore provided easy access for workers. Belen's primacy as the point where

the ERNM would join AT&SF's original north-south line from Albuquerque to El Paso was determined mostly by geography, population, and the willingness of its citizens to donate land. James Dun asked F. M. Jones to approach John Becker and other prominent businesspeople and leaders about providing land for repair shops, right-of-way, and a possible division point (SFS 26 September 26, 1902). Unlike two decades earlier, when the Perea family, wealthy residents of Bernalillo, effectively refused to sell AT&SF land for their facilities, Belen's civic boosters saw the benefits of having frequent rail traffic come through town and donated more than 100 acres. This placed Belen on two major rail lines and eventually earned it the nickname of the Hub City.

There were ways to bypass Willard or Belen, but no cost-effective route was going to avoid Abo Canyon, which allowed for passage from the Rio Grande Valley to the eastern highlands at the fairly reasonable grade of 1.25 percent (Figure 3.5). Even when most of F. M. Jones's survey crews moved all over during the latter half of 1902, the difficulties in the canyon required engineers to live there permanently and plot the area in fine detail, eventually compiling a nearly 15-foot-long

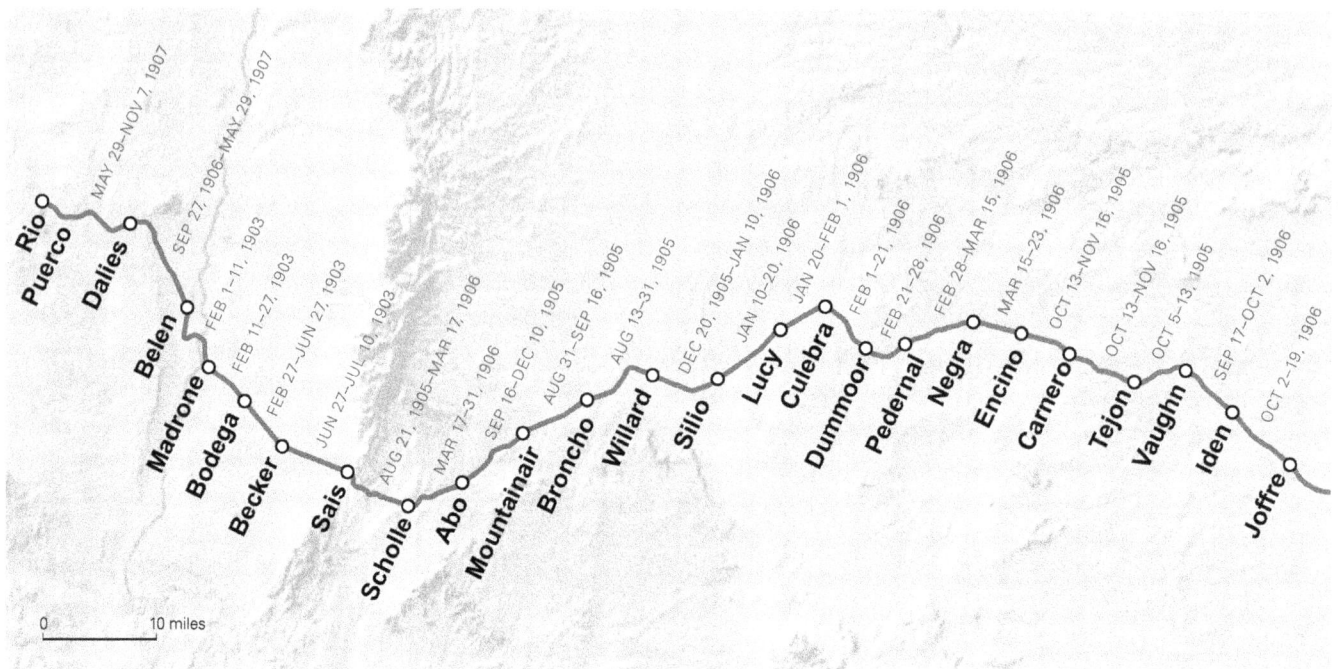

FIG 3.8
Construction dates on the Belen Cutoff

topographic map (SFS 26, F. M. Jones to J. Dun, October 21, 1902). Abo Canyon's geographic constraints seemed to mandate constructing several tunnels. Indeed, when AT&SF put out a request for bids on building the line from Belen to the summit of Abo Pass, one of the assumptions was that the route might include a tunnel almost 3,500 feet in length because of the advantages in grade and curvature (SFS 27, J. Dun to Messrs B. Lantry Sons, October 10, 1902).

Exactly where these engineers stayed in Abo Canyon is unknown, although it appears that most of their supplies, including groceries, were shipped in from AT&SF offices in Chicago. Problems with this scenario caused Jones great consternation, who wrote back to headquarters repeatedly that he just wanted to buy his materials from local merchants: "Scarcely a day passes but that I, or my men, have to go to Mr. Becker for accommodation, and we always get what we want" (SFS 26, F. M. Jones to E. S. Rice, November 1, 1902). AT&SF kept tight control of the supply line, workforce, and built environment throughout the process, including the construction phase that began early in 1903.

Constructing the ERNM: we fashion with our magic art the steel-shod pathway of the trains

On February 1, 1903, work started in Belen on the Cutoff. The ERNM had already been formed as a separate corporation to insulate AT&SF from any potential financial liabilities, teams of railroad engineers had laid out stakes to the southeast, and the firm of B. Lantry and Sons from Strong City, Kansas (also known as Lantry-Sharp Construction Company and hereafter referred to as Lantry), was engaged to build the line on up to near Willard and the juncture with the Santa Fe Central Railway. From this point forward, construction happened at a rapid pace in multiple locations—from Belen heading east and Willard heading west.

Lantry had years of experience working for AT&SF in Kansas and other locations (SFS 25, P. Smith to L. Kingman, April 30, 1888). Building railroads was a well-established industry with specialized contractors who had developed to fill the need. AT&SF sent the request for cost proposals on the ERNM to 14 firms located across the west-central United States in rail centers such as El Paso and Chicago. The successful bidder was expected to furnish "steam shovels, locomotives, cars,

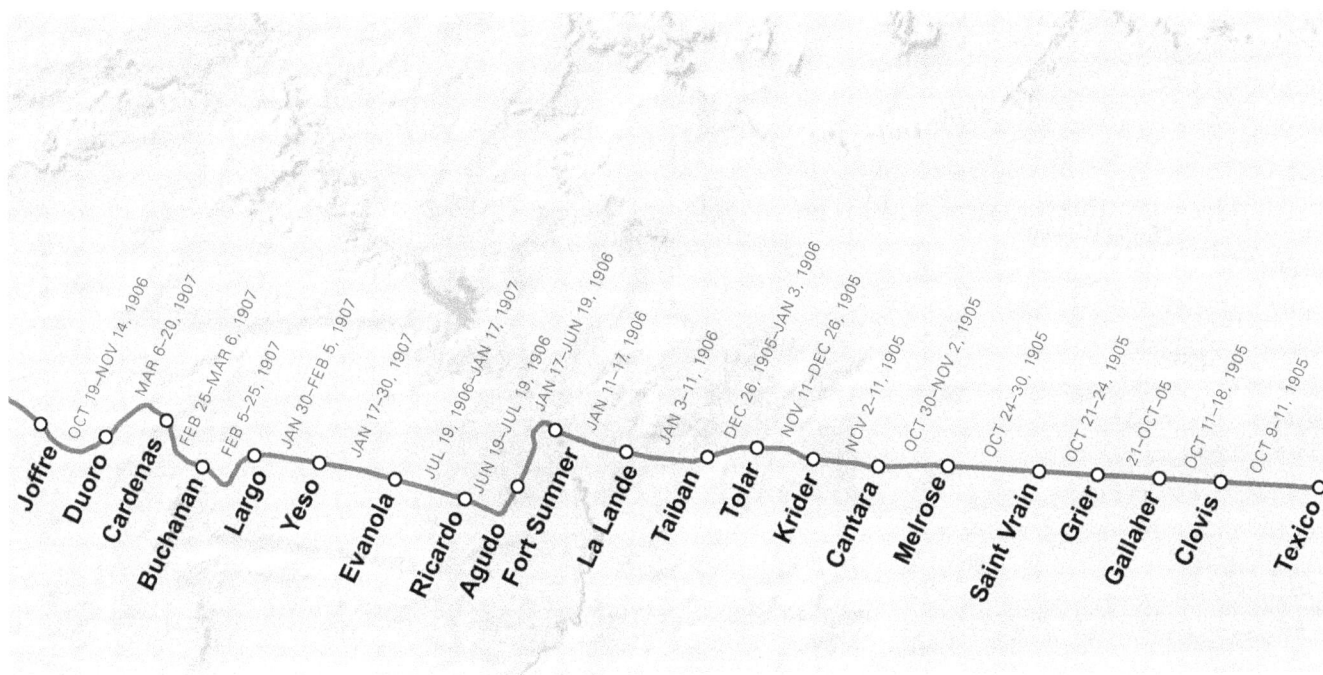

Joffre OCT 19–NOV 14, 1906 · Duoro · Cardenas MAR 6–20, 1907 · Buchanan FEB 25–MAR 6, 1907 · Largo FEB 5–25, 1907 · Yeso JAN 30–FEB 5, 1907 · Evanola JAN 17–30, 1907 · Ricardo JUL 19, 1906–JAN 17, 1907 · Agudo JUN 19–JUL 19, 1906 · Fort Sumner JAN 17–JUN 19, 1906 · La Lande JAN 11–17, 1906 · Taiban JAN 3–11, 1906 · Tolar DEC 26, 1905–JAN 3, 1906 · Krider NOV 11–DEC 26, 1905 · Cantara NOV 2–11, 1905 · Melrose OCT 30–NOV 2, 1905 · Saint Vrain OCT 24–30, 1905 · Grier OCT 21–24, 1905 · Gallaher 21-OCT-05 · Clovis OCT 11–18, 1905 · Texico OCT 9–11, 1905

unloaders, spreaders, and all other equipment [and personnel] necessary to do the work" (SFS 27, J. Dun to contractors, December 6, 1902). ERNM would furnish water for the steam engines; wood, cement, steel, and other materials for the ties, culverts, and bridges; and the rail to actually build the line.

For almost six months, construction went along more or less according to schedule (Figure 3.8 provides the dates that each segment of track was completed). A temporary wooden bridge went up across the Rio Grande, and materials and workers began moving onto the llano stretching out toward the Manzano Mountains. By late July 1903, the road was laid all the way to the mouth of Abo Canyon, and it looked as though much of the heavy work of blasting cuts, creating fills, and building bridges could be done by the end of the year. Unfortunately, national economic conditions had deteriorated enough at this point that it was difficult for railroads and other industries to borrow money. Not wanting to continue with large capital expenditures in uncertain times, AT&SF halted all work on the ERNM. The hiatus (and associated financial problems) lasted for almost two years until construction restarted in the summer of 1905. Abo Canyon and Willard continued to be the primary locations for work gangs, although by the fall other groups had begun to build west from Texico. At the close of 1906 only two sections remained unfinished—Ricardo to Duoro and Belen to Rio Puerco—and these were done by July 11, 1907 (SFS 27, S. E. Ross memorandum, February 8, 1941). Partial train service on the ERNM from Texico to Sunnyside (later known as Fort Sumner) was initiated on March 12, 1906, and the entire line became open to traffic on December 18, 1907, albeit with relatively slow travel times. Passengers leaving Texico at 11:40 a.m. would not arrive in Belen until 9:30 that evening—an average speed of 24.7 miles per hour (SFS 27, ERNM Employes' [sic] Time Table No. 2, December 18, 1907).

Organization, methods, and design

Knowing the detailed construction timeline is insufficient for understanding how the ERNM came to be built. Many questions arise about the ways AT&SF mobilized so many people. Did they all come from Kansas with Lantry, did AT&SF hire local workers, or was it more haphazard? How were they deployed and used with such effect that rigorous standardization could be maintained at some distance from the corporate offices? Given that the construction used very little mechanized

FIG 3.9
Rock drilling the Big Cut
Lantry-Sharp workers using tamping bars for
blasting the Big Cut in Abo Canyon sometime in
1906 (Courtesy of KSHS).

FIG 3.10
Engineers on the ERNM
Courtesy of NMSU ASC.

FIG 3.11
Steam shovel at work along the ERNM
Courtesy of NMSU ASC.

FIG 3.12
Collapsed falsework at the Pecos River Bridge
Bridge with falsework partially destroyed while
under construction (Courtesy of NMSU ASC).

FIG 3.13
Concrete construction on the Pecos River Bridge
Cement mixer and men dumping buckets of concrete
from crane sometime in 1906 (Courtesy of NMSU ASC).

FIG 3.14
Mule teamster in Abo Canyon
Teamster packing up a mule sometime around 1905
to 1906 (Courtesy of KSHS).

FIG 3.15
7th Crossing Abo Arroyo
Photograph taken in 1905 or 1906, view east at
Bridge 871.4 (Courtesy of KSHS).

equipment, how is it possible they built the line in around 30 months, a schedule fairly similar to that for the parallel route BNSF constructed in 2011 in Abo Canyon?

Answering these questions required disparate historical sources, each with their own strengths and weaknesses. AT&SF records focus on engineers and contractors employed, cubic yards moved, pounds of steel and wooden railroad ties purchased, and miles of track completed. Archival photographs provide tantalizing clues about the ethnic composition of the workforce and types of equipment commonly in use. Oral histories let us know that local families helped with construction in various ways. The few remaining pieces of correspondence allow the reader to imagine more fully the human beings who worked long, hard days to realize the new route. Often the relationships between the data are unclear, but a composite picture does emerge.

Organization of the engineers was a reasonably simple affair. AT&SF had a well-defined hierarchy that ranged from Chief System Engineer James Dun on down to the Engineers in Charge for the Eastern and Western Divisions of the ERNM, A. J. Hemstreet and J. V. Key, respectively. In turn, Hemstreet

and Key had resident engineers from AT&SF working for them, Messrs. McCoy, Mudge, and Tulley, to name a few (SFS 27, List of Engineers ERNM). These engineers often had worked previously all over the AT&SF system and came from a variety of backgrounds (Ducker 1983). It was their job to lay out line, check on the quality of contractors' work, and make important strategic decisions—success was theirs, but so was any failure. As construction progressed, AT&SF brought personnel from their Oklahoma and Kansas divisions to run the trains that moved personnel and equipment where necessary (SFS 27, J. Dun to J. W. Kendrick, November 9, 1905). The majority of workers, however, came from the contractors (with their various specialties) that actually built the line, for example:

» Lantry-Sharp: constructing the line from Belen to Texico
» A. Moore: grading portions of the line and terminals
» Nelson & McLeod: erecting engine and boiler houses, water treatment plants, Harvey Houses, depots, and other facilities
» Roberts & Schaeffer Co.: coaling facilities
» McVey Brothers: well drilling
» Gross Kelly & Co. (Gross Kelly): ties and timber

FIG 3.16
Blasting the Big Cut in Abo Canyon
Photograph taken in 1905 or 1906, view west-southwest
at the Big Cut (Courtesy of KSHS).

Most individuals worked for Lantry, which maintained large construction camps at the critical points along the line, including Sunnyside and Abo Canyon. Lantry's records are no longer available, but it is apparent that they employed both skilled and unskilled laborers. Even though specialized equipment was rare, there was a great need for masons, bridgemen, carpenters, and blasters (more commonly known as powder monkeys). At Sunnyside and the long span of the Pecos River with its 14 piers, AT&SF required "a large force of bridgemen and masons [as] it is one of the most important things [on] the Eastern Railway of New Mexico" (SFS 27, J. Dun to Lantry-Sharp, December 28, 1905). Hundreds of people worked at Sunnyside laying falsework for the temporary bridge and track (shoo-fly) and using pile drivers, pumps, and derricks to excavate and build the piers. Concrete was even placed underwater with equipment such as the "Cyclopean Deep Sea Bucket" created for just that purpose (ibid.).

In Abo Canyon, another very large camp included a variety of individuals: carpenters who built the massive forms for the piers, the many people who excavated the cuts and created the extensive fills, quarrymen working at the Sais crusher

to create ballast, and the hundreds of mules that helped the entire process. The heavy rock work and significant amounts of consequent blasting required Lantry to hire a number of powder monkeys. Among this group were a few Kaysers (mentioned elsewhere in Chapters 2, 4, and 5) who lived nearby in Mountainair and had experience using black powder for blasting (P. Kayser 2007 and G. Kayser 2007). Local residents also rented their mule teams and fresno scrapers or acted as teamsters running supplies from Belen to camp (Padilla and Padilla 2008).

A variety of business other than wage labor occurred between AT&SF and New Mexico families and companies. Obtaining water for steam engines was always a concern, and members of the Sisneros family residing at Abo sold rights to use their *ojo* (spring), which proved critical for the trains heading up the steep grade through Abo Pass. Benjamin Spencer contracted with AT&SF to provide 240,000 board feet of timber from his mill at Eastview a few miles to the northeast (SFS 26, F. M. Jones to J. Dun, August 6, 1902). Additionally, Gross Kelly supplied most of the ties for construction from the Manzano Mountains and their other mills in Glorieta and Las Vegas—an average of 3,500 ties per mile and 247,000 alone for the

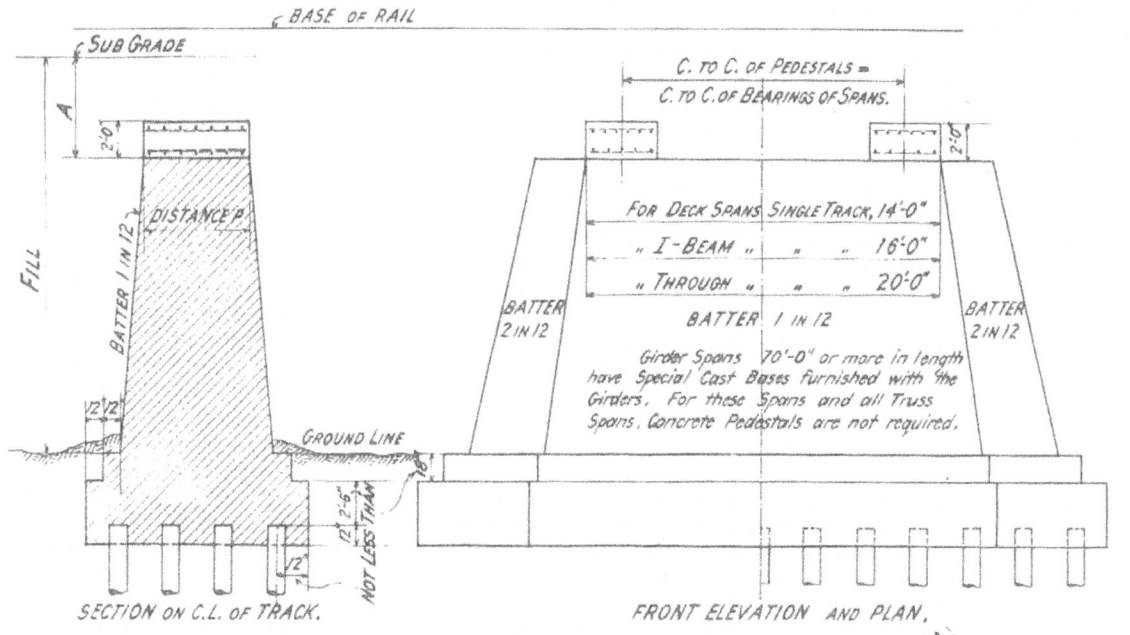

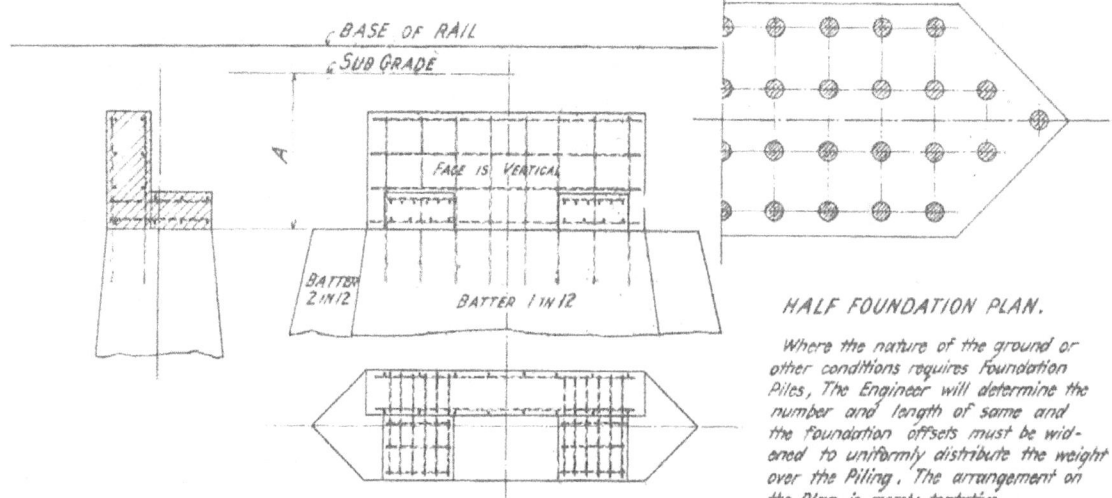

FIG 3.17
Standard plans for concrete abutments and piers
Adapted from AT&SF plans, July 1910, AT&SF (1978).

FIG 3.18
Swinging the last girder into place
Photograph taken in 1906, view northwest at Bridge
871.5 in the east end of Abo Canyon (Courtesy of KSHS).

72-mile segment between Vaughn and Sunnyside (SFS 27, J. Dun to W. E. Hodges, March 27, 1906).

All work on the Cutoff had to be completed to AT&SF's rigorous specifications that allowed for running a rail network covering thousands of miles. The new line was expected to be permanent, well built, and ready for service, differing from the early Union Pacific and Central Pacific Railroads that emphasized speedy construction (which would need almost immediate replacement) to ensure the companies promptly received loans and subsidies from the federal government.

Despite the need for accuracy, Lantry was able to lay an average of 1 mile of track per day in most of 1906 with only the benefit of mules, wagons, and a few steam shovels, (SFS 27, J. Dun to W. E. Hodges, May 12, 1906).

Design standards applied to everything from culverts to coaling stations, and switches to signs. An engineer may have ended up working in California one week and Kansas the next; seeing a similar piece of equipment facilitated those transitions. The bridges in Abo Canyon and at the Pecos River provide good examples of standardized structures that varied greatly in their construction techniques—100-foot-long, prefabricated

steel girders from American Bridgeworks atop concrete piers designed for use in watercourses and proportional to the length of spans (Figure 3.17). Just a few plan sets provided sufficient guidelines for construction, except for variations dictated by local geology and the bridge engineers' expertise.

On the ground and in the camps

Determining what life was like for individuals building the Belen Cutoff, or who they were, is difficult. When did most workdays begin and end? What were people eating, and how much did their experiences differ based on race, class, job skill, or other factors? Much of the information that could help address these complex questions is lacking, but we do have photographs, letters, interviews, newspaper articles, and pieces of stories passed on from one railroader to another. Three individuals provide the dominate narratives of life on the Cutoff: Al Keener, Tom Seery, and F. T. Tulley. Close association with the railroad is common to all of these men. Keener became a locomotive engineer after working on the construction, Seery grew up at the largest Lantry-Sharp camp in Abo Canyon where his father ran the commissary, and Tulley was employed by AT&SF as a resident engineer.

FIG 3.19
Placing a 100-foot girder on the Pecos River Bridge
Photograph taken in 1906, view west-southwest at the Pecos
River Bridge and shoo-fly track (Courtesy of NMSU ASC).

FIG 3.20
Construction camp at the east end of Abo Canyon
Photograph view east-southeast toward the Big Cut and
a Lantry-Sharp construction camp near milepost 871.7,
sometime in 1905 or 1906 (Courtesy of KSHS)

FIG 3.21
Work crew constructing bridge piers on the Pecos River
Photograph of construction crew (with a steam boiler, cement
mixer, and shoo-fly track) building Pier 10 on the Pecos River
Bridge sometime in 1906 (Courtesy of NMSU ASC).

It is worth repeating here the immense debt our research owes to Randy Dunson (himself a third-generation railroad worker on the Cutoff) for recording the experiences of Keener, Seery, and other AT&SF employees when they worked together in the 1970s and 1980s. Dunson forms the end of a lineage for direct transmission of oral-historical knowledge on the railroad: he worked as a fireman for the engineer L. P. Clay, who in turn had fired for Carl Peverly, an engineer who ran a work engine during construction of the Cutoff. Further, Randy's scholarship and interest in the Belen Cutoff, together with his collection of photographs and associated materials, is without parallel. Unless otherwise specified, much of our discussion below is drawn from Randy's work with former AT&SF employees.

These primary narratives, however, present limited viewpoints, particularly for Seery, who was a small child at the time, and reflect an existence of at least partial privilege. Keener, Seery, and Tulley were not local or Hispano and therefore provide no information about what happened to those residents who needed a job and tried to hire on to the numerous labor crews. We are fortunate to have these accounts, although it is important not to extrapolate from them some kind of universal experience. What was likely common to all were harsh conditions with long hours outside in the rain and snow, constantly exposed to the wind and sun.

The need for hundreds of workers to construct the Cutoff exceeded the supply of locally available labor in eastern New Mexico. Few people lived in the area along the ERNM's route, and many were already at work on other nearby rail projects such as the Santa Fe Central. As a result, a significant percentage of the workforce came from Kansas following Lantry. Many of them also stayed on to try their luck at homesteading or to work on the railroad they would help build. Al Keener provides a good example of this process.

He came out from Kansas to New Mexico as a young man, thinking he had found a low-cost way to see the world. Signing on with Lantry covered the price of transportation to the territory but also meant Keener had to work for a while just to pay back his advance wages. Armed guards were on patrol to ensure nobody left without honoring his debt. Keener started at the main camp in Abo Canyon near the bridge at milepost 872.9. His job consisted of pouring concrete into the

FIG 3.22
Mule teams moving fill near the Sais crusher
Photograph of mule teams loading up fill from a cut in Abo
Canyon, sometime during 1903 to 1906 (Courtesy of KSHS).

large piers under construction. With the assistance of a mule and block and tackle, Keener ran loaded wheelbarrows all day for weeks on end, but the rigors of the job eventually got to him. Keener and a friend used a gun to try to force a teamster to smuggle them out of the canyon. More amused than concerned, the teamster relented, hid the boys under a tarp, and transported them to Belen. Ironically, Keener returned only a few years later, having been hired in 1909 as a fireman on an AT&SF locomotive running along the ERNM.

Conditions were much easier for Tom Seery, growing up at the age of four or five in Abo Canyon. His father's position running the commissary must have afforded him special treatment, and the camp would have seemed more a source of excitement than drudgery. During a recorded interview with Randy Dunson in 1983, Seery recalled his impressions of life in Lantry's main camp in Abo Canyon.

We had a wood floor. I remember Dad had charge of the commissary and there was quite a camp. When I was a kid, they'd come in at night, feed the horses and get them ready, and then they'd eat and they'd go to

bed. And they'd get up the next morning and feed the horses and get ready and then hitch 'em up and take off. Each fella had a scraper and a team of horses that he handled. And that was the way they moved the dirt outta those cuts.

They had quite a gang there. They had a big cook tent and cooks and tables. Oh, yeah, they had to shoe those horses and take care of them and all. Yeah, I wouldn't doubt if there was a blacksmith's shop. And then outside of the cook tent, they had a duck farm [platform?] probably as big as this divan is square, and a pool right in the center with steps comin' up to it. They would buy their meat down in Albuquerque, put it on a rope, and pull it up. I can remember the coyotes and wolves fighting around there trying to get to that meat.

Well, I can't remember too much about building the cuts, because they wouldn't let me go up in there. I can remember them going out in the mornings and coming back at night. Oh, they must have had thirty-five, forty horses there at the tents, you know. They fed them in the tent, and they had to have the hay, and the grain,

L-S Con. Co's Corrall, Cam 2

FIG 3.23
Mule corral at the main Lantry-Sharp construction camp in Abo Canyon
Photograph view northeast at the mule corral at the main Lantry-Sharp
construction camp in Abo Canyon, sometime in 1905 or 1906,
(Courtesy of KSHS).

*and the water, and they had a creek down there. The
bank was about eight, nine feet higher at this time, and
they'd get out and go down and take their animals down
there and let them drink and bring 'em back.*

*There was a young fella there that he wanted to
kill a coyote or a wolf and send the hide back to his folks
someplace in the East. So one evening after they got the
horses all put up for the night he'd saw a coyote across
the canyon over there, and he shot it and he hit it. And
it just started goin' round and round. So he rushed in,
got his coat on, and his hat and his gun, and he took off.
He was goin' over there to get it. Well, by the time he
got over there, the coyote or the wolf, whatever it was,
had run away. And he followed the blood, and he got
lost. And he had sense enough to stay where he was
until morning, so he could see again. So he did. And of
course, everybody in camp was excited about him; he
hadn't got in. Anyway, he never did find the animal, and
the next morning, here he come in. He stayed out all
night. But it was pretty wild up there.*

*One morning there at Camp 2, we got up—'course
I didn't, I was too young to know, I heard the folks bab-
bling about it later—but there were two coyotes killed
right by our wall, right outside the camp wall. Shot 'em
one morning, and I can remember the coyotes and
wolves fighting over this platform. Tryin' a get up there
to get that fresh meat, ya know?*

*Another thing there was a little cow and she had a
calf, and the little one was born and the wolves killed it.
The next night, she come down through the camp there
just bellowing and hollerin' for the calf and everything
else and that evening the men decided that they were
gonna have to put a stop to that 'cause, uh, between her
and the wolves, nobody got any sleep. So I think there
were about six men that had guns and that night they
went up to where this little carcass was—that calf—and
they just laid down waiting. I think they killed five or six
wolves that night there and that put a stop to some of
the noise. Finally the mother gave up because bellowing and calling for the calf didn't produce anything, so
we got some sleep* (Seery 1983).

FIG 3.24
Helping survey the Cutoff
This photograph was taken sometime
in 1905 or 1906. The dog pictured
belonged to Bert Day, instrument man
for F. T. Tulley (Courtesy of NMSU ASC).

FIG 3.25
Dr. Lovelace at the AT&SF hospital in Sunnyside
Photograph of Dr. William Lovelace in Sunnyside some-
time in 1908 (Courtesy of NMSU ASC).

Specific details about the construction and workers' lives are somewhat lacking in the accounts of Keener and Seery. This contrasts with the vivid recollections in several letters F. T. Tulley sent to Lee Myers, a Carlsbad journalist, who wrote an article on the Belen Cutoff for *New Mexico Magazine* in April 1964. These letters help us understand labor conditions and also provide information on early settlement and boosterism in the region (discussed further in Chapter 4). Tulley was 82 when he described his experiences, but his memories of being a young engineer appear to be excellent.

I arrived at Texico in June, 1905, with [a] box car along a cinder platform for a depot. [There was] one house and several saloons with wide-open gambling in full sway. We had a field party staking the center line westward to Vaughn 140 miles. We were the [AT&SF] construction resident engineers [and] by October [I] headed for my new residency 100 miles west of Texico with seven wagons of camp equipment, groceries, and water. We had an office, field tent, commissary, cook and stable tent. We had [a] team and spring wagon for transportation of the surveying party, farm wagons for handeling [sic] supplies, and [a] wagon for water; no wells or streams near my camp.

We were on the edge of Gillespie Draw and near a contractor's construction camp where we boarded until our camp could be set up. We found no water in the wagon and the only place was to drive the sheep out of the sink holes and dip up a whitish colored liquid which our native driver cleared up for us by burning grocery boxes and making charcoal which [was] deposited in the barrels [and] became clear spring water, [although] later we learned to use alum.

We hauled coal from Santa Rosa. After the winter broke we had newspapers and magazine delivery by a man with three burros. He would stock up at Albuquerque, come down to Belen and through the Abo Canyon, Mountainair, Willard, Vaughn, my camp, Sunnyside, McFarland camp, on to Texico & Amarillo, 370 miles each way, so you see, we did not get the late editions.

Besides our engineers in charge of all the work, we would have an occasional visit from two sisters

FIG 3.26
AT&SF engineers' camp in Sunnyside
Photograph of AT&SF engineers at the Sunnyside camp
sometime in 1905 or 1906 (Courtesy of KSHS).

with [a] driver, driving from Amarillo to collect for the hospital which was where at first all our casualties had to go until the track was finally laid to Suunyside [sic] and Lantry-Sharp set up a hospital with [a] doctor (Dr. Lovelace) and two nurses (very popular [as they were the] only white girls closer than 70 miles).

The camp at Sunnyside was a huge affair with the dinning [sic] tent as large as a circus tent. Immediately sprang up tent saloons and gambling of all kinds, long tents, narrow. First on the left was roulette, then on [the] right a [illegible] and on back any other game you could name. Eventually came a tent [with a] small dance floor on front of the bar and several bedroom tents in a string behind them. The women [there] were older & rugged looking but the men laborers were rugged too. Later a two-story frame was built not far from the building you mentioned, bar and dance floor below and an outside stair & bedrooms above.

In the morn[ing] you saw a group of men, you went over and there would be a dead body. There was not any law closer than Santa Rosa, Portales, or Roswell.

The Lantry-Sharp commissary man came over, examined him for name and valuables; never any valuables and generally no name. Being sandy, a gang would dig a hole there, roll him in, and drive a stake. There were 200 or 300 men [in Sunnyside].

While camped at my residency we sent a team and wagon to Santa Rosa for coal and groceries. He got caught in a blizzard coming back and arrived a week late with 500 pounds of coal, very few groceries and nearly all the wagon gone, chopped up to build fires with and the mule feed [was] played out [so we] ate flour, grape nuts, and canned corn warmed at the fire. [The team and wagon] had to start right back and we lived in our overcoats until he came back.

Those were wild days at Sunnyside. I played roulette one night and won $2000 but only got out of the tent with $560. The hoboes [sic] crowded around me so tite [sic] I could not move and when I would be putting a winning in my pocket, someone was [already] robbing it. So I could not leave (I'd of been one of those dead men) until a bunch of engineers went looking for

FIG 3.27
A Blast
Blasting a cut somwhere on the Cutoff during 1905 to 1907
(Courtesy of NMSU ASC).

FIG 3.28
Pouring concrete on a pier
Pouring concrete on the 5th pier at the Pecos River bridge
sometime during 1905 or 1906
(Courtesy of NMSU ASC).

Pile Driver
June 13th

FIG 3.29
Driving pilings on the ERNM
Driving pilings for a bridge pier near Ricardo on June 13, 1907
(Courtesy of NMSU ASC).

me and escorted me to the stone house. There were
five saloons very soon at Texico where our home office
and material yard was. The gambling tables were [so]
crowded you could hardly squeeze in or out (NMSU ASC, F.
T. Tulley to Lee Myers, February 3, 1963).

The temporary settlements that sprang up near railroad construction in the West during the nineteenth and twentieth centuries had reputations for being wild places. A combination of gambling, prostitution, rampant alcohol consumption, and periodic violence led some to call these locations hell on wheels. Conditions appear to have been similar along the Belen Cutoff; with the camps came the camp followers. Problems with a saloon near Epris became significant enough for Grant Brothers Construction that they wrote a letter to the territorial governor in June 1906 asking him to close the establishment because it is "a serious detriment to our work" (Dunson collection, Grant Brothers Construction to H. J. Hagerman, June 14, 1906).

Murder was not uncommon, although it was infrequently mentioned in newspapers. For example, some Swedish workers killed two of the camp's prostitutes in Abo Canyon, most likely for giving them a venereal disease. Others in the Lantry

camp did not approve of the Swedes' actions and responded by hanging them under the bridge at milepost 872.9. (The bridges are commonly associated with death in stories about construction [some apocryphal], either by hanging or accidental burial in the concrete piers. Bridge stories continue to be told by railroad workers to this day.) The April 9, 1903, edition of the Santa Fe *New Mexican* did detail an incident that occurred in Lantry-Sharp's grading camp.

On Sunday night a man named Campbell, with several
companions, went into the saloon of Everitt & Reed [in
Abo Canyon]. After taking a few drinks, a quarrel arose
between the men and Everitt. Campbell finally went
behind the bar and commenced to beat Everitt over the
head with bottles. . . . Everitt secured [a] revolver. He
fired, but claims he did not know anyone was hit until
after the saloon was closed. Fearing he would be mur-
dered, Everitt struck out across country and went 40
miles with his face covered with blood [until] he reached
Belen, and from there drove to Los Lunas, where he
gave himself up to the sheriff.

FIG 3.30
Teamster holding a wagon somewhere on the ERNM
Teamster holding a wagon and mule team under a culvert
somewhere along the ERNM (Courtesy of KSHS).

One incident of violence indicates the workforce was ethnically diverse and subject to a variety of tensions. In 1905, a number of African Americans were employed as teamsters in digging the cut and fill near Tolar. One of them got into a fight with the AT&SF engineers' camp cook at Taiban. After being kicked out of the kitchen, the teamster went and got Atlantic Red, a friend with a reputation for fighting. Red lay in wait for the cook (Mr. Stout) and cut open his gut with a large knife. Stout retaliated despite his injuries and, finding a pick handle close at hand, "scattered [Atlantic Red's] brains in all directions" (Santa Fe *New Mexican*, August 22, 1905). The conflict led to a race riot in the camp that caused the death of at least eight individuals, who are allegedly buried in the huge fill at Tolar. This echoes another common legend among railroaders (with little supporting evidence) that combines bridges and racial unrest in rumors of possible lynching.

After the Cutoff: shout across the chasms wide the war song of the engineer

Building new lines for the railroad, even normal employment with the AT&SF, was more than a regular job for many. In his study of workers on the AT&SF from 1860 to 1900, Ducker (1983) comments on the pride railroaders had in their vocation and the significant amount of esprit de corps. The work was dangerous, romantic, and associated with speed and travel in a time when these qualities were not common. By the early twentieth century, AT&SF and its employees had absorbed a certain sense of messianic purpose, as exemplified in Figure 3.31. Even after the ERNM was only partially complete, there already was settlement in its wake. F. T. Tulley commented on this, noting "as soon as track was laid, homeseeker excursions were run every two weeks.... A little town sprang up, [and] lawyers came in" (NMSU ASC, F. T. Tulley to Lee Myers, February 3, 1963). The process really started to accelerate after the Belen Cutoff was officially complete (as commemorated by driving a golden spike at Rio Puerco on May 14, 1908) (Socorro Chieftain, May 16, 1908).

F. M. Jones, Chief Locating Engineer on the Cutoff, was aware of the importance of building railroads and the changes they could cause. In May 1907, just after building the ERNM, he wrote an article about locating railroads in the *Santa Fe Employe's* [sic] *Magazine*.

FIG 3.31
Westward the star of empire takes its way
AT&SF poster (dated approximately 1870 to 1890) promoting travel
on its lines in the western United States (Courtesy of KSHS).

*The subduing and settling of the great West has
extended along lines parallel with the railroad development of the country. The building of a railroad through
a sparsely settled district is usually followed by a
heavy influx of population. New conditions are brought
about, new values created, new towns built and old
ones abandoned or moved to the railroad.*

*Where new towns are required it is better that
the company should handle them, not for all that can
be squeezed out of them, but for the building up of
a compact community which will create business for
the railway. Every endeavor should be made to keep
out speculators, and lots should be sold at a reasonable figure to those who would improve them. Such
a policy would recommend itself to any community
and would inspire a friendly feeling toward the railway company which would head off many a piece of
adverse railway legislation.*

Jones' perspective was not particularly unique or revelatory;
many others voiced similar sentiments. As we consider in the

following chapters, the paternalistic tone of the AT&SF—the
railroad's interests are the country's interests—had positive
and negative regional consequences. Surveyors such as Jones
began the process that brought hundreds of individuals to the
area for work on the ERNM. These men all had different agen-
das and pursued a variety of occupations after the Belen Cutoff
was built. Many of them stayed on in New Mexico to homestead and helped fulfill the prediction of a heavy population
influx following construction. Jones' idea of new settlement
benevolently managed by AT&SF for its interests, however,
would prove a little messier and be subject to various forces
and narratives from inside and outside territorial New Mexico.

4TH OF JULY CELEBRATION

Mountainair, New Mexico

Everybody invited.   Something doing all the day and long into the night.   Governor Merritt C. Mechem and other noted speakers will address the people.   The Mountainair Military Band of 23 pieces will furnish the music assisted by community singers and quartets.

RODEO

Big Purses for the best bronco riders; the most expert in roping; tieing and bull dogging the wildest steers obtainable in these parts; for the person who can rope a goat, do a clown stunt on a burro, or catch a goose. Fat mens' race, Baseball, Dancing all day and long into the night. A wild west show with the restraint of modern humanitarianism.   Parking space for automobiles within the inclosure. Remain in your cars and see the whole performance.

Women and Girls, and Boys under 15 will be admitted free to the Rodeo

FREE BARBECUE

Two thousand pounds of barbecued beef; 600 loaves of bread; gallons of the choicest Mocha and Java coffee; barrels of pickles and great cauldrens of the Pinto Beans which has made Mountainair the most celebrated bean shipping point in the United States, and cooked in that inimitable way known to those who first planted the seed and used them for food.

BOXING MATCH

By followers of the manly art, properly staged.

Baby Show And Beauty Contest

Will be held at the Auditorium.   The county Health Officer and County Nurse will be judges. Prizes for the most beautiful girl.   Come and see the ex-service men put to route.

Come up and join us in the celebration of this, our National day.   Help us sing America and Star Spangled Banner.

HELP US CELEBRATE IN MOUNTAINAIR

4 | Ho! To the land of sunshine: the beginnings of large-scale settlement, boosterism, and agriculture

The first few decades after construction of the Belen Cutoff brought deep changes to east-central New Mexico. Populations increased as Hispano and Anglo families began to claim large amounts of land under the various Homestead acts. Villages and towns such as Scholle, Mountainair, Willard, and Clovis grew up along the rail line and formed communities of influence and interest, eventually coming to pursue their own goals and aspirations. Boosterism was the secular religion of the time, and civic and business leaders were expected to rally in support of their municipality. Several key factors allowed for expansion: homesteading, the railroad town in its many forms, and a developing agricultural industry, including the mighty pinto bean in Mountainair. This chapter looks at these issues and considers the narratives employed in support of homesteading and boosterism using newspapers of the period as primary resources. Of particular interest is the audience for these periodicals and who was excluded from the stories used to explain these communities to themselves and the broader world.

As described in Chapter 2, the mid-nineteenth century in east-central New Mexico was subject to significant change and population movement. Hispano family groups were splitting off from their parent villages in the riverine valleys and establishing new settlements such as Abo and Cienega. In time these communities spawned others while retaining their ties to the extended family networks through compadrasco. The trend of expansion eastward from the Rio Grande corridor onto the plains and south along the Pecos River would eventually intersect with what historian Richard White (1993) called a "stream of migration" flowing westward, mostly following the new rail lines, including the ERNM. Further complicating the story in the twentieth century is the small flood of Mexican migrants who moved north to escape political uncertainties during the Mexican Revolution. These currents may have been complex and often conflicting, but many politicians, newspaper editors, and other luminaries saw the new rail lines and settlement and predicted good times for the territory of New Mexico in the early twentieth century.

The promotion industry: every day the wonder grows

New Mexico's civic and business leaders were not content merely to prophesy about the territory's imminent success, they also hedged their bets and were complicit in trying to bring it about. Newspaper editorials and advertisements repeated news of growth many times over and amplified (or even invented) positive results. This process functioned on a broad level where New Mexico and companies such as AT&SF developed materials for potential immigrants and locally where boosterism for individual communities was the norm. A September 30, 1905, editorial from the Socorro *Chieftain* summarizes many of these sentiments and notes that the right kind of people are coming, a slightly enigmatic opinion considered in greater detail later in this chapter.

The tide of emigration has at last turned toward the great Southwest and New Mexico may as well get ready for such an era of prosperity as she has never

New Mexico's Growth: Never in Better Condition

I never saw the Territory in better condition. It has been a good year for cattle, sheep, and agriculture. The railroads are adding more miles to the trackage in the Territory each year, and at present the Santa Fe is hard at work on the cut-off between Texico and Belen [where] about 2,000 men are employed. In about three months, work will begin upon a line 300 miles long which will open up a part of the Territory hitherto not easily accessible.

The sheep raisers have had the best season they have ever before experienced since they began to keep records. There are now 6,000,000 sheep in the Territory. . . . The tourist travel is greater than ever before, and the country is awakening to the fact that New Mexico is one of the most delightful spots in the whole United States.

Colonel Max Frost, editor of the Santa Fe New Mexican, the premier territorial publication, commenting on New Mexico's excellent fortunes in an October 21, 1905, article from the Socorro *Chieftain*.

yet experienced. The half of the story of the Territory's natural resources has never yet been told. This favored land is already known to be rich in possibilities in all lines of agriculture, stock raising, mining, and manufacturing, but every day the wonder grows. The right kind of people and the necessary capital are coming this way, and the next few years will see a gratifying development here in all lines of industry. New railroads will be built, new areas opened to agriculture, new towns established, old towns built to metropolitan proportions, and, in short, the population and wealth of New Mexico increased to many times their present number and value. The fact is that all this movement is now in progress and those who are already here will do well if they are prepared to witness and to profit by its consummation.

Opinion makers like the editor above found voice in New Mexico's newspapers and other periodicals. They employed a variety of rhetorical tools to support their arguments, but none was so frequently used as statistics describing growth in population, agriculture, and other efforts. This mania for

quantification produced a series of similar articles that extolled the territory's success by tabulating different data. For example, in 1906, New Mexico broke the record for the total number of homestead entries made over a "large area" within a three-month period (a record so oddly constructed it might yet stand to this day) (Socorro *Chieftain*, March 24, 1906). The popularity of scientific agriculture (discussed elsewhere in Chapter 4) would eventually bloom in this context, where information and statistics were used to support previously held assertions.

In this spirit of celebrating data, it is worth considering here the population census for the area of the Belen Cutoff, which includes Valencia, Socorro, Torrance, Guadalupe, DeBaca, Quay, and Curry Counties (Figure 4.1). New Mexico's population increased around 30 percent per decade for 70 years, with the counties along the ERNM doing roughly the same thing. There is one major exception: from the 1900 to 1910 census, New Mexico grew by 67 percent and the area along the Belen Cutoff grew by almost 140 percent. Some of this increase on the ERNM is a result of shifting county boundaries and Hispanos moving from river communities up to the highlands (although often these individuals were just moving

	1870	1880	1890	1900	1910	1920	1930
Population in New Mexico	91,874	119,565	160,282	195,310	327,301	360,350	423,317
Growth in New Mexico since the previous decade	–	30.1%	34.1%	21.9%	67.6%	10.1%	17.5%
Population in the counties on the Belen Cutoff	15,696	20,970	23,471	31,519	75,482	70,478	71,623
Growth on the Cutoff since the previous decade	–	33.6%	11.9%	34.3%	139.5%	–6.6%	1.6%

FIG 4.1

Populations in New Mexico and counties along the Belen Cutoff (1870 to 1930)
Data compiled from decennial census reports from the United States
Census Bureau (USCB) 1932a; 1921; 1913a; 1901; 1895a; 1882a; 1872

to a different location within Socorro and Valencia Counties). This decade of growth represents a historically significant influx of newcomers from outside the territory.

The stories of how this many people came to the region are complex and not easily summarized, but White (1993) identified three dominant modes of migration: kinship networks, the utopian settler, and the "modern" immigrant with access to communication networks. Most of the settlers who came to east-central New Mexico in the wake of the ERNM were of the third category, and we now turn to considering the types of mass media—newspapers, advertising, pamphlets, etc.—that they would have been exposed to on a frequent basis.

Newspapers and immigration bulletins: homesteaders have come to stay

Thomas Jefferson (1819 [1903]) once notably wrote that "advertisements... contain the only truths to be relied on in a newspaper." That sentiment could easily be retooled to describe New Mexican English-language newspapers of the early twentieth century—advertisements were the only thing one could expect and rely on. Journalism and accurate reporting were present in periodicals of the time, but often boosterism made many of the stories read like sales pitches. At one point in the 1920s, the Belen *News* functioned exclusively as a publication for syndicated material, legal notices (such as homestead applications), and advertisements. The system did have a certain elegant logic where ads for railroads and budding towns ran concurrently with stories on the success of the people who just recently had taken these same immigrant trains and helped to found new settlements. Of particular interest is how the newspapers, farmers, government agencies, and railroads interacted and amplified each other's message.

Many of the newcomers came from Kansas, Texas, Oklahoma, the Indian Territory, and other midwestern locations that had only recently been homesteaded and opened to farming. Arthur Curren, United States Land Commissioner, noted that the "homesteaders have come to stay. They have purchased land and are erecting houses. They will build New Mexico just like their fathers developed the great territories to the east" (Santa Fe *New Mexican*, November 13, 1905). Settlers were attracted to dry-land farming along with irrigated lands, although these opportunities were limited on the Cutoff to Fort

FIG 4.2
Kayser homestead near Eastview
The Paul Fredrick August Kayser VI homestead near
Eastview in 1921 (Courtesy of Frank Wimberly).

Sumner and the area along the Pecos River. J. M. Connell, general passenger agent for AT&SF, noted that "New Mexico and Arizona have also secured their share of immigrants, the New Mexico Immigration Bureau having done good work to advertise the territory" (Santa Fe *New Mexican*, November 20, 1905).

Newspapers frequently discussed new settlement in eastern New Mexico counties during the early twentieth century. One particular article from January 15, 1903, illustrates the nexus of interest in attracting people to the territory. The Santa Fe *New Mexican* (owned by Max Frost) celebrated the issuance of 130,000 bulletins by the Bureau of Immigration (whose secretary was Max Frost) and mentioned how "railroads running through New Mexico aided greatly in advertising the resources and conditions.... The members of the bureau are deserving of the thanks of the people of the territory for their unselfish labors for the advancement and prosperity of New Mexico." It was not just the newspapermen, government, and railroads who participated in this effort; homesteaders and settlers were also engaged, as shown in this item from the December 5, 1905, edition of the Santa Fe *New Mexican*.

SETTLING RAPIDLY: Roosevelt County Attractive to Many New Settlers—Fifty Miles of Cut-off Built.

Roosevelt County is evidently one of the most rapidly growing sections of the Sunshine Territory and more facts come daily to hand to prove this. Portions of that country which five years ago supported nothing but a steer, a few jack rabbits, a prairie dog or two and some of those mottled rattlesnakes, are now dotted with homesteads and the homesteaders who are living there with their families and whose numbers are constantly on the increase, are raising good crops of cereals and vegetables, and are redeeming these deserts from its arid condition, more and more satisfactorily daily.

The Bureau of Immigration of the Territory has done much in bringing immigrants to Roosevelt County and in calling attention to the fact that with good intelligent farming and timely work the vast plains there can be made productive and will furnish comfortable homes and a living to many settlers.

A letter just received from one of the new settlers in that section by the Bureau of Immigration explains the situation.

Brownhorn, N. M., November 25, 1905

Dear Sir: The supply of literature you sent me is exhausted and [I] could have used three times as many booklets. Would you please send me as many "Ho! To the Land of Sunshine" and bulletins on Roosevelt County as you can spare me? Could use 500 of each as I am going east in a short time in the interest of immigration.

The Brownhorn country is developing rapidly— many homestead entries being made every week and the influx of homesteaders is on the increase. Track laying on the cut off has reached fifty-one miles and they are pushing it rapidly. This is the heart of agricultural New Mexico and the people are now finding it out.

Very respectfully,
W. D. McBee

The promotion industry in territorial New Mexico was helped by railroad efforts such as pamphlets on immigration and homeseeker excursions. By the early 1900s, AT&SF already had a long history of advertising land and settlement. One of their booklets published during construction of the ERNM was titled *Free U.S. Government Lands along the Santa Fe: Where They Are and How to Get Them* and described available areas near the railroad and the applicable homestead laws. Many of the illustrations were borrowed from *Ho! To the Land of Sunshine* (New Mexico Bureau of Immigration 1907) and prominently displayed such common sights in New Mexico as an artesian well spouting water above the heads of nearby onlookers (Santa Fe *New Mexican*, July 25, 1906).

Homeseekers' excursions: tell your friends in the east

A frequent sight in newspapers was advertisements for homeseeker excursions; twice a month, trains left Iowa, Missouri, Kansas, and Nebraska for round-trip passage to points in New Mexico. People were already there in the territory waiting to greet the newcomers and ready to make some money

FIG 4.5
North Main Street in Clovis
Postcard of North Main Street in Clovis sometime
from 1906 to 1910 (Courtesy of William Penner).

off their situation. Among the members of these informal "welcoming committees" were former construction workers on the Belen Cutoff, such as surveyor F. T. Tulley (previously introduced in Chapter 3). His experience provides details of the early industry that sprang up to help homesteaders along the ERNM.

It was a wonderful time of life in this part of a growing city (Clovis). At first people came in on trains, every 2 weeks excursions and we took them in spring wagons and showed them their ¼ section, charged them $25 each and they paid the land office $16 and thus filed on their claim. There were not any stone corners, roads or any land marks, just a vast expanse. The surveyors, 25 or more years before, were supposed to burn some wood (a match generally) which was put on the corner and four pits dug, one in the east ¼ section and the dirt mounded up on the charcoal for the corner. Well they were hard to find, but I [previously] had to locate all [sections] adjoining the railroad to tie in [to] our survey [on the] constructed line, so I had had several months experience. I soon learned to...pick out the green pits
(where water was retained and the grass subsequently greener), also I had the railroad maps to measure from so I did not have much trouble finding either. Then when you got a location [you left] a red handkerchief.... Every body [was] selling lots [in town] every day [at] a better price. I got some hand bills printed and went up as far as Wichita and met the trains, passing out the bills telling of the prospects of this Santa Fe developing point (Clovis). I shot for 7000 people [but] I missed it, must be 25,000 there now (NMSU Special Collections, F. T. Tulley to Lee Myers, January 4, 1963).

As more people came to live along the Cutoff, certain locations grew from sidings to towns and towns to cities. In the process, each settlement sought ways to make it easier and more desirable for people to come live in their town. Mountainair residents complained to AT&SF that they needed special homeseeker rates so they could be on an equal footing with neighboring communities (Mountainair *Messenger*, July 30, 1909). Competition grew fierce and led to editorials decrying unscrupulous tactics.

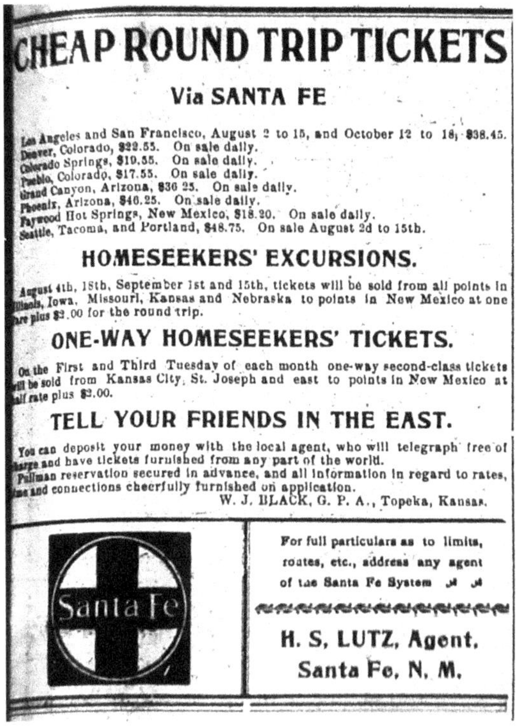

FIG 4.6
Advertisement for excursions to New Mexico
Ad appeared in the Santa Fe *New Mexican* on August 28, 1903
(Courtesy of Zimmerman UNM).

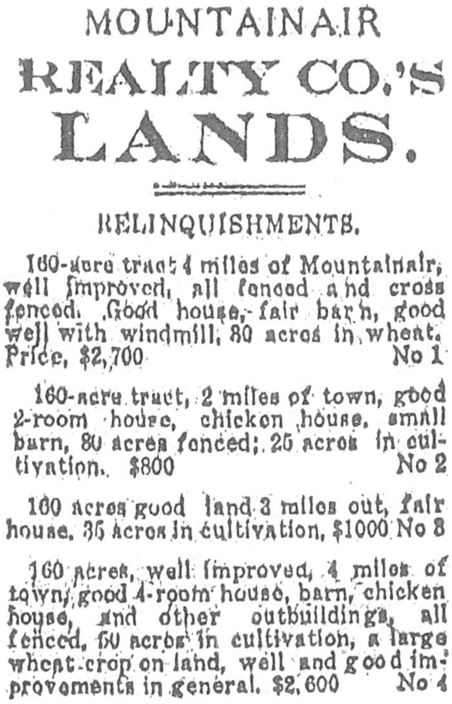

FIG 4.7
Sales of relinquished homesteads
Advertisement appeared in the October 29, 1909,
edition of the Mountainair *Messenger* (Courtesy of
the New Mexico History Library).

Nonresident gentry…are attempting to turn the tide of immigration from the Mountainair country by misrepresenting those citizens here who are engaged legitimately and honorably in the real estate business. There is evidently an organized band of men up and down the Santa Fe and its connecting lines projecting into Texas and Oklahoma to buttonhole people coming this way and divert prospective settlers to less favored localities by unfair means…. The representative citizens of Mountainair do not encourage, and will not tolerate, outrageously unfair and unjust treatment of people who come here to locate. Public sentiment is for a square deal and truthful and honorable treatment. It is a question in which all are morally and financially interested (Mountainair *Messenger*, August 27, 1909).

Newspapers, bulletins, and homeseekers' excursions succeeded in bringing people to eastern New Mexico after construction of the Belen Cutoff, but that was not enough to keep them in the territory. On December 11, 1914, the Fort Sumner *Leader* noted the return of settlers from Oklahoma

and Texas, many of whom were "homesteaders who left here after getting title to their claims, and are now mighty anxious to come back to New Mexico…. Seven years ago the first rush of homesteaders hit eastern New Mexico, and through ignorance of dry farming conditions, became disgusted and the majority trecked [*sic*] back to the cotton patch." Whether by design or default, not everyone stuck it out and sales of relinquished 160-acre tracts with improvements were a common sight in newspapers (Figure 4.7).

Much of the easily accessible land along the Belen Cutoff was settled by the 1920s, leading the Mountainair *Independent* (May 13, 1920) to declare "the time of 'free' homesteads is gone forever [but] it is a fact that land can be purchased more cheaply in this vicinity than any other place in the United States." The editorial may have overstated the diminishing opportunities for homesteads (as discussed previously, many local residents continued to add to their holdings by claiming lands under expansions of the original Homestead Act in 1909 and 1916), but things were changing as communities formed and the promotion industry began to yield to local civic boosterism. Developing towns started to get their own newspapers,

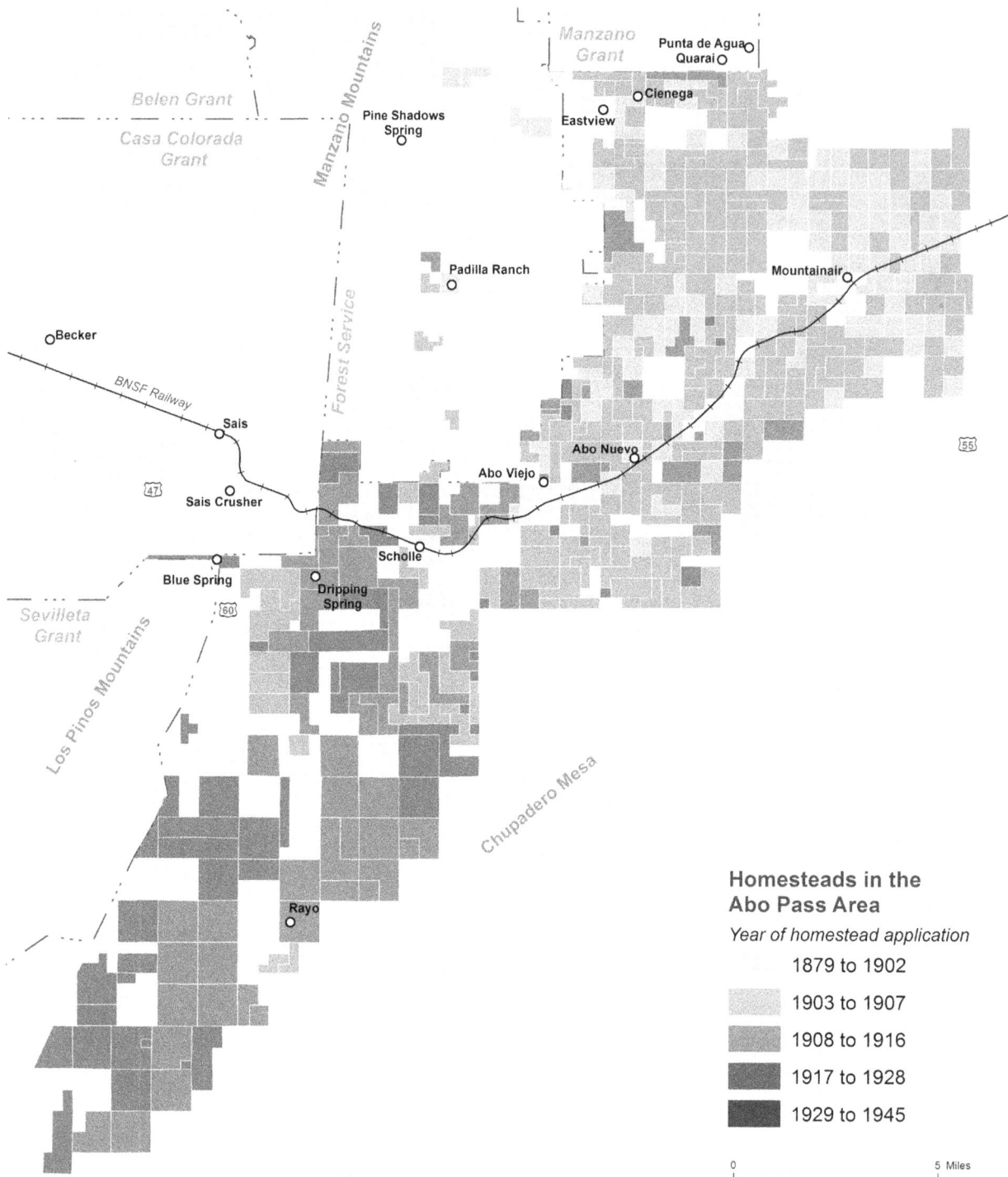

Homesteads in the Abo Pass Area

Year of homestead application

1879 to 1902
1903 to 1907
1908 to 1916
1917 to 1928
1929 to 1945

0   5 Miles

FIG 4.8

Homesteads in Abo Pass

Homestead application dates based on General Land
Office homestead patent information (BLM 2009). Prior
to 1912 it took five years of residency to prove up on a
homestead and after 1912 it only required three years.

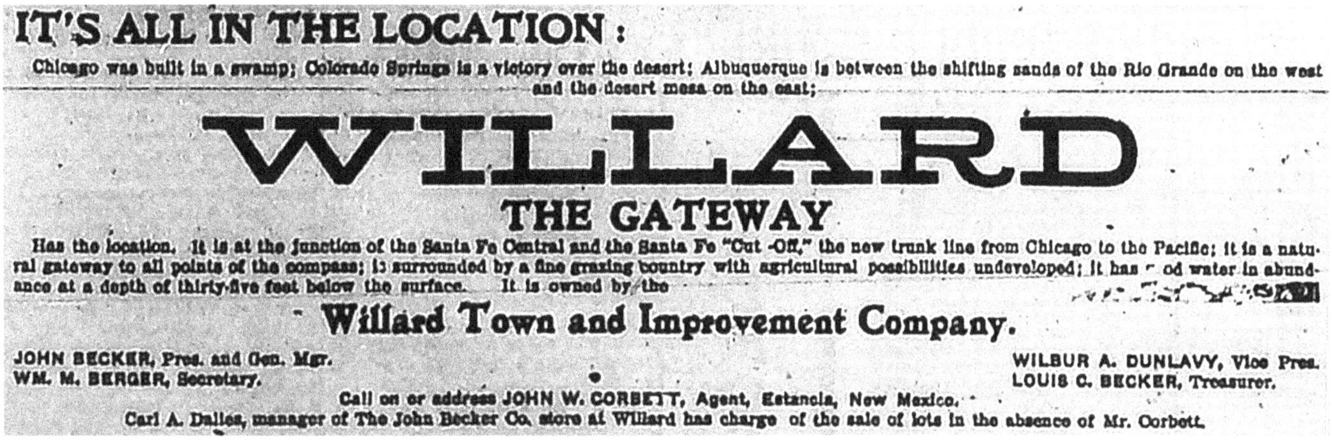

IT'S ALL IN THE LOCATION :

Chicago was built in a swamp; Colorado Springs is a victory over the desert; Albuquerque is between the shifting sands of the Rio Grande on the west and the desert mesa on the east;

WILLARD

THE GATEWAY

Has the location. It is at the junction of the Santa Fe Central and the Santa Fe "Cut-Off," the new trunk line from Chicago to the Pacific; it is a natural gateway to all points of the compass; is surrounded by a fine grazing country with agricultural possibilities undeveloped; It has ~ od water in abundance at a depth of thirty-five feet below the surface.   It is owned by the

Willard Town and Improvement Company.

JOHN BECKER, Pres. and Gen. Mgr.
WM. M. BERGER, Secretary.

WILBUR A. DUNLAVY, Vice Pres.
LOUIS C. BECKER, Treasurer.

Call on or address JOHN W. CORBETT, Agent, Estancia, New Mexico.
Carl A. Dalles, manager of The John Becker Co. store at Willard has charge of the sale of lots in the absence of Mr. Corbett.

FIG 4.9
Willard: the gateway
Advertisement appeared in the September 8, 1905, edition of the
Santa Fe *New Mexican* (Courtesy of Zimmerman UNM).

resident businessmen, and groups variously interested in their collective success. People were looking forward to growing communities, and the accepted wisdom was that things never looked better for eastern New Mexico.

Community development and boosterism: there can't be nothing but prosperity ahead

As construction began on the ERNM, Belen was the only established town of any significance along the 270-mile route, but when train service started four years later, AT&SF had established 44 sidings/sections that formed nuclei for growing settlements. Some sections were obvious choices for towns, for example, Fort Sumner's location on the Pecos River. Merchants such as John Becker anticipated growth and formed companies to plat townsites in places such as Belen and Willard. They predicted big things in newspaper articles and touted the potential of these "cities," even when little had been built and the communities existed primarily on paper. The development of these places followed their own trajectories but was guided by advertising and the boosterism that followed.

Developing communities: it's all in the location

Some towns' success was due to their locations and natural advantages while others' was because that is where AT&SF chose to site certain facilities. Melrose provides an early example of the consequences of failure. It had a mushroom-like growth as it expanded to almost 600 people within a year and its "future [was] roseate" after AT&SF designated it the division headquarters (Santa Fe *New Mexican*, November 6, 1906). Unfortunately, AT&SF discovered there was not enough water, and Melrose's prospects evaporated as its population moved to Clovis and the new division location. Towns and investors knew they needed to succeed and attract people and business, but it was difficult enough that the Mountainair *Independent* noted "making people believe the truth [is our] greatest handicap (Mountainair *Independent*, September 9, 1920). Advertising, however, provided one way to get the word out about the superior qualities of a community.

Nascent communities' desire to attract attention sometimes led them to exercise some freedom with the truth. One prominent example is Willard and Clovis, which frequently published maps showing their locations at the nexus of multiple

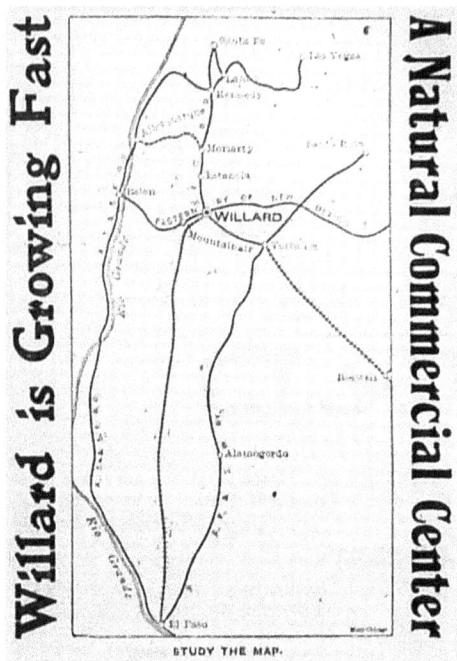

FIG 4.10
Willard is growing fast
Advertisement appeared in the February 9, 1907, edition of the Santa Fe *New Mexican*. The rail line shown heading roughly south of Willard was never built and was never really feasible (Courtesy of Zimmerman UNM).

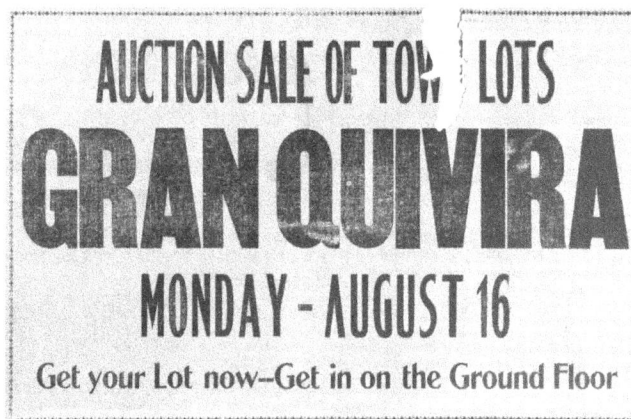

FIG 4.11
Gran Quivira town lots for sale
Advertisement appeared in the August 12, 1920, edition of the Mountainair *Independent* (Courtesy of Center for Southwest Research, University Libraries, University of New Mexico [CSWR UNM]).

rail lines. Not content with being at the intersection of two routes, boosters felt the need to distinguish the towns further by including in each map additional railroads that were never built (Figure 4.10). Willard's success was argued to be inevitable (one headline trumpeted that Willard must become a great trade center soon), and an advertisement called it *the* natural point on the Cutoff: "Willard is a growing town, Willard will make a city, study the map, your opportunity is there" (Santa Fe *New Mexican*, February 9, 1907).

The prospectus for sale of townsite lots in Gran Quivira, a small community south of Mountainair, employed narratives of abandoned pueblos and health seekers—both persistent New Mexico images—in their appeals to potential buyers. It states that local settlers lived in jacal structures and had persevered through early difficulties and "were not easily discouraged, because they had lived long enough in Texas to know that agriculture usually induced moisture" (Mountainair *Independent*, August 12, 1920). Charles Lummis's treatment of the myth of Tabira Pueblo (Gran Quivira) in *Land of Poco Tiempo* is quoted at length and said to provide as faithful a description "as can be known be known of the pueblo [and] the surroundings" (ibid).

Arguments are put forward for Gran Quivira's logical inevitability as a center and county seat, and the climate is described as the "finest in the world, where you can work all day during the hottest weather without fatigue, sleep all night and feel refreshed in the morning, [and] eat your meals each day with unusual relish" (ibid).

The indefatigable F. T. Tulley was there at the beginning of Clovis' rapid rise, and he again played a pivotal role. Here is his description of what actually was happening as a town started:

As the town began to grow, R. C. Reid, the Santa Fe land agent was instrumental in dividing Roosevelt County. [He] made the east part Curry County and Clovis the county seat. At the 1st meeting of the new organized town of Clovis, I was the first city clerk. I was...keeping the books for the Santa Fe Land Improvement Co, managing and constructing the water, systems, putting in all the plumbing through the water company: bath tubs, sinks, cesspool and trench and 4" pipe. Opened up books for the water company, collected all the fees. This company was known as the Craig Mater Height and

FIG 4.12
Belen roundhouse
Belen roundhouse around 1908
(Courtesy of Randy Dunson).

FIG 4.13
AT&SF storehouse in Clovis
Inside the AT&SF storehouse at Clovis in 1909
(Courtesy of Randy Dunson).

FIG 4.14
Clovis roundhouse employees
Clovis roundhouse force around 1915 (Courtesy of Randy Dunson).

Level Co. owned by R. C. Reid and Mr. Craig, the man who drilled the deep wells for the Santa Fe terminal.

We…installed 2" black iron mains in the alleys as the houses grew, [and we] were making money and paying for every thing from profit when we had a couple disastrous fires and Mr. Reid decided the city should own the water works and put in fire protection. We were offered $40,000 by some Independence, Kansas operator, but Mr. Reid, who was also Mayor, wanted Clovis to have it and they sold [the water company to] Clovis for $27,000 in bonds (from an original investment of $5,500.00). R. C. Reid was a wonderful man, he later moved to Roswell and I continued to act for him. He had all the town sites along the line on our 140 miles. It was a wonder[ful] time of life [in] this part of a growing city (NMSU Special Collections, F. T. Tulley to Lee Myers, January 4, 1963).

Significant developments were occurring along the Cutoff, particularly for towns with railroad shops such as Clovis and Belen, and this growth needed no editorial embellishment. Through traffic to California and local business had increased enough by 1912 that 500 people were employed in AT&SF's shops in Clovis; half the city's workers (Clovis *Weekly Journal*, July 18, 1912). In May and June, the shop workforce grew again by 20 percent just to handle the load. Additionally, Harvey Houses were constructed at Belen, Vaughn, and Clovis. This trend of expanding AT&SF employment continued on the ERNM and extended to even the smallest communities, such as Agudo and Scholle, where section gangs and foremen were needed to maintain the tracks. Both Anglos and Hispanos moved to areas on the railroad for work. The family of Fidel Padilla (2006) provides a typical example of Hispano migration within central New Mexico. His father, Eulalio Padilla, was from La Joya originally and went to Kelly to work in the mines in the early twentieth century. As opportunities and ore quality diminished, Eulalio relocated in 1919 to a 160-acre homestead along the tracks near present-day Abo Nuevo. Along with others in the area, he was able to pick up enough work making 10 cents an hour with a section gang to earn a living when combined with subsistence farming. The significance of this employment system in these smaller villages can't be overstated, but most of the stories were not told in local newspapers and

FIG 4.15
Masthead of the Clovis *Journal*
Masthead of the December 26, 1912, edition of the Clovis *Journal*
(Courtesy of Zimmerman UNM).

are consequently only discussed in detail in Chapters 5 and 6, where our interviews with residents are able to provide locals' perspectives in their own words.

It is hard to fault some of the enthusiasm of this period because watching towns come into existence almost instantaneously must have seemed miraculous, the arc from pioneer to village or town so simple. The masthead of the Clovis *Journal* illustrates this journey perfectly, albeit perhaps out of sequence, with oxen and wagons leading to well-fenced farms and thence on to trains, cities, and industry (Figure 4.15). Much of this change was not subject to influence by civic leaders—increased shipping to California did not result from an editorial in a local paper—but that is not the way they presented things. In the era of the booster anything was possible as long as everyone believed enough. Force of will and a positive attitude were all that were needed.

Boosterism: it's bigger than money

By the time boosterism came to eastern New Mexico, it already had a long history. It had been mocked for years, most famously in the "Untold Delights of Duluth" speech delivered in the U.S. Senate during 1871, but that did not stop its popularity in the new towns along the Cutoff. In the period from 1910 to 1925, boosters found much to be pleased with in the region as agricultural and land prices rose and settlement and rail traffic increased. Dr. Campbell's scientific dry-farming methods (coupled with adequate rainfall) seemed to have perfected farming in an arid climate. The price of boosterism was constant vigilance to keep things positive about the community. Newspapers ran advertisements about their towns in almost every issue, typically listing the healthful climate, rich soil unsurpassed in productive capabilities, and industrious people. An advertisement for John Becker's Belen Town and Improvement Company even stated that Belen would grow based solely on residents' energy and efforts to talk up the town at every opportunity (Figure 4.16).

The Clovis *Weekly Journal* focused slightly more on conditions in their area, but their rationale for boosting in a July 26, 1910, editorial was much the same as Belen's—if we don't, the town will not succeed.

FIG 4.16
Why Belen will grow
Advertisement appeared in the May 19, 1914, edition of
the Belen *News* (Courtesy of Zimmerman UNM).

Boost!

There are a great many people on this earth that we don't need and that we wish we could just easily push off. Knockers, for instance . . . a knocker is a knocker, a Pest and a Destroyer. Here is the way to push the Knocker into Oblivion—

Boost!

Boost your Town. Boost your Business. Boost your Friends. Boost your ideas. Boost everything that helps You. Be a Booster and you can't help but be a Builder.

Boost!

The man who Boosts is a Leader. He is always followed by a crowd. His philosophy at once becomes contagious. And he leaves a trail of Boosters in his path. While those who follow him put his name in Bronze.

Boost!

When you don't know what else to do—Boost. It makes little odds what you boost so long as you Boost something. Once you form the habit you need have no fear for lack of things to Boost. They will spring up from every direction.

Boost!

If you want to be happy—Boost. If you want to get higher in the world—Boost. The Busiest and Wisest men that live will be glad to listen to you if you are a Booster. Learn the knack of Boosting. It's a great Knack—more important than any "Pull," or "Influence"—and it's bigger than Money.

Poem by George Matthew Adams appeared in the May 15, 1913, edition of the Clovis *Journal*.

We should boost because we have something to boost first and secondly because of the fact that the two past years of droughty conditions throughout the Southwest has diverted the mind of coming immigration, and we MUST boost if we are to get our share of the immigration of 1912 that is rightly ours and to which we are justly entitled.

Write about conditions here, send your home paper back and let them read about conditions here. Conditions were never brighter, a better season was never more in evidence, and a Bumper Crop was never surer. Boost and help Clovis and New Mexico grow.

Boosterism was probably more popular with the mercantile class and people selling real estate and newspapers than the average citizen, but it also had benefits for regular townspeople. Resultant efforts such as the Mountainair Chautauqua and other community celebrations probably outweighed the more maniacal promotional strain (as in the poem's injunction that "it makes little odds what you boost so long as you Boost something"). The Chautauqua held at Mountainair from 1908 to 1915 shows the type of aspirational tendencies that informed boosterism. The original Chautauqua began in 1874 at the lake of the same name in New York as training for Sunday school teachers. Later versions such as the one at Mountainair (sometimes termed "little Chautauquas") rose to popularity in the late nineteenth and early twentieth centuries and attempted to capitalize on culture, self-improvement, and educational betterment (Gould 1961). Eminent local personages were often invited in an attempt to increase visitorship, a practice copied by Mountainair, which made sure New Mexico's Governor Curry attended in 1909. Despite the limited facilities—tents appear to have been the most sophisticated accommodations—members of the Commercial Club felt their movement was going to "prove to be one of the chief factors tending for good in the great southwest." Mountainair's Chautauqua fell short of that lofty goal, but it did fit within the widespread practice of civic leaders boosting their towns to improve business and people's perceptions.

Promoting towns also included elaborate celebrations such as the one Mountainair threw on the Fourth of July in 1920. Governor Mechem spoke, and many activities were

FIG 4.17
Mountainair Chautauqua
Mountainair Chautauqua Party in 1909 that included
Mountainair founder John Corbett and New Mexico
governor Curry (Courtesy of Jack Hewett).

planned, including rodeos, goose chasing, a fat man's race, and a Wild West show with "the restraint of modern humanitarianism." Two-thousand pounds of barbecue were promised along with "cauldrens [sic] of [the] Pinto Beans which have made Mountainair the most celebrated bean shipping point in the United States" (Mountainair *Independent*, June 22, 1922).

The excitement for commerce and boosterism covered in local newspapers did have less pleasant aspects. In Clovis, competition between hotel proprietors got heated while they were waiting for a train from Amarillo and soliciting business at the rail depot. One man stepped in front of the other to steal a potential customer and an argument broke out, resulting in a fatal shooting at close distance (Santa Fe *New Mexican*, February 1, 1910). Journalistic boosterism did not typically produce this type of violence, but as we will consider, it did systematically omit and ignore what civic leaders would have termed the wrong kind of people. The Mountainair *Messenger* put it succinctly on April 16, 1909: "If you are the right kind, Mountainair wants you and will give you a welcome. If you are not in harmony with the prevailing ideas, you will not find the atmosphere congenial."

Reading between the lines: the hombres under their charge

New Mexican English-language newspapers published in the early twentieth century along the Cutoff were almost as notable for what they did not discuss as for what they did. These omissions can produce dissonance for the modern reader when periodicals include both advertisements and inducements to the "right kind" of settlers from the promotion industry but the legal publications of homestead applications and patents show a large majority of individuals with Spanish surnames. On the western end of the Belen Cutoff, Hispanos were there before the railroad and made up many, if not most, of the settlers moving into the area, yet they were marginal to local publications that overwhelmingly spoke to a Protestant and Anglo audience and often omitted Hispanos, Catholicism, and the Spanish language and periodicals. There was, however, a strong tradition in New Mexico of Spanish-language newspapers that spoke to Hispano concerns, but unfortunately none of these were published along the Cutoff.

FIG 4.18
Hispano section gang in Willard
David Pascal Childers and "his nine men" on the Willard
section gang in 1920 (Courtesy of William Penner).

Ethnic tensions and divisions were present along the ERNM on into the twentieth century and were commented on by people we interviewed. The Cutoff itself presented a spectrum of diversity with predominately Hispano communities on the west end grading into majority Anglo settlements on the east end and communities such as Scholle that came together for mutual support (considered in more detail in Chapter 5) complicating easy definitions in between.

Sometimes when Hispanos were mentioned, it was with a paternalistic tone as in the *Railroad Notes* section of the Clovis *Weekly Journal* (December 5, 1913) acknowledging the ubiquity of Hispano railroad workers and necessity of learning some Spanish.

Santa Fe section foremen, it is understood, are going to be taught the rudiments of the Spanish language in order that they may be able to carry on a conversation with the "hombres" under their charge or at least be able to make the foreman "hombres" understand when they are told that a low "lint" is to be raised, that a rotten tie is to be replaced with a sound one, and other

lingo pertinent to section work. The Santa Fe employs Mexican section help almost exclusively throughout the west and section foremen have labored at a disadvantage with the men under their charge, an interpreter often having to be employed for this purpose. As a starter, little books containing about one hundred words and phrases ordinarily used in track work have been distributed to the foremen, the English and Spanish being in parallel columns in order that the latter pronunciations may be learned by the foremen.

For the Mountainair *Messenger* (and later the *Independent*) in the first few decades of the 1900s, Hispanos infrequently appeared as subjects of editorials or articles, except when reluctantly referred to as "natives." This seems amazing given the proximity of large Spanish settlements such as Manzano but proceeds as part of the logic of marginalization—how can or why would you talk about people who don't really have any social standing? Most times the editorial racial calculus was implicit and required reading against the grain, but occasionally it became obvious as in a discussion of Election Day in 1911.

Abarrotes,
Frutas,
Verduras

Pidan nuestros precios para ahorrar
dinero
Vengan a vernos

MOUNTAINAIR CASH STORE

N. Geo. Tabet, Propietario

Raised by Campbell method.   Raised by common method.
Cut of Pomeroy Farm corn. 1901. Campbell system
vs. adjoining farm.

FIG 4.19
Advertisement for Mountainair Cash Store
Advertisement appeared in Mountainair's *El Independiente* on July 19, 1924 (Courtesy of CSWR UNM).

FIG 4.20
Corn raised by the Campbell method
Figure appeared on page 13 of Campbell's 1905 edition of the Soil Culture Manual (Courtesy of the Library of Congress).

Mountainair hears that Punta is still voting. A voting box with a judge who can neither read nor write is liable to keep open house until Christmas and never knows when it kenoes (sic). *Ask Colonel Imboden and Sam Edwards what they think of 'lection day at Punta and have it framed and decorated with stereopticon snaps. It will sell to posterity for a dozen fortunes. Sam Moss countersigning the blue ballot as a requisite to voting is worth a thousand dollars to start with. But to think of men being elected to office by the votes of such cattle as conducted the Punta and other native voting boxes! Let us hope that by the time another election rolls around we have enough white men in this new state to elect officers over the heads of ignorant rabble* (Mountainair *Messenger*, November 11, 1911).

Discontent was not limited to a single group, and the local chapters of the Alianza Hispano-Americana, a Mexican-American fraternal organization, condemned the tide of homesteaders moving into the area and reducing traditional land uses and overall opportunities for advancement (Francisco Sisneros, personal communication 2010). Eventually the situation began to change with a journalistic compromise where Spanish-language papers were published as companions to the main newspaper; Mountainair had *El Independiente* and Belen had *El Hispano-Americano*. These inserts consisted of legal publications and syndicated material, often with a focus on Mexico during the Revolution and, of course, advertisements. Hispanos bought groceries just like other people, and someone had to buy their beans when they brought them to town. As we will see, the importance of agriculture and beans in particular for Mountainair and the surrounding region was one thing most people could agree on.

Scientific farming, promotion, and the pinto bean: crops were never better

Scientific farming, also known as dry farming, rose out of the ashes of the climatic theories espoused in the nineteenth century by popular scientists such as Nebraska's Samuel Aughey (commonly summarized as "rain follows the plow"). The idea that planting trees and raising crops somehow raised moisture levels and rain lasted up until the late 1890s, when

FIG 4.21
Plowing new ground near Broncho
Plowing new ground near Broncho right next to the Belen Cutoff
sometime in the early 1900s (Courtesy of Dorothy Cole).

overwhelming evidence and changing opinions led to its downfall. Some felt the theory endured because "many of the great railroad corporations have vast areas of land to sell in the Far West [and] they desire to induce European people to go there…so that their business lines may be increased" (Kutzleb 1888 [1971]). Excessive ties to promotion were also a criticism of Hardy Webster Campbell's *Soil Culture Manual*, first published in 1902 and revised many times thereafter, which became the bible for the new scientific farmers (Hargreaves 1958). The pinto bean in Mountainair provides a good example of the dry-farming system and its close relationship with boosters.

Perfecting the dry-farming system

Scientific farming found a convenient fit in the early twentieth century's popular love of statistics and quantification. It offered the opportunity for a perfectible world that would yield sufficient crops once farmers understood exactly what system to employ. The search for this new method played out in the newspapers, such as this editorial from the Mountainair *Messenger* on July 15, 1910.

As to rainfall and agriculture: it is proved by statistics that rainfall does not increase with agriculture and tree planting; although generally supposed to do so, but what is equivalent or better, as the soil is tilled deeper it absorbs and holds sufficient moisture to keep crops growing through an ordinary drouth and the actual absence of rainfall is not so apparent.… The more we stir the rich lands of the Estancia Valley, the more and better crops we will grow, call it what you like. One writer declares that land broken six feet deep would catch and hold moisture enough for a crop with no summer rain. Will someone please try this?

An industry sprang up to help answer the questions of farmers and communities as they looked for assured success in their agricultural efforts. "Dry-farmer Campbell" was perhaps the most famous proselytizer, but there were others who were also popular speakers, such as Thomas Shaw, an agent for the Great Northern Railway (Hargreaves 1948). Underpinning these spokesmen were institutions such as the Dry Farming Congress and various federal, state, and private experimental

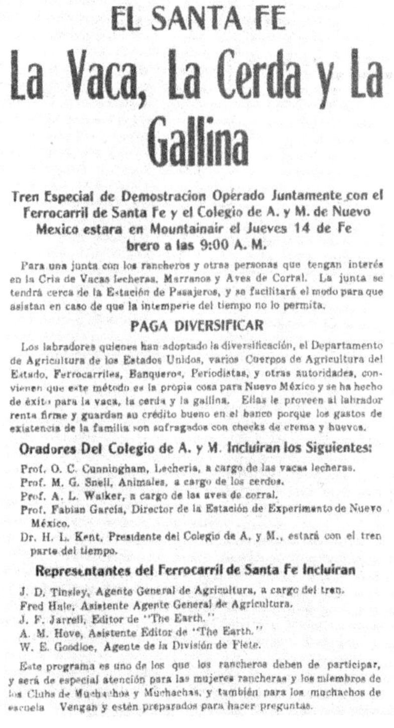

EL SANTA FE

La Vaca, La Cerda y La Gallina

Tren Especial de Demostracion Operado Juntamente con el Ferrocarril de Santa Fe y el Colegio de A. y M. de Nuevo Mexico estara en Mountainair el Jueves 14 de Febrero a las 9:00 A. M.

Para una junta con los rancheros y otras personas que tengan interés en la Cria de Vacas lecheras, Marranos y Aves de Corral. La junta se tendrá cerca de la Estación de Pasajeros, y se facilitará el modo para que asistan en caso de que la intemperie del tiempo no lo permita.

PAGA DIVERSIFICAR

Los labradores quienes han adoptado la diversificación, el Departamento de Agricultura de los Estados Unidos, varios Cuerpos de Agricultura del Estado, Ferrocarriles, Banqueros, Periodistas, y otras autoridades, convienen que este método es la propia cosa para Nuevo México y se ha hecho de éxito para la vaca, la cerda y la gallina. Ellas le proveen al labrador renta firme y guardan su crédito bueno en el banco porque los gastos de existencia de la familia son sufragados con checks de crema y huevos.

Oradores Del Colegio de A. y M. Incluiran los Siguientes:

Prof. O. C. Cunningham, Lecheria, a cargo de las vacas lecheras.
Prof. M. G. Snell, Animales, a cargo de los cerdos.
Prof. A. L. Walker, a cargo de las aves de corral.
Prof. Fabian García, Director de la Estación de Experimento de Nuevo México.
Dr. H. L. Kent, Presidente del Colegio de A. y M., estará con el tren parte del tiempo.

Representantes del Ferrocarril de Santa Fe Incluiran

J. D. Tinsley, Agente General de Agricultura, a cargo del tren.
Fred Hale, Asistente Agente General de Agricultura.
J. F. Jarrell, Editor de "The Earth."
A. M. Hove, Asistente Editor de "The Earth."
W. E. Goodloe, Agente de la División de Flete.

Este programa es uno de los que los rancheros deben de participar, y será de especial atención para las mujeres rancheras y los miembros de los Clubs de Muchachos y Muchachas, y también para los muchachos de escuela. Vengan y estén preparados para hacer preguntas.

FIG 4.22

La Vaca, La Cerda y La Gallina

Spanish advertisement for the AT&SF special educational train for agriculture (headed by J. D. Tinsley) appeared in the February 9, 1924, edition of Mountainair's *El Independiente* (Courtesy of CSWR UNM).

agriculture efforts. The people working in the various US Department of Agriculture programs were interested in what actually worked, but they were generally unsuccessful in publishing their results, especially when those contradicted the popular theories of scientific farming (ibid.). The inability to stand against the promotional and propaganda phenomenon of dry-farming was due in large part to the movement's alliance with the railroads.

> *Whatever we may say about the soulless corporations, there is no doubt about the broad mindedness of the policy which the great transcontinental railroads are carrying out for the benefit of the farmer—and eventually the benefit of the railroad—in the southwest. The work of the Santa Fe company, through its industrial department; the work of Professor Tinsley, its field expert in New Mexico, is showing the farmers how to get the best result.... Other railway systems are pursuing the same policy; a dry farming special train, manned by some of the best known experts in the country* (Clovis *Journal*, April 22, 1911).

AT&SF's "broad minded" policy of providing experts to help farmers proved to be popular. Twenty years after the above editorial, J. D. Tinsley was still running agricultural education trains so that people could "learn new and practical ideas pertaining to soil improvements; crops in general; livestock of all kinds; boys and girls club work; and home economics" (Willard *Record*, March 21, 1930). Railroads and dry-farming experts proposed a wide variety of techniques that would ensure success. The methodologies were often so divergent and partially adopted that the entire movement could only be categorized as "agriculture without irrigation in semi-arid regions" (Hargreaves 1977). Some of the more popular system components, however, included alternating fallow fields to bank annual soil moisture through capillary action, packing the subsoil and using dust mulch, and deep plowing.

> *It is lamentable that many homesteaders have made a failure in establishing a home in the semi-arid portions of the United States by using the wrong methods of farming. Many of them tried to use the same methods they used in the Eastern and Northern states, but the*

	1900	1910	1920	1930	1940	1950	1960
New Mexico pinto bean production	36,022	85,795	850,334	1,624,842	817,527	749,794	138,922
Growth since the previous decade	—	138.2%	891.1%	91.1%	−49.7%	−8.3%	−81.5%
Torrance County pinto bean production	Unavailable	14,985	244,930	733,486	315,088	291,232	26,155
Percentage of total NM production	Unavailable	17.5%	28.8%	45.1%	38.5%	38.8%	18.8%
Growth since the previous decade	Unavailable	—	1534.5%	199.5%	−57%	−7.6%	−91%

FIG 4.23
Bean production in New Mexico and Torrance County (1900 to 1960)
Data compiled from decennial agricultural census reports from the USCB
1960; 1952b; 1942b; 1932b; 1922a; 1922b; 1913b; 1902b. All figures given
in bushels of dry beans.

different climatic conditions made their experiments a life-long regret. There are today, mute, but unmistakable evidences of their failures in the vacant "shacks" that are to be seen in traveling thru the country. These little empty houses tell a pitiful story of hardships and sacrifices of the former occupants. There were some that came with a great store of ambition, energy and confidence in their abilities to cope with the environments that were thrown around them when they made settlement upon the rich and level acres that held out such great promises of wealth and happiness.

Some of them "stuck it out" and proved up on their homesteads, but as soon as they could leave they went sorrowfully away to find a land of greater promise that they had read about in literature sent out by the ton telling of the opportunities for accumulating a fortune in some specially selected part of the country where crop failures are unknown (Mountainair *Independent*, June 10, 1920).

In years of good rain the proponents of dry farming had an easy time explaining why their system worked. When

droughts occurred, you could always blame the farmer's inability to "stick to it." The Santa Fe *New Mexican* (August 16, 1909), in a moment of inadvertent journalistic prescience and honesty, perfectly summarized the dry farming movement in a headline:

DRY FARMING IS A SUCCESS
Provided That Farmers Supplement It with Pumping

Pinto beans and boosterism

The homesteaders that moved to the Mountainair region in the wake of the Belen Cutoff grew a variety of foodstuffs such as potatoes but had few suitable cash crops. The search for the right product that would be adapted to the dry, high-elevation climate and still command decent prices eventually found the pinto bean. Pinto beans were already cultivated for subsistence by farmers in land-grant communities such as Manzano and Punta de Agua, and a market for the beans was found in the lower Rio Grande Valley and cotton-growing areas of Texas (Culbert 1941). Initial experiments were very successful, and the industry increased from 1910 to 1950, most dramatically from 1910 to 1920 (Figure 4.23).

PINTO--The Bean King!
Rules in Mountainair
Saturday, October 25th

BEAN DAY

The Compliments of

MOUNTAINAIR

Exhibit your Best Beans

In connection with the Exhibit
of the Boys' and Girl's Clubs

Come One - Come All

The Eats are on Mountainair

FIG 4.24
King Bean Day
Advertisement appeared in the October 23, 1919, edition
of the Mountainair *Independent* (Courtesy of CSWR UNM).

TO BEANGROWERS

❖ ❖ ❖ ❖ ❖

The Association is the growers friend and every one
should stand by it and do everything possible to keep it alive.
It was organized in order to help them and to save them
from the local buyers and no grower should sell his beans only
thru it. It should be as strong as the "Rock of Gibralter" and
can be made that way if all of the growers will become interested in it and work to that end.
California Pink beans are being quoted at 7.25 fob Cost.
Why not the Pinto at the same price here? California only has
a 50 per cent crop this year. Colorado only has a 20 per cent
crop and is just about shipped out. Our Pinto is supreme and
there is no reason why we should make any sacrifices.
Most of the growers in the Association are holding for
7 cents or better and we have the best of reasons for believing
that they will get it. Everything points to better prices and
just as soon as the local buyers are out of the way we can con-
fidently expect to see it come. I am quoting out six cars at 7
cents fob shipping points and when they are sold or with-
drawn will quote out at 7 1-2 fob.
Sit tight in your boat and everything will come out to
your satisfaction. Cut the local buyers out of your end of it.

New Mexico Bean
Growers Association

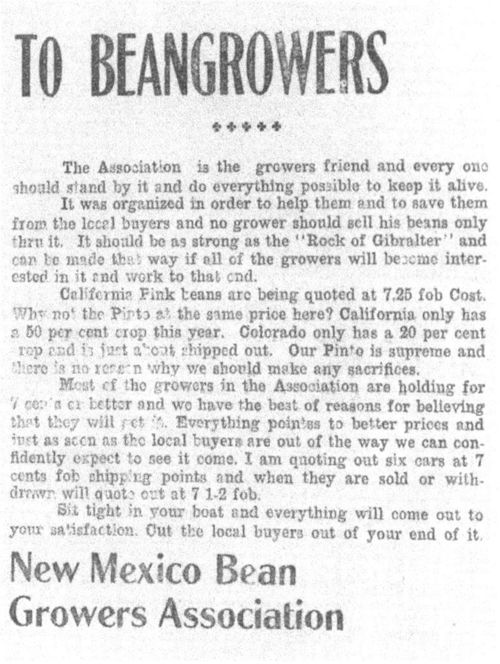

FIG 4.25
A message to bean growers
Advertisement appeared in the February 19, 1920, edition of
the Mountainair *Independent* (Courtesy of CSWR UNM).

Once the pinto was shown to be a viable crop, the Mountainair newspapers rarely had an issue without some mention of beans. Testimonials were common, and the editor of the Mountainair *Independent* (November 6, 1919) included a letter from someone who had recently visited town and had "read an article…about that 'King Bean Day' to be pulled off… on the 25th. I regret very much that I cannot be in attendance and only wish that I could be there with my big spoon to show you how I could sample your beans." AT&SF publications such as *The Earth* even ran an article on the phenomenon.

Buyers are no longer satisfied to specify Mexican pinto beans, but demand quality New Mexico pinto beans, which is distinctly a native production of that state…. The crop has been taken over as the particular crop of the New Mexico "dry farmer." The pinto bean…is the surest un-irrigated crop which New Mexico has at its command. Many farmers are extending their land holdings with profits from their 1916 crop and are planning to increase their acreage this spring (Belen *News*, January 8, 1917).

In the boom years of the pinto bean from just before World War I up until the mid-1920s there was a lot to celebrate in Mountainair, and at the end of each harvest season there was always a new crop of articles on how well the area had done.

That Mountainair is the "Heart of the Bean District" is shown by the fact that there has been over eighty carloads of beans shipped from here this season and the shipping has only begun…. The local warehouses are full of beans—most of which are being held in anticipation of a better market…. In driving through the country one is struck by the number of beans awaiting the coming of the thresher…. Kayser Brothers have already threshed over a million pounds of beans and have as many more contracted to thresh. And this is but one thresher. Verily there are beans galore in Mountainair (Mountainair *Independent*, November 13, 1919).

A large portion of the bean industry's significance in Mountainair came from the amount of infrastructure required to support the farmers, for example, the sale of specialized

FIG 4.26
Trinidad bean elevator
Trinidad bean elevator in Mountainair, NM, constructed
sometime after 1918 (Courtesy of Dorothy Cole).

mechanical equipment, use of threshers, and bean storage facilities. Booster efforts became more sophisticated, and farmers banded together in response to fluctuating prices, forming organizations such as the New Mexico Bean Growers Association. Member farmers were asked to pool their beans to maintain "better prices for the entire crop than can be obtained under the present system of handling. By this method an average sales price can be arrived at, at the close of the season, and each grower will realize the same price for his crop…. The expense of hauling, cleaning, and selling will be kept down as low as possible" (Mountainair *Independent*, May 20, 1920).

Boosterism of the pinto bean was an easy thing when prices were rising and yields grew every year as during World War I. Significant effort was made to perfect systems of agriculture, and for a while there was enough rain that it seemed everyone knew how to grow to beans in a semiarid climate. What proved more difficult and less easily addressed with the system of scientific farming or the promotion industry was the issue of prices and production.

The problem of marketing farm products is probably the most perplexing problem that now confronts the agricultural population of the state. Less is known of how to approach this problem than any other, because during the past the farmers of the state and the leaders of agriculture have devoted the larger portion of their time to the study of the problems looking to larger production rather than to the problem of marketing that production advantageously and profitably (Mountainair *Independent*, April 22, 1920).

Price fluctuations were confusing to most people, and newspapers dedicated a fair amount of effort to explaining how farmers could compete as their products entered a commodities market that was increasingly global, industrial, and impersonal. A typical response to low prices was to plant and harvest, fueling a cycle that would lead to the Dust Bowl, as we consider in the next chapter. Alternately, prices would go way up and people would put still more land into production to reap the rewards. As in the formation of the New Mexico Bean

FIG 4.27
Hauling beans to the thresher in Mountainair
Hauling beans to the thresher in Mountainair, date
unknown (Courtesy of Dorothy Cole).

FIG 4.28
Rags.ol' Iron
Frank Lowden's syndicated column Rags-ol' Iron appeared in the
Belen *News* on January 1, 1925 (Courtesy of Zimmerman UNM).

FIG 4.29
Follow the leader
Cartoon depicting irrationally high commodity prices appeared
in the May 18, 1922, edition of the Mountainair *Independent*
(Courtesy of CSWR UNM).

Growers Association, many felt organization and corporatization was the only way farmers could fairly compete in difficult economic climates. Frank Lowden, the onetime presidential candidate, lamented what he perceived as the "American Farm on the Junk Heap" in his syndicated column that appeared in the Belen *News* on January 1, 1925.

Agriculture has emerged from its primitive state. It must therefore conform to those practices which have been found necessary to the success of other great industries. In all other fields of commerce, unrestricted, free and open competition in the marketing of products has been gradually disappearing. Agriculture, therefore, finds itself with its millions of members freely competing among themselves in a highly industrialized and commercial world. If farmers are to put themselves upon terms of equality with the great industries of the country they, too, must organize.... This is not the problem of agriculture alone. It is the problem of all (Belen *News*, January 1, 1925).

The initial era of the homesteader and booster came to a close by the mid-1920s, when most towns and villages along the Belen Cutoff were fairly well established. Although they did not know it, the best days of their communities lay ahead, when they would come together during challenges such as the Great Depression, low crop prices, and reduced yields. The people of the Cutoff were made of stern stuff, and the Mountainair Independent (October 21, 1920) description of the Annual Bean Dinner, conducted when beans weren't going for much on the open market, summarizes their attitude.

The Annual Bean Dinner on last Saturday proved a humdinger as an attraction. The big crowd began gathering early in the morning and apparently they kept a comin' all day long. Autos, trucks, wagons, buggies—all come in loaded. The big warehouse was none too large to accommodate the large number who attended the jollification. And evidently the people thought, if they could not sell their beans for a decent price, they could eat them, and eat them they did.

**The growin'-up days:
life and work on the Belen Cutoff**

The previous chapters discussed east-central New Mexico and changes brought with the Belen Cutoff, primarily through newspapers, archival materials, and letters when available. These sources provide excellent vantage points to look at broad issues and themes but do not always tell the stories of individuals and families. In contrast, Chapters 5 and 6 focus on presenting a multivocal perspective from those who have lived and worked on the Belen Cutoff. Informed by our extensive oral-history work with over 70 participants, we include long excerpts that range from family histories to the experiences of the interviewees. This approach allows the people of the region to tell their own stories—accompanied by historic materials and photographs–about the period that included such significant events as the Great Depression and World War II. Not withstanding the terrible difficulties experienced by many, these were looked on as the good times.

Community dynamics

A number of settlements in east-central New Mexico were built on a strong sense of social obligation in its most positive sense. Many of the people who came first to these places, both Hispano and Anglo, had to rely on networks of family, neighbors, and friends to survive. Living off the land and creating or maintaining social capital to weather difficult times began a process that formed the communities on the Belen Cutoff. The heyday for these villages and towns came close on the heels of the original homesteading boom and included the years between approximately 1925 and 1949, when agriculture and commercial exchange, if not population, were at their height. An example of this process is provided by the community of Eastview.

As mentioned in Chapter 2, B. B. Spencer moved to the southern Manzano Mountains from White Oaks, New Mexico, in 1887 and established the first sawmill. After contracting with the AT&SF to provide ties for the Belen Cutoff, his sawmill eventually employed almost 70 people. Many workers lived in the nearby communities of Cienega and Eastview. These settlements were similar to others in the area, with small-scale

subsistence farming and ranching, often on 160-acre homesteads. Here Richard Spencer (2008), the great-grandson of B. B. Spencer, talks about how the community of Eastview functioned during his grandfather's time and on into later decades, along with the importance of local churches and schools.

You probably could equate it—and I haven't been to Alaska—but I would guess that it was like Alaska is now in the smaller communities, where people were helping each other, those kind of things that were goin' on. The harvest was done as a community, neighbor helping neighbor kind of thing. It was a subsistence living as far as they were thinking about the winter and food, and money was not necessarily the commerce that was goin' on. You traded a chicken for a goat, and they killed a beef in the wintertime because they had no refrigeration, so when they killed a beef, everybody got a little beef around [to] the neighbors and those kind of things. So the community aspect of that day is gone. It totally changed, compared to today. I mean, there's a little bit of neighboring going on, and there's a little bit of helpful folks around, and whatever. But back there, they had to

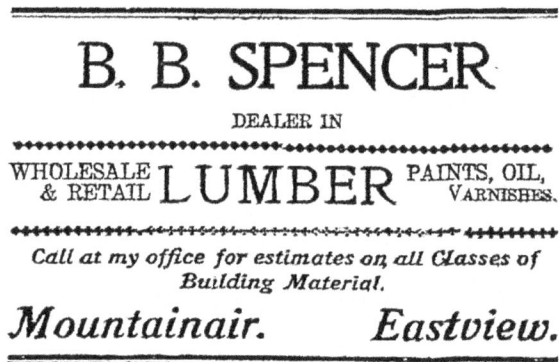

help each other. They talk about the flu, my dad talked about the flu when everybody died. And they just put them out on the porch because they couldn't bury them yet. It was wintertime, the ground was frozen. And how when the funeral happened, then everybody was there and helped the family. And maybe it was the dad that died or whatever, so there were kids. Yeah, the helpful part of that community was there, that I think we've lost. And again, the subsistence part of it, there was no money, and so it was basically a trade, and labor for trade kind of society. My dad talked about his dad paying off those guys, the 60 or 70 that were working up there, in silver dollars, and they got a dollar a day. So the economy was totally different, and the society was totally different.

The recreation part of it, which you think, "Oh, those guys, all they did was work." But the recreation part of it was centered back around the church, and church activities. You know, the old ice cream social thing. The dances that they had was either in the school or the church. And they danced all night, they literally danced all night, and everybody went home in the morning. And so those community things were centered around the church and the school, but primarily the church. So that, of course, has changed now; society doesn't acknowledge that much.

You had one church—well, you had two, basically. You had a Protestant church and a Catholic church. And of course the Catholic churches were here at the community, so Punta and Manzano and Mountainair. As an example, Mountainair got, somebody said, eight or ten churches one time. But the Methodist church was the first church that was there. And the Methodists and the Baptists both met in the same church house, and it was also the school at the same time. So that's kind of the influence of the community at that point. You know, they really didn't have a community, like as far as you're talking about the designated area. As they were building up, there was only one guy and his family or whatever, and then they got two or three or four or whatever, and that's when they needed a schoolteacher, and so my grandpa went to get a schoolteacher, and then you had

SPEND THE FOURTH
IN THE COOL SHADE
AT BARRANCO CAÑON

PROGRAM

Commencing at 10 o'clock a. m.

Band Concert.
"America," - - - - Everybody
Invocation.
Address, - - - Rev. O. A. Crowder
"Tramp, Tramp, Tramp, the Boys are Marching" Everybody
Address, - - , - - Rev. W. E. Henson
"A la Lucha," - - - Mexican Sunday School
Spanish Oration, "George Washington," - Julian Salas
"Battle Hymn of the Republic," - - Everybody
Address, - - - - - Rev. S. S. Bussell
"The Star Spangled Banner," - - Everybody
Benediction.

Dinner---Everybody Eats

2 o'clock p. m.

Boys' Rodeo and Wild West—R. F. Snapp, Director.

Act No. 1. Form in marching circle of about 20 rods diameter, hand every left loose in ring; each boy given chance to rope same. Rope around neck 10 points; anywhere else than neck, 5 points.

Act 2. Trick Riding, 1 rider; Best, 10 points.

Act No. 3. Trick Riding, 2 riders; Best 10 points.

Act No. 4. Burro Race, 3 to enter; Winner 10 points.

Act, No. 5. Burro Polo.

Judges: Hoyland, Mitchell and R. V. Shaw.

Animals must be treated humanely and riders act cautiously or will be ruled out by judges. Boy entrants to be not over 17 years of age.

Races and Games under auspices of Committee.

Baseball Game—Baptists vs. Methodists—No regular players.

FIG 5.2
Advertisement for July 4th celebration
Advertisement appeared in the June 26, 1924, edition of the Mountainair *Independent*.

a school.... The process of building that community was not streets and businesses, like we think of a community, I guess, at this point. But it was people, and then people gathering. You know, the horse racing, that was a gathering part. The celebrations, the 4th of July things, were races: people races, horse races, those kinds of things that now things are so commercialized that we think of Disneyland as a recreational site and a place to go. And of course those guys were thinking, "This 4th of July celebration, let's have pie and race horses.... It was all local.

Eastview was not right on the Belen Cutoff, but it experienced many of the same changes as the section towns. These villages, located about every 6 miles along the ERNM, constituted the dominant type of community that flourished in this period. Other settlements along the Cutoff varied from larger cities such as Clovis and Belen with their railroad machine shops and ample employment to smaller towns such as Mountainair and Willard with diverse economies primarily supported by nearby agriculture. Scholle, located at the head of Abo Canyon,

provides a good example of section-town development, and its history encapsulates the dynamics of these years.

Scholle: a portrait of a railroading/ranch town

Seems like we were all related, we were all one; it wasn't many families, it was one family—Polly Sisneros (2008)

Like most communities in east-central New Mexico, Scholle was a new town compared to those in the Rio Grande Valley. The history of settlement at the head of Abo Canyon began in the late 1800s. A number of Hispano and Anglo families patented land near La Salada, where a local spring provided water and pastures for good grazing. When the AT&SF constructed the Belen Cutoff, settlement increased rapidly in this area, which had been sparsely populated with isolated ranches and a few nearby villages such as Abo and Punta de Agua. Growth coalesced around the Scholle watering station, siding, and depot, established in 1906 by the AT&SF on land the railroad obtained from the federal government (Figure 5.3). The siding and resultant settlement were named after a local merchant and Belen resident, Frederick Scholle, who had a homestead

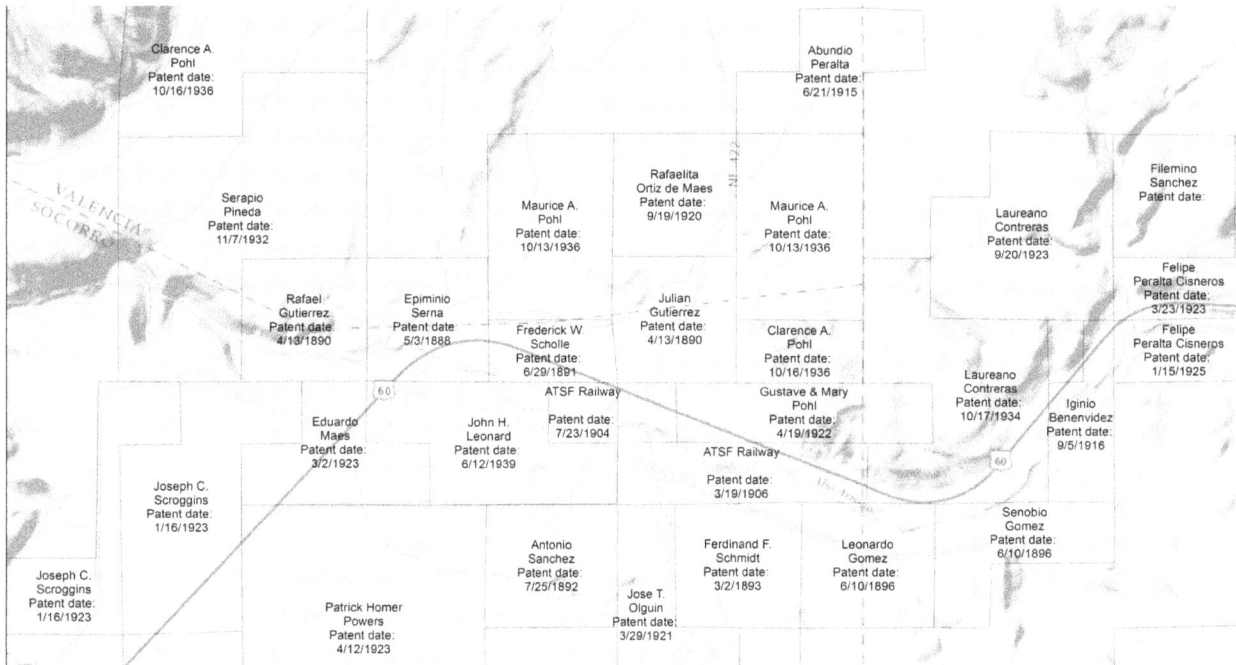

FIG 5.3
Homestead patents in the Scholle area
Map developed by William Penner from BLM General Land Office
(GLO) data. Patent dates are shown rather than application dates.
Prior to 1912 it took five years to prove up on a homestead, and
after 1912 it only took three years.

and orchard in the vicinity (Julyan 1996). Because minerals in the water at Scholle made it unfit for steam engines, the railroad piped in good, mineral-free water from the spring at Abo a few miles to the northeast.

Scholle had a post office by 1908 and the beginnings of a community for dozens of families, including the Brazils, Contreras, Garcias, Kaysers, Pohls, Sisneros, and others (Pohl 2008; P. Sisneros 2008; Julyan 1996). Many of these families worked for the railroad on the local section gang that maintained the tracks. Over the next few decades, the settlement grew in size to include a school, various stores, a hotel, a ballroom, a freight depot, station, and scales and loading pens for livestock. Much of this increase was due to the relationships between Scholle and other outlying properties.

Scholle was not just a railroad town. It served the outlying ranches and functioned as a center of commerce, communication, transportation, and social activities for a number of years. This was particularly true after 1916, when local residents often increased their holdings through the expanded homesteading laws and led a second wave of settlement into more remote locations to patent 640-acre parcels. People used these new

lands for mixed subsistence strategies that included ranching and small-scale farming, sometimes doing this while still working for AT&SF on the section gang. Local ranchers came to town for their mail, supplies, and, critically, to sell their livestock and load it onto the railroad.

Families with children sent them to Scholle because it had the only schoolhouse in the area. When in the 1930s the community outgrew the two boxcars that had always served as the school, they used Works Progress Administration (WPA) funds to build a new masonry structure. This effort had the added benefit of employing many local residents. Martina Brazil Franklin (2008) grew up in Scholle, where her father was a prominent sheepman and member of the community. She recalls how it was.

When we moved to Scholle in 1922, I was just a baby—maybe a year or a year and a half. They built our house out of sandstone rock. It was a very nice house, had wood floors and high ceilings—you know how they built them then—the rooms were large. Of course, we didn't have electricity and we didn't have running water. Oh,

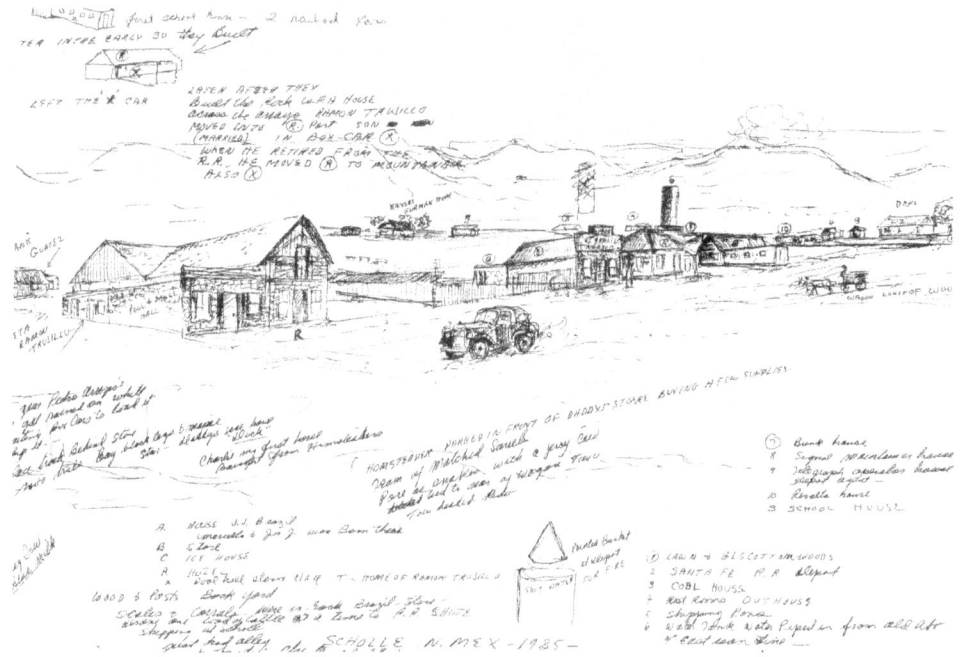

FIG 5.4
Scholle as it looked around 1935
Sketch drawing of Scholle around 1935 as remembered
by Joe J. Brazil (Courtesy of Martina Brazil Franklin).

the Santa Fe Railroad provided water for the community; they brought it from Abo, from the spring at Abo—and at no charge. Yes, I think it was a very nice area to grow up in. Most of the people in town worked for the railroad—except the ranchers' families.

I went to school in a boxcar. It was converted into a schoolhouse and painted yellow, just like the depot. It was a very comfortable schoolroom. Scholle was one of the biggest taxpaying areas, but we always got the leftovers. Mother always said the blackboards they sent us were old, the erasers, everything—we seemed to get the old, nothing new. All of us feel we got a good education in that little two-room schoolhouse. My mother was one of the teachers. Now, it didn't happen where we lived, but I understand over there in Catron County and Socorro, if a kid spoke Spanish, they punished them. In Scholle it was too small a town; the Pohls and the Kaysers all spoke Spanish, they learned it.

My dad would sell and buy—he was a trader. We had a general store in Scholle—Brazil Mercantile Company. You know, Scholle was also a big shipping center. We sold wood and they'd ship bagones—that's boxcars—of sheep and cattle. When the terrible drought occurred in Kansas and Oklahoma, those folks left. The times were terrible and they came through going to California. My folks were very charitable, gave them gas and food to go on because, you know, they were destitute. When people talk now about hard times and the cost of gas, they don't know anything about hard times. We had enough to eat, and clothes, but a lot of people coming in from Kansas and Oklahoma were destitute.

We ate leg of lamb all the time, and cocitas—ribs. We had a lot of soups and roasts and ate well. From the river communities we traded meat for vegetables and fruit. We had goats, my mother made cheese, and you know, none of us liked it, now it's a delicacy!

My mother made bread to last all week. We had chickens and turkeys—Christmas and Thanksgiving. We canned both meats and vegetables in pressure cookers, because we didn't have electricity. And we dried green pinto beans, blanched them, and then strung them up. They taste just like fresh green beans.

FIG 5.5
Scholle schoolhouse with Mrs. Brazil and her pupils
WPA schoolhouse in Scholle sometime in 1938 or 1939 with Mrs.
Marie E. Brazil and her pupils (Courtesy of Frank Wimberly).

The community dynamics of Scholle, being a small settlement serving a rural population of Hispano and Anglos, required people to depend on one another. It does not mean everyone always got along, but people helped each other, children went to school together and shared some common experiences of what life was like in Scholle (Brazil Franklin 2008).

Polly Sisneros was born in Scholle near La Salada, where her family originally herded sheep in the nineteenth century. Her father, Canuto Sisneros, reluctantly worked for the railroad because it was the only locally available job. Below, Polly Sisneros (2008) recalls the dances and religious celebrations and ceremonies that occurred in Scholle and the surrounding areas.

They used to have parties! Scholle was a party town. Oh my God! My dad worked in this pool hall. That's how come we came to Scholle, because Mr. Brazil wanted my dad to manage the pool hall. They used to have the dances there on a big ol' patio between the Brazils' home and Frank Gómez's. All the old dances, the raspa, the varsiliana, baile de la silla, they used to

dance a lot. We used to sweep the patio real good and water it, so it would be nice and hard and wouldn't lift the dirt. Dance till midnight. It was so much fun! Pedro Olguin was an accordion player. Frank Gómez played the guitar. One of the Peraltas also played the guitar. Pedro's brother, Beltrán, played the harmonica. God that was a lively town!

And then at the Bibianos' house, we used to have a wake on Christmas Eve. They were the Mexican people. They had a velorio (wake) every Christmas, and the whole community got together, and we had a dance of the Comanches. That's a holy, well, Catholic dance, you could say, I guess. We had the Comanches and Mama and Daddy were the padrinos (sponsors) for that velorio. So we had that every December. My dad used to collect flares from the Santa Fe [Railroad] the whole year round, so he had enough to put from our house over here to the Bibianos' house. He used to line them up, and put them all in rows and light them for Christmas Eve. We used to line up all the people and process in the middle of the flares carrying the

FIG 5.6
Polly Sisneros at her family's home
Polly Sisneros in 2008 at her family's home in Scholle.
The home was occupied mostly in the 1930s.

baby Jesus to the Bibanos' house, where we danced for him. It was nice. It was a big, big religious celebration. That was fun.

People depended on one another to survive in this isolated area and became close-knit. Scholle was made up of both people living near the tracks and others living on the periphery, where the "community" stretched for miles. The boundaries were influenced by the post office and school. If Scholle was where a family picked up their mail or sent children to school, it was their community no matter how far out they lived from town. Certain families and individuals did their part to create a sense of belonging, and their roles are still remembered. All of this made Scholle an important focal point.

Clarence (Bill) Pohl's grandfather, Gustave Pohl, moved to the Scholle area in the early 1900s. Gustave worked on the original construction of the Belen Cutoff, established the first store, and in 1917 was killed by a train in Abo Canyon while working as a special agent for the railroad. The Pohl family homesteaded in Scholle and operated the post office for many years. Here Bill Pohl (2008) describes what his family did

to make a living as well as the importance of local women in the community:

We were tin can and hardware people I guess you'd call us. We did odd jobs for anybody and everybody. Our main profession during the growin'-up days was building fences. And my daddy was a horse trader. He bought wild horses by the hundreds. He was a trader; he would trade flour and beans, honey and stuff like that, for wild horses. And then he had finally wound up with a market in Oklahoma for a lot of these mustang horses, and they were starting to open up riding academies and riding stables and stuff in Oklahoma. Well, that was a market that he had for three or four years. And then along about that time, one of the big droughts come in '35. A lot of this country grew up in loco [weed] and killed off hundreds of those wild horses. So that kind of put a stop to that horse-tradin' business.

So Daddy built fences, and of course he farmed here. We always had two or three cows; we always raised our own meat. Even at one time, we had a bunch

FIG 5.7
Bill Pohl at abandoned homestead in Scholle
Bill Pohl in 2008 visiting an abandoned homestead in Scholle just north of
the juncture of US 60 and the Belen Cutoff (Photograph by William Penner).

*of those big white ducks in a surface tank over there
north of the schoolhouse. We always had turkeys and
chickens. We always raised our own meat, had plenty
of eggs. For a long, long time, Mother would trade eggs
for some of the people that helped her to clean house
or something' like that. Or she would give eggs for birth-
day parties and stuff like that, to do the cake baking'
and stuff like that because she had a bunch of beautiful white Leghorn chickens, and they all laid. We always
had plenty of eggs. So anybody knew; if they needed a
dozen eggs to make a cake, why, they could get it.*

*Well, we had a women's club during World War
II, and they were like all the rest of the people, they
got together, had dances and stuff, a fundraiser to send
stuff overseas to the service people. And that was the
nucleus of the people there in Scholle. In fact, Mrs.
Brazil, who was a schoolteacher, was the one that kind
of ran that show. She was the leader because she was
a schoolteacher; she was the principal of the school. So
she actually kept the nucleus pretty well together.... And
she's also the one that put together the school hot lunch*

*program with the commodities from the WPA days. So
she was just normally the leader in the households.
Mrs. Brown (they were all Baptists from Texas) used
to contribute to the school, because they had gardens
and a beautiful orchard. About once or twice during the
late summer and early fall, they'd bring a wagonload of
stuff down and give it to the people down here. But they
never were a part of it [the town]—they were always up
on the mountain, you know. But they did those things
for the people down here. So everybody got along, and
it's been much different in the last 40 or 50 years, I'll tell
you. But that's what Scholle was.*

Scholle flourished until World War II, when many people moved
in search of better-paid employment. Some vitality remained
during the late 1940s—the height of livestock traffic for one,
when more cattle were shipped from Scholle than any other
location in New Mexico. Drought, hard times, and changing
technology all eventually affected the dynamics of the region.
The section gang at Scholle closed and the town dissipated
in the early 1950s; it now has only a few residents and exists

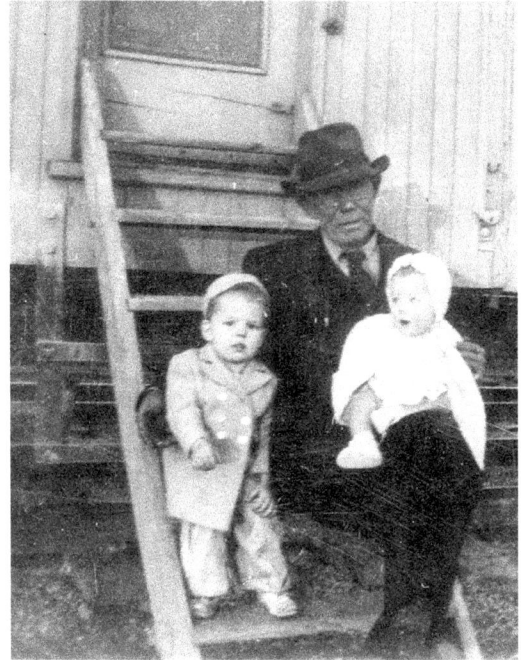

FIG 5.8
Living in a boxcar
August Kayser, longtime Scholle section foreman, in front of a
boxcar converted to a residence with his grandchildren Frank
Wimberly and Deborah Kayser sometime in the early 1940s
(Courtesy of Frank Wimberly).

mostly in memory. The forces of change that caused this will
be discussed further in Chapter 6. Martina Brazil Franklin (2008)
describes how Scholle changed in the 1940s:

*I lived in Scholle until I went away to school at the
University of New Mexico. It was hard times, so I
only went two years. I used to take the train from
Albuquerque to Scholle. The train would stop at Scholle,
although the depot wasn't there anymore by 1939 when
I went to college. The passenger train doesn't go that
way anymore—just freight. The railroad took out the
section houses after I left. Before that, they had all
these boxcars for the crews and their families. I wanted
to live in a boxcar. It looked like such a fascinating world.*

Before this dissipation, however, Scholle formed a unique
position on the Cutoff, something of a balance point that is
worth mentioning. It was not the terminus of the east-flowing
stream of Hispano migration, nor was it the wrack line of the
Anglo flood coming west. Both movements of these people
extended well beyond Scholle, but everyone interviewed about
the town mentioned how integrated and cohesive it was, how

everyone got along in some form of equipoise. This was not
always the case for other communities, as we will consider
further. The larger towns and cities along the Cutoff also tried
to come to some resolution of what they were as they experienced significant changes with new people coming together.

Division points and developing cities

Although the 38 section towns along the Cutoff constituted the
most common and widespread form of settlement, the cities
of Belen and Clovis (and to a lesser extent Mountainair, Willard,
Vaughn, and Fort Sumner) probably seemed more influential
due to their size, diverse economies, and local newspapers.
This primacy has led to them being more frequently studied
than section towns such as Scholle. In particular, there is little
we can do to improve on the excellent scholarship Margaret
McDonald (1997) conducted on Belen's cultural transformations
in the wake of Anglo settlement and the railroad. There are,
however, some elements specific to the larger cities/towns on
the Cutoff that are worth considering.

The bigger communities in east-central New Mexico did
not have quite the same level of boosterism in the late 1930s

FIG 5.9
Engine in the Vaughn rail yards
Engine in the Vaughn yards sometime from 1920 to
1940 (Courtesy of Steve Haines).

that was so prevalent in the preceding decades. Some of the difficulties were beyond their control: mounting droughts and depression, lack of rail facilities, groundwater buried too deep to use easily. Nearly two decades of newspaper publication and attempts at farming meant most people knew what opportunities were like in an area, and no amount of clever advertising was going to compel someone to move to a place because of a fictional railway. The cities and towns each had some clear advantage—Belen and Clovis had their rail shops, Mountainair was the bean capital, Vaughn had a Harvey House, Fort Sumner had irrigation from the Pecos River—except for Willard. The early promise of a great town located at the center of New Mexico's rail traffic was already evaporating by 1929, when the New Mexico Central Railroad was partially dismantled due to lack of shipping (Myrick 1990). An editorial in the Willard *Record* captured some of the regret about this failure to grow.

Willard has failed to hold its own commercially with surrounding towns and so far the writer is not in a position to state just how this situation has been brought about. It is possible for a community, or a person, to be located at the wrong place. Is our location wrong? Are we in a poorer, less fertile part of the county than Estancia and Mountainair? Apparently not.

Are the citizens of Willard ultra-conservative? Have they failed to take advantage of the opportunities that must have been offered them at various times? Has Willard outlived its usefulness? It is possible for towns, as well as people, to do this. Or have the people of the community lain dormant to their opportunities? Possibly so. Perhaps the time is come when we will awaken to glorious opportunities that will make Willard a thriving, cultured community.

Change, constant change is necessary to keep abreast with the conditions of our country. We must profit by past experiences and adapt ourselves to new conditions or give way to those whose progress cannot be stayed (Willard *Record*, November 28, 1930).

Despite some challenging conditions on the ERNM, local commerce reached a zenith in the pre–World War II period during that brief historical moment when automobile ownership was

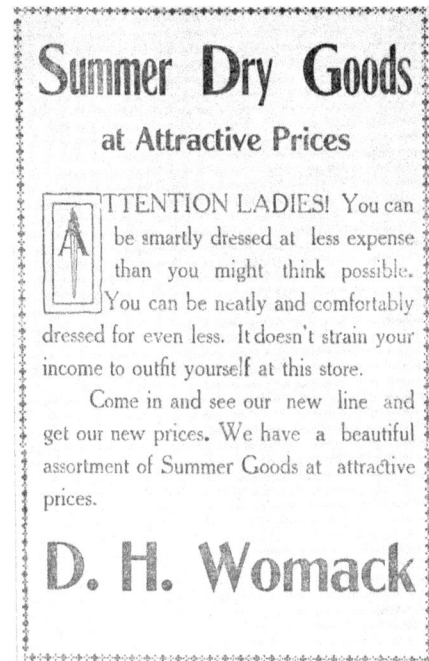

FIG 5.10
Advertisement for D. H. Womack
Advertisement appeared in the September 8, 1923, edition of
the Mountainair *Independent* (Courtesy of CSWR UNM).

not widespread and the majority of products were bought locally. Eliseo R. Sisneros (2008) remembered how many businesses were in Mountainair in the 1930s and early 1940s.

Mountainair used to have a lot of big grocery stores. They had the Mountainair Trading Company, the Tabet Mercantile, the Mountainair Grocery and Bakery. That was the darnedest thing I ever saw, the Mountainair Bakery and meat market would make their own cakes, their own bread, their own ice and everything. [The town had] Brokol's, Womack's, Redfern's, and Blake's. Mountainair used to have a tailor shop. Used to have a central office for telephone, you know, where the operator would say, "Number, please." They [had] the utilities plant, the Inland Utilities…and a bank too (of course the bank got robbed in the thirties). Mountainair had a ball diamond that was fenced in [with] wooden bleachers and [there was] a little miniature golf course.

Belen and Clovis occupied unique positions on the ERNM, bookends to the Belen Cutoff that grew together in the early 1900s. They were located at either end of a spectrum that ranged from west to east, new to old, and Hispano to Anglo, respectively. This was not a fixed entity, and there were counterexamples but it was evident enough even to outsiders such as Carrie Hodges, a WPA employee, who inadvertently identified a "midpoint" in a July 24, 1936, memo, noting that West Vaughn was Spanish and East Vaughn was Anglo. Closer to Abo Canyon, interviewees identified a local version of the continuum where Manzano was Hispano and Mountainair Anglo. Developments in the railroad economies and ethnic makeup of Belen and Clovis made things more complex than just this simple dichotomy.

AT&SF had a mixed relationship with their labor pool and unions, such as the Brotherhood of Locomotive Engineers or Brotherhood of Railroad Trainmen. Workers were not always easy to come by in remote and less desirable locations, so AT&SF handled potential conflicts and strikes in a variety of ways depending on who they could find as replacements (Ducker 1983). One successful technique employed in New Mexico when Anglo labor was unavailable was to use Hispanos, in particular on track gangs. Native Americans were later employed in this capacity when it proved difficult to hire enough Hispanos

FIG 5.11
AT&SF's Japanese replacement workers at the Clovis Roundhouse
Employees of the AT&SF Roundhouse in Clovis sometime in the 1920s.
The pictured Japanese workers were brought in 1922 as replacements
during a strike (Courtesy of Randy Dunson).

(Dunson 2009). AT&SF similarly expanded and maintained their labor pool in the shop crews at the division points by using Japanese workers (whom the federal government sent to internment camps during World War II as we later discuss).

Wage labor and gainful employment

In the period between World War I and II, there were few employment opportunities in small towns on the ERNM. AT&SF and the Sais Crusher provided the most jobs, followed by timber operations and the moonshine industry. The Abo Copper Mining Company at Scholle had some promise, but this and other local mining concerns yielded only short-term benefits during construction of ore-processing facilities built mostly to lure less than savvy investors.

Santa Fe all the way

Everybody worked for the railroad—Polly Sisneros (2008)

Since the construction of the Belen Cutoff, AT&SF required section gangs and facilities up and down the line for maintenance and operations. Local Hispanos and Anglos came from

across New Mexico and other areas to bring their families and live along the tracks near this steady employment with the railroad. Sections on the ERNM initially covered 6 miles of track (Figure 3.3) and required roughly six individuals and a foreman for maintenance. Employees established settlements around the section housing, resulting in many small towns along the Cutoff, such as the aforementioned Scholle. For the Scholle section gang a significant amount of work was taking care of the tracks through Abo Canyon—the most difficult grade on the Cutoff. Below, Fidel Padilla (2008) describes what it was like being a section-gang worker in Scholle and what the watchmen did in Abo Canyon.

My father was first at work here in 1919 in Abo and then they hired me after him. He worked for 10 cents an hour. I started to work in 1940 for the Santa Fe Railroad. Then my brother Elfido worked in here. We both worked together in Scholle and Belen. I worked there for many years. When [my brother] retired, he was a machine operator and I was a machine operator too when I retired. I used to have a foreman; his name was Kayser.

FIG 5.12
Scholle section gang in Abo Canyon
Scholle section gang in 1949 working near milepost 872.0. From left to
right: Acacio Trujillo, Canuto Sisneros, Luis Ortiz, Loreto Molina, Hermenes
Sisneros, Fidel Padilla, and José Sisneros (Courtesy of Polly Sisneros).

*Antonio Garcia was another foreman too—in Scholle.
We used to take care of that canyon day and night. We
worked there—just laying some ties—whatever they
need. Anything was wrong with the track we had to fix
it. Sometimes they got a broken rail; sometimes they
got some mess on the tracks.*

*Sometimes they used to put me in Abo Canyon
during the nighttime—like a kind of watchman—
because rocks came down in the cuts when it was rain-
ing. They had a little shack there for [me] if I stayed in
the nighttime. I had to make two trips from the shack to
the Sais crossing; rest and go back again. A dangerous
place, 2 miles or so—I don't know how long that is. The
one [who worked] at nighttime, he was the one that
would have to notify the foreman in case of something
wrong. He called the dispatcher, then the dispatcher
would tell the foreman that the canyon watchman is in
trouble—they got stones on the tracks, rocks, or whatever. The foreman would pick up the rest of the men and
take them and clean it up.*

Many of the interviewees who lived in Abo and Scholle had
worked for AT&SF in some capacity during their life, although
most of them started after World War II and are discussed in
Chapter 6. In addition to direct employment with AT&SF, some
families negotiated business relationships with the railroad.
Sylvestre Sisneros recalls how his family had long-standing
contracts with the railroad to use water from their spring. In
the era of steam engines, this water was critical to eastbound
freight trains climbing out of Abo Canyon (the steepest grade
on the Belen Cutoff) to replenish water in their boilers. Minerals
in the water at Scholle made it unfit for use, so the railroad
piped in good, clean water from the Sisneros' spring at Abo.
The railroad periodically had to renegotiate their lease of the
spring water. Sylvestre Sisneros (2008) recalls one time when
his family went through this process and struggled with the
complex relationship between water, AT&SF, and the national
economic climate:

*By 1905 he [my grandfather] leased the water from
the spring to the Santa Fe [Railway] at $500 a year.
He had a contract with the railroad for 25 years. And*

FIG 5.13
Fidel Padilla in Abo Canyon
Fidel Padilla in 2008 at Culvert 874.5 in Abo Canyon
(Photograph by William Penner).

the reason I say it was about 1905 is because by the end of 1929, just the time the Depression started, that was the end of the contract. Santa Fe then dropped it down to $360—a dollar a day. It went on like that until about 1938. That was a scare tactic there, you know, the Depression was on, and people were afraid to lose the $360. Three-hundred sixty dollars at that time was something! Every time my [family] would ask for more, the Santa Fe powers that be would tell them, "If you don't want this $360, we'll just close the water off." That would never happen, couldn't happen, because the [railroad] still had the steam engines and that was the only source of fresh water in the area. So I knew it wouldn't happen, but that's what they would tell us.

I was 13 at that time and told them, "You guys back me up, we'll get more." My grandfather said, "How you gonna do that?" I said, "Write them a letter, tell them that we're gonna ask for what they want, and then if they want to close us down, we tell 'em, 'go ahead and close it down….' " As soon as I wrote the letter, a guy from Clovis—that was headquarters for the railroad

then—he came down. Him and an attorney came down and wanted to know who wrote the letter. So my dad took them to me, and they said, "You wrote the letter?" "Yes sir." "Well, you tell your folks we can't do that, we'd rather close it" because I asked for $3,600. I told my dad and Uncle Fred, "Okay, close it." Going back, the railroad guys got together again on the side and talked it over. And he came back and said, "Well, the best we can do is $2,800 a year." Of course my dad and my uncle almost fell over backwards. They'd never dreamed that they would get anything like that. And I still think to myself, with the necessity the Santa Fe had for that water, we could have claimed a lot more.

The reason I arrived at that $3,600 a year is because they had two pump men over here in Becker that they paid 'em, I think 24 hours a day to keep those pumps going. I think the rate was about $2.50 an hour or something like that. I came to the conclusion that it was worth at least $3,600. But it worked. Then they came out with a contract for five years. And then after the five years—because they were anticipating that the

FIG 5.14
Work crew at the Sais Crusher
Work crew at the Sais Crusher in the late 1920s or early 1930s. Loreto
Molina is shown at center with the cigar (Courtesy of Julia Molina).

*diesel engines were coming by that time, they kept on
talking about it but there was no diesel engine—they
asked my folks if they could continue on a year-to-year
basis. And that's what happened until 1956 [when they
phased out steam engines].*

The Sais Crusher

The Sais rock crusher supplied rock ballast for the Belen Cutoff
since its original construction. AT&SF hired Lantry-Sharp to
operate everything for them until the closure in 1959. The
facility employed a number of full-time workers, including
Louis McNiel, the foreman from the early 1940s through the
facility's decommissioning. AT&SF stationed some of their
employees at the crusher, including an engineer to oversee
operations and a brakeman responsible for loading boxcars
full of ballast onto trains. Dozens of men would be employed
seasonally during blasting and quarry operations. A number of
workers lived at the crusher in boxcars or crosstie shacks that
served as homes for their families.

Bill Huckabay (2008) spent some of his younger years living
at the crusher, while his dad, an engineer for the AT&SF, over-
saw operations. He describes life at the crusher:

*There were several converted boxcars; people lived in
all those. There was also a bunch of railroad tie shacks
and there were people living in them. The car we lived in
was an old business coach, like you see in the old-time
movies: inlaid walls of mahogany, gas light fixtures, and
windows all across a raised portion on the top. [On] the
wall above the main coal stove that was used for heat
was written "1929," the last time that car was in the
shop for repairs in Topeka. When I first moved out there,
you cooked with coal, you heated with coal. In 1943,
the only electric power came during the daytime when
the power plant was running the crusher and then at
night there was a small generator that you could only
use for lights.*

*Water was brought in from Belen. They put this
water tank up on top and it was all gravity fed. [In the]
early days, there was a communal shower house and
a family would go in at a time—or a bunch of girls or*

FIG 5.15
Lumber truck in the Manzano Mountains
Lumber truck in the Manzano Mountains sometime
between 1920 and 1940 (Courtesy of Dorothy Cole).

FIG 5.16
Kayser Brothers Lumber
Advertisement appeared in the February 16, 1922, edition of
the Mountainair *Independent* (Courtesy of CSWR UNM).

*whatever. You know, it was tough on womenfolk out
there. It was hard living.*

*There was a cook car in the old days; I'm talking
about the '40s and before. Ma Green was the cook
and Al Green was a shovel operator or a drop hammer
operator, so they both worked for Sharp and Fellows
Contracting Company and fixed and furnished meals for
all those contractor workers. Sometime after the war,
the cook car went away and a lot [fewer] people lived
out there. They'd live in Belen or Mountainair and commute. It wasn't that big a deal to commute anymore.*

The rock crusher operated all year long, but the main operations
were seasonal. Albert McNiel (2008) who grew up at the crusher
talks about this and some of the people who worked there:

*They'd load all year, just about. But in the wintertime, a
skeleton crew—five or six or seven or eight of them—
would be the only ones out there. It would be the shovel
operator, and probably somebody running the cat—typically a gentleman by the name of Roy Lawrence. We
called him "Skinny." That was his nickname—Skinny. He*

*was the crusher foreman. And he would typically run
the caterpillar and push the rock up in the wintertime.
X. B. was the shovel operator; he'd load it into the cars.
The welder was Espinosa. He lived in Belen.... Espinosa
worked in the wintertime. And probably the mechanic,
whoever it was. There were several of them [mechan-
ics] from time to time. But the truck drivers and the
guys, the individuals, that worked on the crusher, and
the other guys, they were all laid off in the wintertime.
And a lot of them were from Belen.*

Timber and the white mule industry

The timber available in the southern Manzano Mountains
allowed for a short period of sawmill operations. As discussed
previously, B. B. Spencer started the trend with his work near
Eastview. By 1921, the industry increased enough that three
sawmills were in operation, producing 40,000 board-feet a day.
Much of the lumber obtained by Gross-Kelly in the 1920s was
from this area (Mountainair *Independent*, November 14, 1921; Carroll 1965).

The region's challenging geography, which limited most

FIG 5.17
Bill Pohl at a still near Priest Canyon
Bill Pohl in 2008 at a well-hidden still in a tributary of Priest Canyon. The former operators had blasted a reservoir in the bedrock to capture the spring water in sufficient quantity to make moonshine. The still's location in a box canyon was not visible from more than 50 feet away (Photograph by William Penner).

industries, was turned into an advantage during Prohibition. Scholle is located at the juncture of Torrance, Socorro, and Valencia Counties, far from most local law enforcement. The remoteness, coupled with the numerous small springs in the area, led to Scholle becoming the moonshine/hooch/white mule capital of central New Mexico, and local newspapers frequently ran news items about stills being busted. The operations sometimes were quite large and professional.

> *Hidden away in a wooded pocket in the highest reaches of the Manzano Mountains of New Mexico, and accessible only by climbing trails all but obliterated, what is believed to be one of the principal sources of New Mexico's whiskey supply has been located and destroyed.... The still was one of the largest and best equipped...and 300 gallons of distilled liquor [were found]* (Mountainair *Independent*, July 8, 1920).

The trade was lucrative enough to induce Adolph Becker, John Becker's son, to begin production. Becker denied his involvement in the liquor business but did allow "he never cared for whiskey until after the Volstead Act went into force: formerly he had drunk lightly of light wine and beer, but since old Volstead came into prominence Mr. Becker's thirst for a stronger brew developed. But he had to be cautious as his wife opposed drinking; he therefore kept his 'hooch' in a quart can concealed in the asparagus bushes" (Mountainair *Independent*, March 30, 1922). Protestations aside, he still received six months in jail.

Agriculture: a full circle from ranching to farming and back to ranching.

> *The land blew away, the potential was gone, the farmers left, and it went back to ranching—Richard Spencer* (2008)

Agriculture dominated both the physical landscape and the economic opportunities for the communities along the Belen Cutoff. Raising livestock, which began with sheep and shifted mostly to cattle by the 1940s, was the most typical occupation in the area for decades. Farming grew in importance and scope in the early 1900s with scientific agriculture such as that of the pinto bean industry. Although much of the farming was for personal consumption, many families also supplemented their income with gardens, orchards, and raising other farm animals.

FIG 5.18
A pinto bean farm
A pinto bean farm in east-central New Mexico sometime in
the 1930s or 1940s (Courtesy of NMSU ASC).

In this section we will examine both the history of ranching and farming in the region and how climatic and economic conditions started shifting in the 1930s and 1940s.

Farming the arid uplands

There used to be a lot of farming everywhere, up around Eastview, and south of [Mountainair] on what we call the mesas, and even around Claunch, Gran Quivira; big bean farms—Jack Hewett (2008)

Chapter 4 introduced the rise of dry farming and described the initial experiences of many of the families who moved to communities and homesteads in the upland regions along the Belen Cutoff. The settlers' success was hampered by ill-adapted farming techniques and, more critically, the frequent droughts and lack of rainfall common in New Mexico. This too was the experience of Dorothy Cole's family. They moved to Corona from Texas in 1935 and four years later relocated to the Roundtop community south of Mountainair so the children could be closer to school. At Roundtop, Dorothy's father farmed for one year and then switched to raising cows. As the

nearby bean fields failed, he bought the surrounding places and accumulated additional land. The Coles made a living by ranching and cattle trading with supplemental activities such as selling cream via the railroad. Dorothy Cole (2008) talks about the era of pinto bean farming around Mountainair and what type of people came to the area in the early to mid-twentieth century.

A lot of our neighbors were the original homesteaders in that area. They stayed through the whole bean field thing. Bill Rogers, he and Vernie Wells, they lasted longer at dryland farming than anybody did, up until probably '75 or '76. After the '50s, they really weren't making it, though. It was really just a fluke. It's hard for me to imagine now that there were dryland farms everywhere, because this is ranchland, it really is; probably the soil should never have been turned.

Looking back over the whole thing, there were probably not over eight or ten years out of the whole bean field era that were really any good. But some of them were really good. They made bumper crops and everybody made money. Of course they waited

FIG 5.19
Threshing pinto beans
The Williams family threshing pinto beans during the
1929 harvest (Courtesy of Gorden and Biddie McMath).

FIG 5.20
Farmer with plow
*Farmer in Mountainair area sometime in the
1920s or 1930s (Courtesy of Dorothy Cole).*

for the next year, and the next year there just might not be any rain at all. So it was always really uneven. But there were enough rains during that era, enough years that people moved here, because they thought it was really a gold mine.

I don't know, I am speculating that when the home-steaders started coming here, they really were farmers from east of here, Texas, Arkansas, Oklahoma—a lot of them from Texas. Most of them were not property owners where they were from, they had been more or less sharecroppers, so that's what they knew how to do. And they probably got the ideas of pinto beans from the Spanish people who were here. I guess the homestead-ers noticed that it was a quick crop, and one that would really do well. The railroads were right there and all they had to do, really, was get them [pinto beans] into the depots. They had four bean elevators where they would take them to, to be cleaned. It's like Bill Rogers always said, you could plant your crop and harvest it and spend the money in 90 days, or 60 days even.

In fact, Mountainair sort of battled it out with Dove

Creek, Colorado, to see who was growing the most beans. I don't know if someone awarded the title, or Mountainair just claimed it, but it went as "[The] Pinto Bean Capital of the World" for several years. Dove Creek for sure has that title now.

The 1920s and 1930s were the best years for the pinto bean industry in Mountainair. During this period there were planted fields extending in a nearly unbroken swath from the foot-hills of the Manzano Mountains east to near the New Mexico Central Railroad. Pinto bean farming had begun its decline by the 1940s (see Figure 4.3), but there were still 120,000 acres under cultivation in the Estancia Valley—roughly 78 percent of New Mexico's total production area for beans (Culbert 1941). Mountainair and the bean industry deserved each other in many ways. Mixed agriculture was generally impossible because of the arid environment and lack of other cash crops adapted to the climate. Additionally, the market price for beans was adequate for a little while to make the good years pay for the bad ones (ibid.). James Culbert, an economic geographer, provided this description of the conditions.

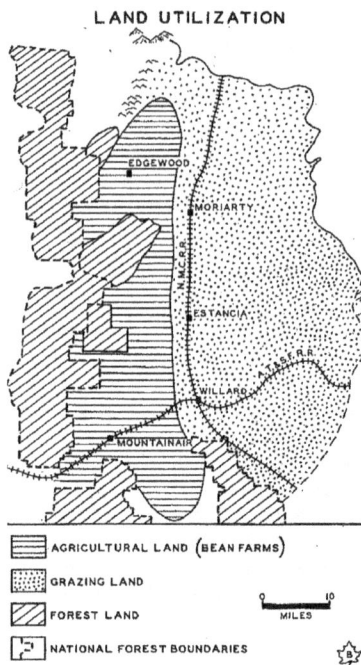

FIG 5.21
Land utilization near Mountainair
Map adapted from Culbert 1941

FIG 5.22
Children outside shack near Mountainair
Children outside shack near Mountainair sometime in
the 1920s or 1930s (Courtesy of Dorothy Cole).

Farmsteads generally consist of three or four unpainted buildings crowded close together near the road. There is usually a windmill, and a few straggly cottonwood trees about it. Barns are particularly small and poorly constructed, being only large enough to keep the family cow, in the rare instances when there is one. Farm machinery is kept in a lean-to nearby or else out in the open exposed to the weather. Dwelling houses appear to be in as poor a state of repair as the outbuildings. Some of the houses are finished inside, and are clapboarded without, while others are little better than shelters consisting of planks nailed vertically to frames, and are entirely unfinished. All of the houses are small and entirely without modern conveniences such as toilet facilities, electric lights, etc. The gray of the weathered boards gives the farmstead an air of desolation and poverty.

The bean country suffers from all of the evils of one-crop farming.... The farmer stakes his time, money, and labor, against the hope that he can make a crop which will be sold at a price sufficiently high to allow him

a profit on the venture. Most of the time, the weather is against him (Culbert 1941).

Culbert's suggestion for improving the situation was a greater emphasis on self-sufficient, mixed agriculture or a switch to irrigation from dry farming. As shown above, bean farming was really only feasible within a limited area near the mountains and above 6,200 feet where rainfall exceeded 15 inches per year (Culbert 1941). By the 1930s, people had realized the difficulties of agriculture elsewhere on the Cutoff, particularly east of Willard. AT&SF commented on this in a 1933 report they commissioned on dry farming on the Pecos Division of their main line, noting, "Twenty years ago there was quite a group of farms in the open flat to the north of Lucy but practically all of them have been abandoned" (NMSU ASC, AT&SF Agricultural Files [AAF]).

People in places such as Scholle already were growing a variety of crops (as described by Al and Joe Padilla below), but they suffered all the same as mono-crop bean farmers when drought conditions in the 1930s and 1950s, along with the lure of outside wage labor during World War II, caused people to

FIG 5.23
Juan J. Sanchez, third-generation rancher in Scholle
Juan J. Sanchez in 2008 on his ranch, which was homesteaded in the late
1800s by his grandfather Elias Sanchez (Photograph by Shawn Kelley).

leave the region. One Mountainair newspaperman also blamed the bean industry for the tough times, but for a different reason: "I maintain that pinto beans have a direct influence on the weather. They are the cause of many dry years. Pinto beans contain 7.4 percent moisture [and] in an average crop year we ship out 14,751,400 pounds of pintos. *This is equivalent to 100,000 gallons of water*" (Santa Fe *New Mexican*, August 9, 1937). No matter the cause, the people that starved out and moved away left room for the resurgence of ranching.

Ranching the land

It was all farming and ranching...everybody did their ranching plus farming—Juan Sanchez (2008)

To understand the landscape of ranching along the ERNM, it is important to look at its regional roots. The Manzano and Los Pinos Mountains were used for summer sheep grazing throughout the nineteenth century. Farther east, cattlemen from Texas ran vast herds of cattle on the unfenced range later in the 1800s. Eventually, families such as the Sisneroses, Sanchezes, and Padillas permanently moved east from La Joya

and other locations along the Rio Grande to the upland areas. Many of these families maintained strong ties to their parent villages and other settlements in the Abo Pass area.

The Padilla family moved from La Joya to La Cienega, a small village west of Punta de Agua and south of the Manzano Land Grant. Later, Gabino Padilla and his three sons, Justo, Jose, and Severo, homesteaded at the head of Priest Canyon, forming a loose-knit community commonly called the Padilla Ranch. In 1905, the Forest Service removed the southern Manzano Mountains from the public domain and lands patented by the Padillas and a few other neighbors became inholdings, thereby limiting growth. Here brothers Al and Joe Padilla (2008) discuss family life on their homesteads. They describe agriculture and sharing aspects of two economies: the long-standing system of barter—mountain villages trading wood or other goods for fruits and vegetables with river communities—contrasted with any available wage labor.

Joe: See, my dad did all kinds of work. My dad worked for the railroad. He worked for that Sais Crusher, and

H-2056 MEXICAN WATER CARRIER ON THE BELEN CUT-OFF, N. M.

FIG 5.24
Mexican water carrier on the Belen Cutoff
Postcard from the Fred Harvey Company depicting a small
Hispano community somewhere along the Belen Cutoff, most
likely in the Manzano Mountains (Courtesy of William Penner).

also on construction of US 60 there. And the reason
for that is because they couldn't make enough money
with the cows that they had. For some reason or other
[on] the leased part of their property, they [the Forest
Service] would not let them keep that many animals,
so they couldn't make a living. If I'm not mistaken, each
one of the brothers and sisters could only have nine
cows. My grandfather Gabino supposedly he was making a living with the cattle that he had, and sheep, and
goats, and stuff like that, because that's what they used
to do. My dad and uncle used to cut wood and deliver
to that little Miller's store near Scholle. The store had
bread, potatoes, beans; it was like a little convenience
store with anything that a person would need. They
used to go out there and pay their bill with wood. Once
in a while, my dad would come to Belen, to the Becker-
Dalies store, and exchange wood for clothing, food, or
whatever he could buy.

Al: Our uncle Jose used to do that very often.
He had a truck, a Model B, and he used to come over
here to the river, and deliver wood for food. Sometimes

when it was ready, they'd exchange the wood for vegetables and fruit.

Joe: I never did go with my dad. At the time I was
too small, you know, and he wouldn't take me with
him. Well, when he was working at the Sais Crusher,
my dad would go horseback every day from the ranch.
He would travel that cañon—Cañon de la Arena, Sand
Canyon—which was about 5 miles. Another thing too,
Uncle Jose would kind of take care of stuff at the ranch.
They used to help each other, my dad and Jose.
Al: At one point they'd leave us there [at the ranch] in the
summer—I don't know if Joe was there—but Joe Gurule,
a cousin of mine, and I had to hoist water from the well
for the cows. We must have been 14 or 15, somewhere
around that age. We didn't have enough money to buy
a little gas motor and pipe it down and bring it up. We'd
have to hoist, dump it into the barrel or whatever, bring it
back down again, and bring it back up again.

Joe: They used to plant corn, so we would go out
there and take care of the crop in the fields. My dad had
18 acres of beans. And even at that, they used to do

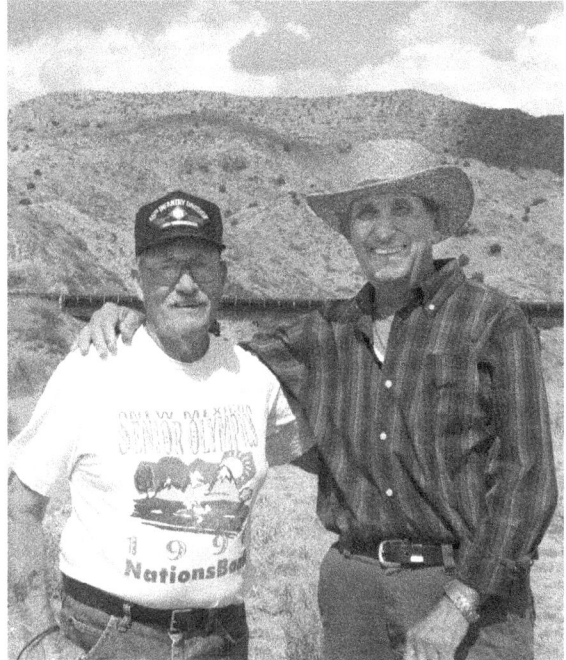

Joe and Al Padilla near Sais Crusher
Joe and Al Padilla at the camp next to the Sais Crusher in 2008 with Bridge 874.2 in the background (Photograph by Shawn Kelley).

some hard work there in the fields. As a matter of fact, when my dad used to work—I mean, when he planted the beans, we'd get up very, very early in the morning. All the kids who were big enough, we'd help my dad hoe the beans, or whatever it was to be done. My mother would go over there [the fields] for a while, until she was ready to go and cook breakfast. We'd be watching over there, it was kind of far, but she would get a white towel and wave it. So here we go, to eat breakfast. But, like I said, women used to help the men in the fields also— my mother would. The women were very capable. My uncle had three girls, the oldest ones he would have them cutting wood out there just like men.

There were three houses there at the ranch and a schoolhouse. The name of it was the Valencia County School. It went up to the eighth grade. It was for the community and I remember one time there was as many as 17 children. I went to that school…. Some of the older brothers and cousins, they would have to rent a place for them in Belen or Mountainair whenever they were going to junior high and high school.

The school closed in 1947, when they contracted my uncle Jose with all his children to go to Colorado to work at the beet farms in Brush. He had a lot of children, so he had help to work these farms. It was very, very hard work and they found out right quick. So the cousins started getting better jobs after they graduated from high school. They quit that labor work there on the farms, you know.

Up until the mid-to-late 1930s, most of the region was open range, where it was easy to move herd animals between pastures and drive them to auction or loading facilities. Residents would utilize loading pens such as those located on the railroad at Scholle, although this decreased as private lands were increasingly fenced (Pohl 2008; Sanchez 2007). Ranching remained an integral part of the landscape in the region. Richard Spencer (2008) summed this up well.

Ranching is kind of an interesting thing: you either like it or you hate it. Is it a genetic thing or not? I don't know. But I've always liked animals, and that was a goal in life, to be a rancher. And I've always liked animals and the

FIG 5.26
Cattle brands from the Fort Sumner area
Cattle brands from Fort Sumner that appeared in the
March 31, 1917, edition of the Fort Sumner *Review*
(Courtesy of Zimmerman UNM).

outdoors and those kinds of things, even though I grew up in town. I spent all of my time out in the country, and so the roots back into this area and into the mountain, because of the grandpas and the uncles and the dads and whatever, was a heritage to me. And I won't say I wanted to emulate it, but I wanted to be a part of it, to be a part of that heritage.

And so I've been a rancher for quite a few years, and enjoy going up to that rock house where Daddy talked about Elfego Baca and those kind of things that are just part of my life…. It's a part of my custom, it's a part of my culture, that goes back to B. B. Spencer [my grandfather]. You've got to respect him—I do—as an individual that did something a little bit different back in those days, and had to have some kind of sand, some kind of ability, and some kind of a strength as a pioneer, that I think a lot of people in New Mexico have—and the West. As progress came this way, they were out in front of it, and it wasn't a polite society all the time.

And again, gringos coming into a Spanish community—those kind of things were tough. And yet there was a bonding with the Spanish culture that was here, from him, and I feel that same thing—rather than a conflict, like some folks have. My grandpa, because he had a little more means maybe, or something, was put in a position to help people—pulling teeth [is] a good example. He had a set of forceps. He pulled teeth for the Spanish folks that were around, for everybody. And those little things like that, that kind of puts a guy in a position of being a community leader or whatever you want to call it. And so I feel a kinship…. I don't have any problem going to Manzano and different places. I've got good friends, people our families have known for years, for generations. That's a good feeling. You know, it's a home feeling. People look at things differently, but home to me is the roots that are here, and the interactions that my family has had over time with different folks. So this is home. You come back to this is home. I was gone for a lot of years and came back. And they say you can never go home. And you can't, to that same situation that you left, but home is the roots that are here, so home was still here. So yeah, I'm proud of our history.

FIG 5.27
Appraising sheep
Sheep in northeast New Mexico in the
1940s (Courtesy of NMSU ASC).

FIG 5.28
Manzano Mountains
View west to Manzano Mountains sometime in
the 1930s or 1940s (Courtesy of Dorothy Cole).

We were never governors and senators and those kind of things, but yeah, I'm proud of our background.

If you look at the evolutionary process of what we're talking about here over time, there was a mountain up here that had timber in it when my grandfather came up here, and the others that came up. And that was the area of wealth [and] opportunity, the [Manzano] Mountains. And they came up and probably cut too many trees and some things like that. And so you go from an era [where] the mountain had value to people—and the hunting and the aesthetics and that kind of stuff was not as important to them, but yet it was. The stillness and the quietness and the nature that was up there, that was important to them.

So you go from that era, then to a bunch of bean farmers that got off of the railroad trains as they came in, and they made their impact here. And the wind came, and the farms blew away, and the potential that was there was gone. The potential, a little bit, at the early point was gone, as my grandfather and others cut the trees out up there on the mountain. And yet

the wildlife and those other intrinsic values were there. The land then changed from the farmer era. The land blew away, the potential was gone, the farmers left, and it went back to ranching. And at that point, the ranchers were the rural community. And depending on their thought patterns and their knowledge, they could either benefit that land or they could rip it off like the farmers had done. And some of them ripped it off, and some of them took care of it.

At that point, if you look at the farmers, it really wasn't the farmers' fault with what they did. They came from the East, they came from Germany, they came from places where it rained. They came out to the arid Southwest and they expected the same kind of circumstances as far as plow [it] up and plant it and it'll grow a crop. And it did that...once in a while when it rained. But basically it was the desert, and it grew dry and it blew away, and so they went away. The rancher then had been here a little bit longer to observe it, and understand it a little bit more.

FIG 5.29
Hispano sheep shearers
Hispano sheep shearers somewhere in eastern
New Mexico (Courtesy of NMSU ASC).

There's almost an automatic thing involved there: as it gets dry and there's too many livestock, they eat off what's there, they have to go, die, whatever. You can't just do like the farmer and plow it up again, and plow it up again, and plow it up again. So some of them had been there long enough to see that concept and say, "Okay, well, we need to move these sheep"— you know, the first guys were the sheep guys anyway. They'd move them up to the mountain, and then bring them back down, and so there was a rotation of sorts going on. Where the problem came in then was with the fencing part of it, after the homesteaders, where everything was fenced, and all of a sudden you had to contain things, and you couldn't move them, and you contained them too long. And so things were over-grazed and hurt that way.

I spent a career telling people how to do it, showing them how to do it. I don't know how many times I've taken people out on my ranch country, and showed them, "Here's what you need to do. Rest this country, let these cool season [crops] grow up, let these warm

seasons grow up, put it back on the calendar, get a plan." And the illustration I always used to use was a horse. You can take a horse and get on him out here in the corral today and go to the top of the mountain, and he'll take you up there pretty well, and you can come back, and he's going to be tired. And you can feed him, and tomorrow you can get on him and he can probably get up that mountain tomorrow, but about the third day, he's not going to be able to do it. And the country is the same way, the land is the same way, it has to have some rest, it has to have some recuperation. And then you can "take it to the top of the mountain," put some cows on it, whatever.

So most people, at this point, have various degrees of knowledge of what land stewardship is, and how to manage country, and how to manage country with cattle. And the horses and sheep are gone. You know, there were a jillion horses running everywhere too, because they let them loose. South of here, on towards Caballo, there was 10,000 horses in there around the turn of the century—not that long ago.

H-2061 A NEW MEXICO SHEEP RANCH ON THE BELEN CUT-OFF.

FIG 5.30
Sheep ranch on the Belen Cutoff
Fred Harvey Company postcard titled *A New Mexico sheep ranch on the Belen Cutoff* (Courtesy of William Penner).

The world intrudes: the Great Depression, starving out, and World War II

Like the rest of the nation and New Mexico, the Great Depression had profound effects along the Belen Cutoff. Many people starved out and sold their homesteads or relied on federal and state assistance to make ends meet. The droughts and storms that caused the Dust Bowl were mostly located east of the ERNM. People fleeing those problems often came west on Highway 60, however, passing through the area and creating a deep impression on the local residents. Conditions on the Cutoff were partially mitigated because many families owned their land outright, in some cases for generations. Sylvestre Sisneros (2008), who grew up with his grandparents next to the mission pueblo at Abo, describes life during the Depression.

We were bad off, but those people [Dust Bowl farmers] were worse than we were, because for one thing their loans that were extended to them didn't exist for us. So we didn't have any loan to pay off; we couldn't lose our property. They would lose their property because it was mortgaged to them. I remember the kids used to come,

one Model T after another, loaded with everything that they had, in real dire straits, really, real poor. We were poor, but at least we had a place to hide.

The idea that having title to land limited New Mexicans' exposure to economic difficulties is challenged by Suzanne Forrest (1998) in her study of New Mexican Hispanos and the New Deal. She argues that the Great Depression exposed Hispano villagers' reliance on outside sources of wage labor (Wyoming sheepherding and Colorado sugar beets, for example), which had been a critical and increasing source of support in the twentieth century. As much of this work disappeared in the 1930s, communities plunged into crisis even if the circumstances seemed mild in comparison to Dust Bowl Oklahoma. Federal efforts such as the Civilian Conservation Corps (CCC) and WPA helped in the area around Manzano as excavations at the mission pueblos of Quarai and Abo provided jobs over a few summers for people such as Fidel Padilla (Figure 5.31).

Gorden McMath's family exemplifies the different ways people made ends meet during the 1930s and the difficulties of farming in a dry climate with variable yields.

FIG 5.31
WPA excavation crew at Abo ruins during the late 1930s
Toulouse's excavation crew at Abo during 1938 or 1939. The group was made up of local residents, including Fidel Padilla (Courtesy of George Lopez).

My dad and mother, six boys and two girls, were raised up out there [in Roundtop]. Nineteen twenty-nine was a tremendous bean crop, and there was just enough crops harvested and sold to get by—pay the grocery bill and get by—until 1941. My dad bought that farm out there (Ewing) in the winter of '33, and he worked it [while also] dismantling [part of] the Sais Crusher and shipping it to old Mexico, and doing this and that. My dad also was the community representative of the farm program. When Roosevelt came into office, we came up with all the farm programs, each community had to have a county supervisor, they called them, to check the farms to see if they were in compliance with the program before they could get their compliance checks or money from the government. And Dad worked at that, he worked at everything. Boys big enough to farm, well, we did the farming. Dad worked out to make a living for us. It was just a scratch and go barefooted, boys. One, two summers, [we] didn't even come to town the whole summer long. The summer of 1935, we didn't even have a car, and Mama only came to town twice a month for groceries. I mean, it was hard. It was bad times.

[In 1941] my dad was at Sais, still dismantling the crusher, [and] we made such a tremendous bean crop that year, we paid up all past debts, Dad bought a new pickup and a new tractor, and Mom bought all new furniture. It's the first time that we had had any money in my whole lifetime,'41. And I was always kind of proud of my dad that he was able to raise a family out there and keep it all together and stay. It was something to be proud of (McMath 2008).

Conditions on the Cutoff were certainly softened by the constancy of railroad work, although that could only help so much. Social cohesion, resilient spirit, and the fertility still remaining in bean fields (now farmed for almost two decades) somehow made up the difference, so that years later almost all the people we interviewed would note how the 1930s and early 1940s were the best times in their communities. These were the individuals who stayed on successfully, however, and those who left would probably tell different stories.

Farming in a harsh climate and a few years of drought or

FIG 5.32
McMath family's bean harvest
Photograph taken of the McMath family in 1936 during their bean harvest. The tractor was an Oliver "80" Hart Parr, and the individuals are (from to left to right).: Gorden, Robert, W. P., Eva, Lee, Jack, Charles, and Bill—Ellis is shown driving (Courtesy of Gorden and Biddie McMath).

FIG 5.33
Square dance
Square dance in Mountainair, date unknown (Courtesy of Dorothy Cole).

misfortune did cause many to pull up stakes and move. They sold their land, often to other local families, who expanded their ranching operations if they had the means. Sylvestre Sisneros (2008) remembers his family patenting additional lands under the Homestead Enlargement Act, the homesteaders who moved into the area, the changes that happened, and the poverty experienced during the Depression.

There was about five sections south of Abo near Chupadero Mesa that they couldn't dispose of it under the original Homestead Act (which only allowed 160 acres), because the land didn't have any water. It was good grazing, but it was far out of water. Juan Jose Contreras, who was my dad's cousin, had a piece of land where he had drilled a well down in the canyon. He had the only water available for about 5, 10 miles there in the area. And Joe Brazil had another piece of land adjacent to Contreras. These two men were sheepherders; at that time there [were] sheep all over the country. Well, what these two men did, they would go and lease all of that land—it was just common then—[for]

the sheepherders. Because they had the only water available, Brazil and Contreras would divide the profits.

So by 1932, these two gentlemen had an out. Brazil, he went and told my dad, my uncle Fred, my uncle Martin, Canuto, and my tío (uncle) Ramon that there was five sections available there, to just apply for them. As soon as they improved them—the requirement was to put up, I think, a corral and a little house or shack, and fence it—then the government would approve the claim. My dad got a deed from President Roosevelt in 1933.

We lived there one summer. My dad built a two-room shack we had to move into and my dad had us fence the whole thing—4 miles around. I was just dragging along, I think, with maybe the hammer and the staples or somethin'. The rest of the kids were too young.

Well, the section [owner] south of my dad, his name was Cocanougher. My family worked with him, they had a bean field. He was a single man, he had tuberculosis and eventually got too sick to be there, and he wanted to go back to Texas. And he went and offered my dad his section—real estate wasn't moving'

FIG 5.34
Kayser and Tarin families at Scholle
Kayser and Tarin children at the section foreman's house in
Scholle sometime in the 1930s (Courtesy of Frank Wimberly).

FIG 5.35
Mountainair street scene
Mountainair parade in 1937 (Courtesy of Jack Hewett).

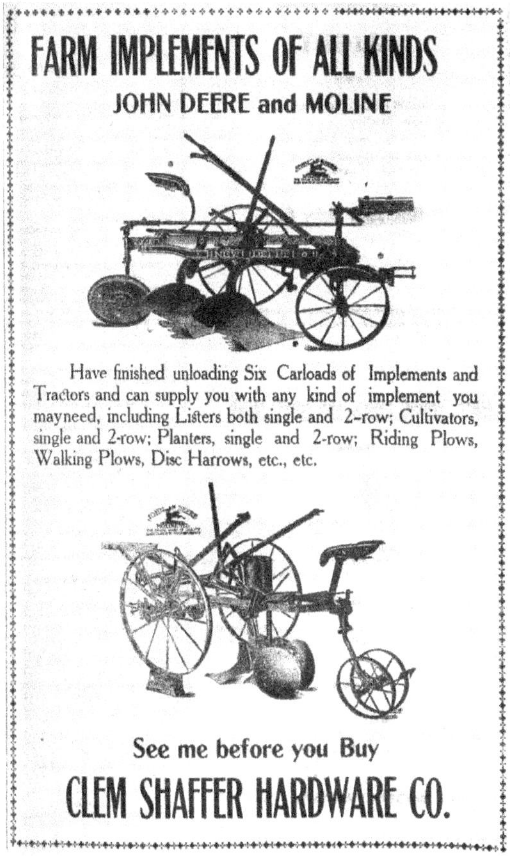

FIG 5.36
Case tractor
Advertisement appeared in the May 6, 1920, edition of the Mountainair *Independent* (Courtesy of CSWR UNM).

very fast—for $150. We were fencing up there between Cocanougher and my dad's [land]. Cocanougher came up and said, "If you can raise $50 and give me $50, then you can pay me the rest, 'cause I got to go back to Texas with the family." Of course during the Depression, he might as well say $500,000, because nobody had [cash]. I said to my dad, "Buy it! Buy it! Why don't you buy it?" I figured my dad could probably borrow $50 someplace, but he finally got fed up and kicked me on the bottom and said, "You guys don't know what you're talking' about."

Well, years went by, I went to California, and when I came back my dad told me to take care of that place there for him—he was getting pretty old. And I said, "Sure, I'll help you out." So we went [to] that place where we had put the fence and I remembered he had kicked me in the bottom. As we were going by the fence, I said, "You remember when you kicked my butt here?" Of course my dad remembered, and he said, "Turn around so you can kick me in the butt; $150 for a section!"

There were other changes happening to the rural landscape of eastern New Mexico. As mentioned previously, the adoption of mechanized equipment was becoming more necessary and widespread to effectively compete in the national economy, and farm and ranch sizes were on the rise (Figure 5.37). Teams of mules were traded in for tractors just as the earliest homesteaders had moved on from using oxen. That had implications for the nearby towns, a phenomenon commented on by Weldon McKinley (2008).

The homesteaders came and Mountainair developed a bunch of little stores. They had some equipment dealers, had a John Deere dealer, and they had a Case dealer once the tractors started. Before that there was an old guy by the name of John Jackson that used to trade horses all the time—teams of horses.

Tractors changed things somewhat for towns and villages on the Cutoff, but the adoption of automobiles had a greater impact (as discussed in detail in Chapter 6). People could drive farther to get their groceries, and children could be bused to distant schools every day. Early on, though, not many people

	1900	1910	1920	1930	1940	1950	1960
New Mexico	417	316	818	982	832	1,139	2,908
Counties along the Belen Cutoff	169	276	1,090	1,436	1,617	2,788	4,021

FIG 5.37
Average farm and ranch size (1900 to 1960)
Data compiled from decennial agricultural census reports from the USCB
1952b; 1942b; 1932b; 1922a; 1922b; 1913b; 1902b. All figures given in acres.
The average farm size along the Cutoff is skewed by DeBaca and Guadalupe
Counties, which have always included large ranches.

had cars except for those with money and a specific need. Martina Brazil Franklin's father traded sheep for a living, and she remembered when he got his first car.

> Mr. Redfern, the mayor at Estancia told me that [my father] had the first car in Torrance County…. He bought a brand-new V-8 Ford, prettiest car, prettiest upholstery. Well, he promised [my mom] he would not put animals in the car. [But soon enough] people talked about it, they looked, there was this car going by with rams and sheep! Mother had a hard time. He did what he wanted to do (Brazil Franklin 2008).

By 1942, the United States had moved to a wartime economy. There were labor shortages, and both Hispanos and Anglos often moved to the cities to work. The *bracero* (a short-term Mexican laborer) program initiated by the federal government helped bring Mexicans to the region to work on farms and the rail systems. Section foremen such as August Kayser at Scholle used several *braceros* during the next few years to fill in labor gaps as local boys left the area to enlist (Wimberley 2009). Agriculture still was important, though, and AT&SF encouraged

people along their routes to grow crops for the country's success (Figure 5.38). Indeed, railroad promotion of farms on the Cutoff almost combined with the fate of Japanese Americans during the war to create an odd legacy.

As mentioned previously, AT&SF employed Japanese Americans in their machine shops at Clovis and Belen to replace Anglo workers striking during the 1920s. These individuals stayed, worked, and raised families in the area for almost two decades until they were rounded up and interned at Fort Stanton at the onset of World War II (Dunson 2008). A Japanese-American businessman in Belen was so well-liked by the community that they successfully fought the removal process and managed to keep him in town (Dunson 2008).

While this was ongoing, Hi Korematsu, acting chairman of the Evacuated Alien Resettlement Program, and others were trying to find locations for Japanese-American farmers outside areas on the Pacific coast, where they were now restricted from living (NMSU ASC, H. M. Bainer to A. M. Reinhardt, March 18, 1942). The Japanese were to establish a nonprofit cooperative farm under federal control, and AT&SF was approached to help in the effort. Their general agricultural agent at Amarillo, Texas,

Vegetables of War

"*MORE HEALTH AND STRENGTH FOR A NATION AT WAR!*" is the War Cry of America's Southwest.

In this land of golden sunshine and fertile fields grow tons upon tons of vitamin-rich vegetables.

Many of its fields are producing one, two, three, and even four crops each year—our Vegetables of War.

To you of the Southwest who are asking more and *getting* more from your acres than ever before—thanks, from all of us! Keep up the good work that means better nutrition for America's fighters and workers!

Santa Fe

SANTA FE SYSTEM LINES
Serving 12 Western and Southwestern States

FIG 5.38
Vegetables of war
Advertisement appeared in 1945 in an undetermined
publication (Courtesy of William Penner).

FIG 5.39
Mountainair street scene
Mountainair's Main Street sometime in the 1940s
(Courtesy of Jack Hewett).

H. M. Bainer, considered this business and suggested the Estancia Valley might be suitable, although nothing ever came of the plan in the end.

> With this area in mind as of first importance in New Mexico for Japanese farm units, I visited this valley yesterday to find out how those residing there would feel towards the establishment of Japanese farm units within their neighborhood. I made contact with seven of the leading citizens of the valley, and was surprised in that very little criticism was expressed against this kind of movement, and on the other hand, all were agreeable to cooperating in a federally supervised program. These citizens have in mind that the Jap farm units would be able to help relieve the farm labor situation, in addition to the farm work on the unit (NMSU ASC, H. M. Bainer to G. L. Goin, March 18, 1942).

AT&SF's transcontinental line, which included the Cutoff, also moved much of the men and military equipment for the war in the Pacific theater. In response, new businesses sprang up in towns along the ERNM to service the troops passing through. In Mountainair, the Abo Hotel and White House Hotel rented rooms to soldiers, as did local residents (E. Sisneros 2008). Abo Canyon's bridges were considered strategically important enough that watchmen were assigned to guard them for the duration of the war (Padilla 2006; E. Sisneros 2007, 2008).

Most young men of the Cutoff served in some way during World War II, and this experience exposed them to a broader world than they had known before. Gorden McMath (2008) was raised on a bean farm in Mountainair and had never even been around an airplane but ended up as a flight engineer due to his mechanical aptitude. He recalls some war stories and a chance encounter in Kunming, China.

> I was in the army air force during World War II. My job wound up to be flying over the hump, the Himalayan Mountains, delivering supplies and gasoline and war supplies over to the Flying Tigers and so on in China. I'd been over there about a year and a half or so, and I was down and out, homesick, and blue, and wanted to come home…. I had my sister send me some pinto

beans, because it rained over there a lot, and I thought they would grow. So I was out behind the barracks there and I made me a little garden; I planted some of them pinto beans. Boy, they popped out of the ground and grew up and got about that high, and the bugs ate them up to the ground.

But anyway, we came into Kunming, China…and I walked over there where they were stockpiling all of the stuff that came in airplanes. There were hundreds of airplanes that were coming in. There was a stack of beans over there. I went over and looked at 'em, and there were 144 one-hundred-pound bags, pinto beans from Mountainair Trading Company!

The events surrounding World War II had far-reaching consequences for the farmers, railroaders, and communities on the Belen Cutoff. Their relationships to land and labor would irrevocably shift over the next decades. Some of the changes reflect trends that began earlier, while others were new. Chapter 6 considers these issues and how the people of east-central New Mexico entered the modern, post-war era.

6 | Drought, diesel, and the almighty dollar: post-war change in east-central New Mexico

During the post-World War II era, three major factors combined to alter the economy and society of east-central New Mexico. First, drought and poor soil conditions in the region's arid uplands continued to reduce agricultural output, a trend that began in the 1930s. Second, employment shifted away from rural areas to urban centers and included industrial production and manufacturing. Third, railroad companies changed the way they operated due to technological advancements. Diesel engines required less infrastructure and maintenance, which caused small railroad settlements to become obsolete. Implementation of automated controls and other advancements further reduced the number of available jobs in the region. These three factors brought the Belen Cutoff full circle from homestead boom to post-war bust. In this chapter we explore how these changes impacted the people and settlements of the region and present brief project conclusions.

Rain didn't follow the plow: drought and the Soil Bank

This country…should never have been put into dryland farming—Gorden McMath (2008)

Drought and changing realities

As discussed in Chapter 5, unstable environmental and economic conditions during the 1930s and 1940s transformed life along the Belen Cutoff. The economic decline caused by the Great Depression dramatically altered community structures as people migrated toward regions with better economic opportunities. The World War II industrial boom attracted workers to urban areas. At the same time, young men and women enlisted into national service to help with the war effort. Food production became critical to national security just as many of the nation's young men and women were away from home in the services or positions supporting the military. Despite drought conditions and irregular growing seasons, a few farming families were able to benefit from the occasional good harvest and the elevated prices of wartime commodities.

Large-scale agriculture along the Belen Cutoff was primarily dedicated to pinto bean farming. During the railroad boom environmental conditions were somewhat favorable, and many people believed that if the area was intensively farmed, the arid land could be permanently greened. The main proponents of this theory were railroad boosters, who had little experience farming. The favorable environmental conditions and the climate of boosterism that drove dryland farming for decades ultimately declined as the drought proved too challenging for farmers. As early as the 1930s, many families starved out, especially families who did not own their land but leased it or sharecropped other farms. Lean years between a few great ones proved to be hard for many who owned property as well, sometimes tying them to land that was hardly worth selling.

After World War II, the agricultural decline of the region only intensified. As farmers struggled to make a go at dryland farming during drought conditions, agricultural extension agents explored ways to improve the situation. State agencies and agricultural experts believed that there were significant aquifers that could be pumped for irrigated farming in the Estancia area.

Behind the scenes, the railroad company continued to

FIG 6.1
The Williams family harvesting beans
The Williams family harvesting beans sometime around 1912 to 1915, from left to right: John Williams, Durey (Dude) Boyd, Lester Williams, and an unidentified neighbor (Courtesy of Gorden and Biddie McMath).

FIG 6.2
Steam engine pulling refrigerator cars in Abo Canyon
View of steam engine pulling refrigerator cars in Abo Canyon at milepost 872.9 sometime from 1940 to 1949 (Courtesy of KSHS).

push for land development, irrigation projects, and any other economic schemes that would foster agricultural production. Rail company profits depended significantly on the transportation and shipment of agricultural goods. H. M. Bainer, AT&SF's agricultural agent in Amarillo, Texas, commented in 1943 on development proposed by a local agent and the possibility of irrigated farming in the Estancia Valley:

> While we realize that carrots, cabbage, etc., can be grown in limited areas in the valley under irrigation by pumping, we are very doubtful of successful production on anything like a large scale (50,000 acres suggested by Engel); however, we do appreciate his enthusiasm and desire to be helpful in such production as the valley is capable of doing. We are hopeful that something can be done to provide funds so the State Engineer can make a thorough investigation of irrigation by pumping possibilities of the Estancia Valley in the near future.... Possibly through our legal solicitor for New Mexico, we can be instrumental in getting such assistance provided by the next session of the legislature (NMSU ASC, AAF, H. M. Bainer to G. C. Jefferies, November 24, 1943).

Four years later, Bainer wrote a memorandum on the crop outlook for the Estancia Valley.

> As you will recall, no carrots have been grown in the valley since 1945 during which season we handled 21 carloads out of the area. Following 1945 it seems that no one has been interested in carrots or any other vegetable for commercial shipping. The usual acreage of pinto beans are being planted at this time. Up to recently the soil has been very dry; however, there has been sufficient rainfall lately for planting of the beans, and the crop is mostly up at this time, but more rain will be required in the near future to keep the crop going.
>
> Comparatively little acreage of grain sorghums are being grown for commercial handling. The grass conditions in the valley are fair to good and livestock of all kinds are in splendid condition. It is reported that a number of new irrigation wells are being developed, all of which are low in capacity and comparatively little acreage is being irrigated outside of acreage of alfalfa (NMSU ASC, AAF, H. M. Bainer to M. Lymen, June 7, 1947).

FIG 6.3
Driving cattle
Driving cattle somewhere near Mountainair in the 1950s
(Courtesy of Dorothy Cole).

For landowners with access to groundwater, such as those in the Estancia Basin, Pecos River valley and Clovis area, farming remained a viable option. However, despite efforts to promote small farms along the rest of the Belen Cutoff, the inevitable result of drought, poor soil, and low commodity prices resulted in land consolidation. Ranching became the most viable large-scale agricultural prospect for the majority of lands in the area. Many local ranchers purchased small homesteads from struggling farmers and slowly began to expand grazing areas (see Figure 5.40).

For example, James Autrey's family homesteaded just north of Mountainair during the early twentieth century. At first, they grew pinto beans and later mostly switched to ranching. Autrey (2008) relates how his family accumulated different ranchlands over the years.

I guess my dad was the one that started it [ranching]. It'd been about the time I was born. Now, I'm not sure about the acreage and everything, but it must have been about '39, because I was two or three years old. He bought that piece of land at Abo, which I think was about 500 acres…. From that 500 acres, he put together

3,300 acres. That was during all my growing-up years. And then in 1954, he got in financial problems, and he ended up selling that [land] at Abo, and buying that at Chupadero. That was my senior year. I didn't go to Chupadero, I went to work for the telephone company. That's the year my dad went to Chupadero…. Well, he bought 14 sections to start with, and he ended up with 55 sections. And then he sold that to my two brothers. He (Dad) would run between 500 to 700 head…. I've thought a lot about it, and it's kind of a marvel to me that he put that much together, through those years, and then raised a family, you know. And he didn't work anywhere, he made it off of cattle.

Although some families were able to adjust to the changing realities of ranching and farming in Mountainair, others were not so fortunate. For example, as community members returned from overseas military service, they discovered shrinking communities and limited economic opportunities. Gorden McMath (2008) describes his experience as a farmer after World War II and the difficulties he encountered.

FIG 6.4
McMath family threshing beans
McMath family using tractors to thresh beans, 1954, from left to right:
Gorden, Robert, and W. P (Courtesy of Gorden and Biddie McMath).

FIG 6.5
Gorden McMath, 2008
Gorden McMath in 2008 with his some of his metal folk-art sculptures
(Photograph by Shawn Kelley).

I got out [of the service] on July 10, 1946, come back here, and started farming beans. Went broke three times after that, farming beans. Bad years and not good prices, and just barely marginal farming. When I came back from the army...we knew that the water was there in this pool from Estancia and down through there— [in an] aquifer. And during World War II they developed pumps that were economical, and that would pump enough volume of water to irrigate with. So that's when they started drilling wells and irrigating over in that area. But it took a lot of money and a lot of work and good luck and everything to get going. A lot of help to develop a farm and drill the irrigation well. They're still doing it... consolidating farms. Instead of with a shovel and getting up at night and changing the water and so on, they have the sprinkler systems and all that now....

One family can handled about what three farmers could earlier, at the time that picture was taken there (1910s). *But it's still very marginal. The price that fuel is now, I doubt that they're going to be able to make it.*

This country here, as a farming enterprise, should never have been put into dryland farming. It probably should have been kept as a ranchland...because there's just not enough rain/moisture to dryland farm out here. So it didn't explain it in this book that you read (The Tale of Three Cities), but the whole fact to the matter is, the railroad and the government encouraged people to come here and homestead and plow up the land and farm. Of course I don't suppose they knew any better. But they should have. This should have never been, and is not now—there's not one acre of dryland farming in this whole bean valley area.

Gorden McMath's experience represents a deeper crisis in U.S. agriculture. Many small farmers throughout the 1930s and 1940s struggled to deal with drought, unstable economic situations, and changing markets with little government support. As a result, the federal government created a series of programs to stabilize agricultural production. The next section explores the impacts of soil banking in east-central New Mexico.

FIG 6.6
Pinto beans in the field
Pinto bean plants in northeastern New Mexico (Courtesy of NMSU ASC).

Soil banking

Americans witnessed the extreme effects of drought and soil loss from extensive farming in many parts of the country during the 1930s and 1940s. The effects of the Dust Bowl were etched into the American psyche through popular media, literature, and lived experiences. John Steinbeck's novel *The Grapes of Wrath* and Dorothea Lange's documentary photos created enduring popular images of the Dust Bowl migration.

In an effort to promote, preserve, and protect American agriculture, the federal government developed a number of initiatives to support farmers. In east-central New Mexico one of the more prominent federal projects was the Soil Bank Program. The Soil Bank Program was created as part of the Agriculture Act of 1954 and was designed to protect soil from further degradation. The program required participating farmers to retire lands from agricultural production for 10 years in return for monetary compensation. The Soil Bank created an economic vehicle through which farmers were able to regenerate the health of their fields without being penalized with a loss of income. Many farmers along the Belen Cutoff took advantage of the program.

Jerry Shaw's family was like many who came to the region during the early twentieth century. His father farmed pinto beans for decades through the good and bad years until finally giving up altogether in the 1970s. Jerry Shaw (2007) describes the drought, the Soil Bank program, and the decline of the pinto bean industry.

[The] Soil Bank came in the mid-'50s and that wiped out the farming completely…. You know the Soil Bank, it was a government program. Until then, a few of the farmers still tried, you know, in 1949 we had a fair crop, and never again after that, it just was so dry. But a few of them [farmers] continued to try until, oh, '53 or '4. It just didn't rain anymore and then the Soil Bank came in and all the farmers put their land in the Soil Bank, and that's the end of it…. A few of the natives up in the mountains try out a little patch once in a while, but nobody [really produces]. My dad's one of the last ones to try it out here. He farmed till about '70…'3…'4, somewhere in there…He didn't farm big but he kept trying. Never had a good year after the Soil Bank.

FIG 6.7
Construction of Scholle's WPA School
Construction of the WPA-funded masonry schoolhouse in Scholle
(Courtesy of Polly Sisneros).

*Down there [Mountainair] was the pinto bean cap-
ital of the world.... From Mountainair east, south and
north. There were all farms—you can see still the timber
is not nearly as tall where the fields were, but it's coming back in old junipers now.*

Although the Soil Bank marks an end of the pinto bean boom, it helped farmers through the painful transition into new liveli-hoods. Many community members continued to emigrate out of the region in search of work in larger urban areas. The next section will trace the impact of the post–World War II economy on the communities along the Belen Cutoff.

The post–World War II economy

*World War II is what jerked the people out of this coun-
try and of course once before that, back in the '30s, it
was the drought—Bill Pohl* (2009)

The post-war economy of east-central New Mexico was shaped by a number of local and national variables. Agricultural decline and drought paired with improvements in railroad tech-nology and reduced the number of jobs in the area. Economic crises in the 1930s were followed by American involvement in World War II, which increased industrial production and pulled community members away from the region into mili-tary service or jobs in urban areas. The mass production of automobiles, improved roads, and cheap gas also contributed to the creation of a mobile society shifting away from railroad dependence. Within the short span of 30 years, life along the Belen Cutoff was drastically altered. Oral history accounts of this period illustrate how the region changed.

Francisco Sisneros, a local historian, grew up in Abo. His family's residence was located near Highway 60, and they ran a small store in front. Although the business provided some income, his father sought out other employment over the years. Francisco was interviewed by Cheryl Foote for an oral history project focused on the Hispano resettlement of Abo and Quarai and talked about how families in rural areas tran-sitioned into the wage-labor economy beginning during the Great Depression and continuing through the post-war era.

*My father, his first job I guess was through the CCC,
the Civilian Conservation Corps, in the 1930s where he
started out as a cook's helper, then later as a cook. This*

FIG 6.8
Drill at Sais Crusher
Drill at the Sais Crusher sometime in the 1940s or 1950s
(Courtesy of Albert McNiel).

was in the Jemez Mountains, and then he transferred to the same program in the Manzanos when they were cutting fire lines in the Manzanos. Then from there he worked as a cook in Mountainair in a café. Not very long. Then he was drafted and took his physical in Santa Fe and here in Albuquerque. And he was sent for training in Ft. Bliss, Texas. There he was in the 200th Coast Artillery, which of course later on was captured in the Philippines and all that. He didn't go. He got hurt during training, and so he spent two months in training and then about two and a half months in the hospital. He had a knee injury.

After that he went to Abo and married my mother in 1941. By later 1941 they were in San Francisco, California, living there. He had gone to work there in the shipyards in Richmond, California, right across the bay from San Francisco. And of course there were a lot of people who were going there from New Mexico, well, from Oklahoma and everywhere else too. But from New Mexico there were a lot of people from the area of Abo… that ended up over there, and a lot of them stayed… [my parents]for two years or so and then my dad came

back and worked for a while for the Santa Fe Railroad on the line. After that he worked for different companies, mostly Sharp and Fellows Company, which crushed ballast (a layer of gravel between ties). He worked there for quite a few years, 11 or 13 years. He was the explosives person for the company and did a lot of the drilling also. Then after that he worked highway construction, doing the same kind of thing, explosives and drilling.

My dad and mom had a store even before I was born in Abo. They had a gas station there too. I remember the old gas pump, it was really a pump where you pumped gas. They had a little store that sold groceries. And then they closed that up, I don't remember the year. But it was around the time our house was condemned by the state [of New Mexico]…to build a new highway. Then my mom did have another store, where my dad now lives. Just a little store [that] sold candy and cigarettes and potato chips…. I don't think she ever made any money, but she had a real time over there (Sisneros 1988).

FIG 6.9
Scholle siding
Unknown individual and Margaret Kayser at Scholle in 1949
(Courtesy of Frank Wimberly).

Similar to the elder Sisneros' experience, many young men from the area were enlisted in the armed services from towns and villages such as Mountainair and Scholle. Community members who stayed in the area sought out the few employment opportunities that remained. Even after World War II ended, the urban economic shift continued to pull workers away from the Belen Cutoff. Community members who emigrated during the war often stayed in large metropolitan areas such as Albuquerque and San Francisco, California, to work wage jobs. Some residents did return home and discovered that their towns were in the midst of transformation.

The section town of Scholle is a good example of this transition. Polly Sisneros (2008) discusses the changes that occurred in Scholle during the war years.

During the war they started [leaving Scholle].... They were still working for the Santa Fe, but they started farming. Mountainair was the bean factory of the county. Everybody started working for the bean factory there. Oh, they loaded all the beans. And then potatoes, they started planting potatoes too. Oh, they had a lot of potatoes in that area. Lettuce, they planted a lot of

lettuce. ...Families moved out, Scholle was deserted. Everybody left. The only ones left there were the Pohls and Brazils. Other than that, everybody moved out. The people in Abo were left there. But almost everybody went to Mountainair to work in the bean fields. [There were] a lot of beans.

Others such as Sy Sisneros went to find work in California during the war. He enlisted in the service and when he returned continued to find wage work in California for a number of years (Sisneros and Sisneros 2008).

Well, there was a double whammy: one was Uncle Sam, when Soil Conservation came with a project that they would pay you, because of the Dust Bowl, they would pay you $2 an acre not to farm. Well, since the bean crop was getting so iffy, a lot of people went for the $2. They had to sign a contract that they wouldn't farm it for so long, and they were going to give them $2 an acre. So that was part of it. The other part was the drought. It started getting too dry, and they might have one good crop and maybe three or four years with

FIG 6.10
Sy and Francisco Sisneros
Sylvestre (Sy) Sisneros and his nephew Francisco Sisneros in 2008 in Veguita, New Mexico (Photograph by Shawn Kelley).

nothing. So they had to do something.

By the time I finished high school, I went to California to work in the shipyards, but I knew that either the draft was going pick you up, or you volunteered, one of the two. And I was in California, working in the shipyards, and I decided to volunteer, because I could select the kind of service I wanted to go to.... So in San Francisco I joined the navy, and then they sent me to Farragut, Idaho, way out close to Canada, for training. Later on I went to Bremerton for indoctrination, and then Astoria. That's where we picked up the first ship, this carrier I was on—brand new. And I stayed on that one all the time in the Pacific. When I came back in 1946, they decided to scrap it. And I ended up with that [ship] in Bremerton, Washington.

I was working in San Francisco before I left, but after the war, that was another picture. Everybody and their brother was getting out, and all these plants were laying off, shipyards were closing, no jobs. I went for two weeks or three weeks, no jobs. There were lines of ex-GIs looking for a job. And you could

see the guy; the receptionist would be shaking his head. There were no jobs.

There was a plant in Oakland, they called it Kit Kay Box Company. About that time, one guy quit. Because, see, the government, everything was cost-plus on all of these companies during the war [effort]. The government would take these companies over, and then they would pay them cost plus 10 percent. So everybody was short of money. But then as soon as they canceled those contracts, these companies had to go on their own.

I went in [the box factory] and [the manager] said, "We work eight hours straight, we give a 15-minute break for lunch, and I'm going to show you how to do it...." There was big, hot cardboard coming off of a conveyor and you have to get it up and stack it up like this on the roller.... I started taking over, knocking out cardboard—you don't know how to handle it, it can slice you like razor blades, the edges of that hot cardboard.... I was already bleeding on my face and my arms. In the evening, I dragged myself home.... When [the manager]

Hunt arrowheads, hike, picnic and take pictures in the land of the cliff dwellers

Where Apache Haunts and Mission Ruins
Bring back Pioneer Days

FIG 6.11
Auto tourism advertisement
Advertisement from an unknown publication circa 1950
(Courtesy of CSWR UNM).

saw me the next day, he couldn't believe it, he said, "I thought you'd never make it back." Once I got use to handling that stuff, it wasn't bad.

Anyway, I worked there for a while, and then I decided I wanted to come to school. I never made it, but I made it on training on refrigeration. I went to a 10-month course in Albuquerque, studying refrigeration. And then after the course, I found out there were no refrigerators in New Mexico! (laughs) You couldn't get a job, period. Right after the war, it was like talking about recession—real rough. So I decided to go in business. In Belen, I put in a restaurant. In three months, I was broke.

Then I borrowed some money, I went to California. My intention was to go to the same place where I had worked in the box factory, because I knew that guy would take me in, I thought. But with $40, I could only get to Barstow. Forty dollars! I got there penniless. I finally got a job at Santa Fe Railroad for a little while. And then those bases were opening around Barstow.... so there were a lot of government jobs coming in and I worked at the marine base.

Tourism gained wide popularity in post-war America because of the growing middle class, greater access to automobiles, and improved highways for interstate travel. By the early 1950s as much as 80 to 90 percent of U.S. tourist travel was done with cars (Zierer 1952). Regions such as the Southwest were popular tourist destinations as well. New Mexico was quick to start an official Tourism Bureau in 1935. The state actively advertised New Mexico as a national tourist destination promoting its scenery and unique culture (Kelley and Reynolds 2010). Highways 66 and 60 through New Mexico were major national travel corridors, and Highway 60 paralleled almost the entire Belen Cutoff. Communities on those highways also tried to demonstrate their sights and attractions and benefit from the increased traffic (Figures 6.11 and 6.12).

Tourists were still taking the railroad, but AT&SF's former dominance over the imagery and experience of the Southwest was in decline. By 1965 the best arguments AT&SF could provide for traveling by rail were the on-board restaurants and "scenic level" of their trains that made for more daytime enjoyment (Figure 6.13). Only five years later, in July 1970, AT&SF issued their final public timetable and completely ceased passenger

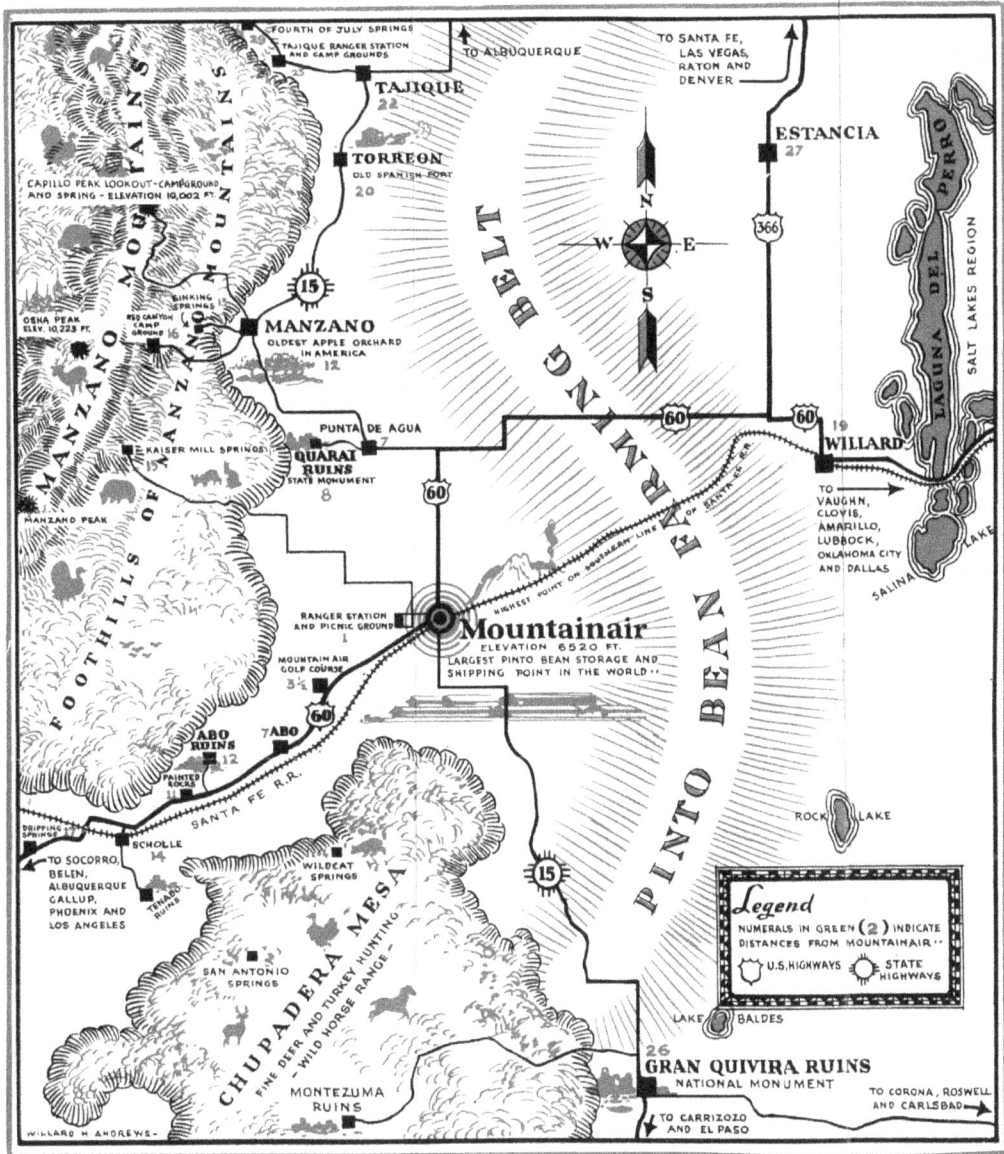

Mountainair is the Center of a Scenic and Historic Wonderland

SPREADING out from Mountainair in every direction is a fascinating wonderland of historic interest and scenic beauty. Probably the best known of these historic spots is the Gran Quivira National Monument, embracing the ruins of the Gran Quivira Mission. About the time the Pilgrims were landing on our eastern coast a valiant Spanish Friar was building a great church to serve the needs of one of the ten cities of the Piro Indians, a tribe now totally extinct. With the aid of these Indians a second church and a monastery were built about 1649. The older church is now fallen completely to the ground, but the massive walls of the newer one, from four to six feet thick, still stand as mute testimony to the zeal and faith of centuries ago. The Gran Quivira is the largest Christian temple in ruins in the United States. It is remarkable no less for the skill of its primitive masons than for its historic interest. This spot was set aside as a National Monument in 1909.

No less interesting than Gran Quivira are the ruins of the Abo and Quarai Missions, shown on another page of this folder, and all over this vast area are scattered the ruins of once thriving Indian villages. Covered by the shifting dust of centuries, these ruins may be stumbled upon by any who venture off the main highways, and even the most casual inspection will turn up shards of pottery and arrowheads from a prehistoric past. Unlike most of the Southwest, lack of rainfall could not have been the reason for abandonment of these villages, since the area around Mountainair is now a fertile farming country, and the town itself is the site of the largest bean warehouses in the world. In the foothills, on the high mesas and in the mountains there is good hunting for quail, bear and deer in season. Mountainair, with two good hotels and several camp-grounds, supplies excellent accommodations for a stay of any length in any season.

FIG 6.12
Mountainair brochure
Advertisement for Mountainair Community Chamber
of Commerce circa 1950 (Courtesy of CSWR UNM).

Look how far above the rail El Capitan and San Francisco Chief chair car seats are. This puts travelers at the scenic level for daytime enjoyment and offers a quieter, smoother ride day and night. Note that passengers board Hi-Level cars at the center.

FIG 6.13
Traveling at the scenic level
Image touting the benefits of traveling on AT&SF in 1965
from the *Travel Agent's Sales Guide of Santa Fe Rail Travel*
(Courtesy of William Penner).

traffic in May 1971 due to massive financial losses (Bryant 1974).

It seems amazing that the railroad that introduced the United States to the West through advertising and iconography could have stopped all passenger service, but the market had moved on. AT&SF made most of its money through long-haul freight and selling off its vast land empire (ibid.). During the same period, the railroad was competing with trucking companies for shipping business. Along the Cutoff agricultural enterprises were increasingly relying on trucks for hauling goods. Even if they wanted, people couldn't drive their animals overland to load on the trains because the depot and pens had often been dismantled. As we discuss later in the chapter, ranchers were particularly affected by the shift away from rail traffic.

The railroad made it, and the railroad destroyed it: diesels, abandonment, and automation

> *That was the death blow.... [The steam engine] was rough on the track and the diesel was easy.... They could almost immediately cut off half the section crews—Randy Dunson* (2009)

The railroad that facilitated large-scale settlement in the region decades earlier also started experiencing economic stress during the Great Depression. Rail lines in some places were abandoned or track was taken up. By 1943, the New Mexico Central Railroad was reduced to a fragment of its former length and trains ran only on the 28-mile line from Estancia to Moriarty. The railroad decline was temporarily abated during World War II as the AT&SF transcontinental line moved great amounts of supplies across the country. The high volume of freight during the war years was tough on the tracks and required a great deal of maintenance. For many who stayed in the region or returned after the war, the railroad remained the largest employer along the Cutoff. However, for the rail company this time of economic stability would be short-lived.

Fixing the rail

World War II freight traffic strained the railroad tracks because of its frequency, quantity, and mass. AT&SF needed laborers to repair the tracks, but workers were in short supply due to the number of men enlisted in the armed services. In some places, the AT&SF used a workforce of Mexican laborers.

FIG 6.14
San Francisco Chief in Abo Canyon
San Francisco Chief headed east over Bridge 874.2 near the mouth
of Abo Canyon in April 9, 1969. This train operated in the last years
of passenger service on the line (Courtesy of Randy Dunson).

These *braceros* were allowed to come and stay by the federal government, which issued temporary visas to Mexicans who wanted to work in the United States. Across the country, *braceros* labored in critical sectors such as agricultural and the railroad. Along the Belen Cutoff, braceros were employed by the railroad. In particular, Scholle siding supported a large group of braceros. Bill Pohl (2009) recalls the Mexican laborers that lived and worked in the community.

We had anywhere from 200 to 300 Mexicans in here working on the railroad on contract—braceros. They had them sidetracked there at Scholle. They had two big cook cars, had a complete deal for the guys. They didn't have to go anywhere. But they would leave a steak dinner over there and come over here and get a baloney sandwich and get soda pop over at our place (store). And they would buy soda pop by the case and take it back with them, and they would put it in the cooler over there. They had a place there they got water out of the pipe, coming from Abo, and there was a big hole there. And it was [an] honor system; nobody took anybody else's soda pop.

They were redoing the railroad in the 1940s...for the better part of two years—they re-tied this whole thing. [The braceros stayed] at Scholle on the side tracks. They laid special side tracks around their trains out there. They had bunk cars and everything.

Although the braceros were employed in large numbers, local New Mexican work crews continued to fill the various positions along the Pecos Division to maintain railroad operations in the post-war years. Then, as earlier, a key component of the work force was Hispanos laborers. The social and racial dynamics in post-war New Mexico shifted, and Hispano employees began to obtain specialized positions within the railroad company hierarchy.

Opportunities for New Mexico's Hispanos and Native Americans

Since the arrival of the AT&SF in New Mexico, numerous Hispanos were part of the railroad workforce. Along the Belen Cutoff, Hispanos were employed primarily as laborers on section and extra gangs while specialized positions such as engineers, conductors, and telegraph operators were held

FIG 6.15
Fidel Padilla and Eliseo R. Sisneros
Fidel Padilla and Eliseo R. Sisneros in Abo Canyon in 2008
(Photograph by William Penner).

by Anglos. As discussed in Chapter 5, racial and ethnic discrimination within east-central New Mexican communities varied and was reflected in geography, employment, and social interactions.

In the post-war era some of these institutionalized race lines began to change. Telegraph operators were critical components of the railroad communication system, ensuring trains were running safely and that freight and passengers arrived at their destination on time. Previously, only Anglos held the position of operator in east-central New Mexico. Felix Gabaldon (2008) briefly describes what it was like to be the first Hispano operator working in the Mountainair depot in 1950.

My first job was in Abo, about three weeks, maybe, and then I bumped somebody in Mountainair. I was there three, four years, then I went to Fort Sumner, worked there another maybe six, seven months. From Fort Sumner, I went to Roswell, then to Dexter. From Dexter, I came back to Willard, and I ended my career there. I worked in a depot, worked the teletype, typing orders like freight and the mail. In those days, the

mail train would be coming through at 50 miles an hour with the long pole for the mail hanging up, very scary at first. In Abo it was mostly a little freight, ranchers would load cattle, I just did the paperwork on where they were heading to.

To start off, like in Mountainair, I wasn't accepted. I was the first Chicano working in a depot in the Pecos Division from Belen east; I broke the ice. I had to learn by records, old records of how it was done, like the freight, selling tickets there in the depot. It was unheard of, I guess. Here, in Willard, it was no problem. I think it was mostly Anglo people in just certain places; other places were Spanish people. So it made a difference, yeah. They were used to having Hispanics on track gangs, but I was the first Hispanic telegraph operator. I knew I needed that paycheck; otherwise I would have never made it.

Felix Gabaldon, along with other individuals who broke color lines, paved the way for later Hispanos to take higher-ranking jobs within the railroad along the Cutoff. Although racial dynamics varied from place to place in east-central New Mexico,

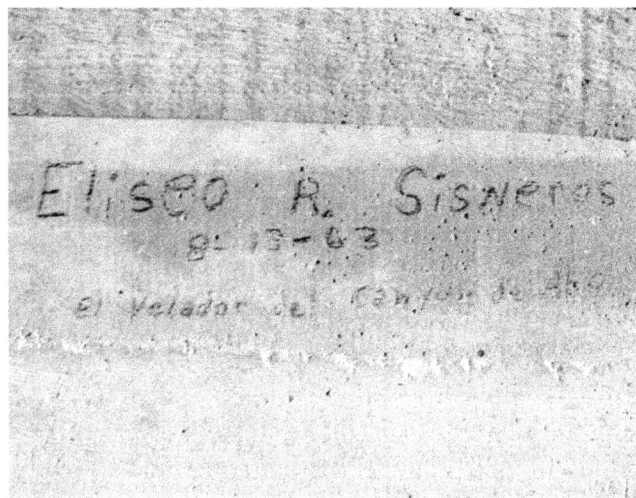

FIG 6.16
Inscription at Culvert 871.2 in Abo Canyon
Eliseo R. Sisneros wrote his name on this culvert in Abo Canyon in the 1960s.
Many other railroad workers did the same during the twentieth century
(Photograph by Shawn Kelley).

overcoming boundaries in employment remained a challenge.

Another railroader, Eliseo R. Sisneros, made a career working up the ranks in AT&SF. Eliseo began his first railroad job in 1951 on labor gangs. Over time he moved through the ranks as a machine operator, rail rider, assistant foreman, foreman, and eventually spent the last 18 years as a track supervisor. His career spanned a significant social transition from when many people lived along the Belen Cutoff and maintained the tracks to a later time when improved technology meant fewer laborers were necessary for a functioning railroad. Here Eliseo R. Sisneros (2009) talks about an incident in Abo Canyon when a man was injured and reflects on changes with the railroad.

One night a rock come down in Abo Canyon and it hit the electric warning fence and knocked a hole in it. They called the Belen Section and couldn't find a foreman. So I went up there with the assistant foreman and a bunch of men to help that signalman. We got the rock out of the track and then I told the assistant foreman, "Well, leave one man here with the signalman to help him fix that hole in the fence and you go to the east end and

wait on him and go on in back to Belen." Then I got in my pickup and I went off, but I didn't have my radio on.

This signal maintainer had a little motorcycle that holds a basket and would go on the track. You put on the rod with the high rail wheel on one side and it had two little wheels on the other side, and you pull the lever and start. So, he got on the motorcycle and the men that they left over there to help him got in the basket, but they put in a railroad jack—it's heavy, all the tools in there and that little basket and the section man—then they took off. It would have been all right, but there was a little crossing, and you know how them crossings had that plank in the center. I guess he was going as fast as that little motorcycle was going, but with that rod he had so much weight that when it hit that plank, both of them flew up and it broke the section man's collarbone.

The assistant section foreman tried to get a hold of me on the radio, but I didn't have my radio on. When I got to Belen, I noticed my radio was off. So, I turned it on and the first thing I heard he was still hollering that he had a man was hurt. I waited for him on the

FIG 6.17
Navajo railroad worker
Navajo railroad worker in Winslow, Arizona, March 1943. Photographed by Jack Delano (Courtesy of the Library of Congress).

highway and yeah, he was hurt, so I took him straight on to the hospital. I got demerits over that because I was the head man; my section foreman didn't get nothing. And the hurt guy got five demerits and the signalman got five demerits. I told them to give them to me, but they wouldn't do it. The railroad said that the men had a lot of responsibility too. Railroading is a tough job—a lot of people don't know—they just think it's a pick and shovel. And it's not just that simple my friend.

I think they got a better railroad now because I will tell you a story. The old man I learned to railroad from, his name was Tony Garcia. He used to be the section foreman at Scholle. When they cut out Scholle section, one day he said, "Sis"—they use to call me Sis—"they will never hold this railroad without sections." Well, they cut out Scholle section and cut out other sections. The last time I saw Tony, he was a section foreman at Vaughn and I was a track supervisor between Vaughn and Ft. Sumner, and we were both standing there by the depot. And I bet you a train was going at 65 or 70 miles an hour when it went by. I looked at Tony and said,

"I thought you told me one time, they wouldn't hold it." I said, "Look at that train. It goes faster, it's got more tonnage, and they got a better railroad." He said, "You know what, I never thought they would hold it."

Native American railroaders

Although the AT&SF started to close a number of its sidings and section gangs in the region, it continued to require labor. Track maintenance was vital for efficient and safe operations. Extra gangs with no geographic affiliation moved up and down the line as needed to maintain the railroad. Some of these gangs consisted of Native American crews.

Native American employment for the railroad extends back to the construction of the first railroads in the New Mexico. In order to lay track through Laguna lands, the Atlantic and Pacific (later the AT&SF) made a deal with the Pueblo of Laguna to employ its men as long as the railroad ran through Laguna lands. The name of the understanding is known as "Watering the Flower of Friendship" (Peters 1994 and 1998). Over the years this arrangement placed Laguna employees in positions all over the southwest United States. So many people

FIG 6.18
Randy Dunson growing up on the Cutoff
Hazel Carter Dunson with her son Randy in their
converted boxcar living somewhere on the Belen
Cutoff in 1950 (Courtesy of Randy Dunson).

from Laguna were living and working for the AT&SF away from their community that the Pueblo of Laguna established colonies in cities as far away as Winslow, Arizona, and Richmond and Barstow, California. Other groups, such as the Pueblo of Acoma and the Navajo, also have a long history of working for the railroad, especially during the post-war period.

Randy Dunson (2009) spent a number of years living with his family in a boxcar when his dad was a foreman. He recalls a childhood along the railroad and what the first Navajo work gang in the area was like.

The first eight years of my life were spent in a 40-foot wooden boxcar converted for living quarters. Up and down the Belen Cutoff; just wherever the work took us that's where we went. I made every school between Clovis and Belen, except Yeso—we were there in the summertime. Sometime in the probably '54 to '55 era, the Santa Fe hired the first Navajo gang on the division and my dad got them. They just about gave him ulcers until he got them figured out. It was kind of politically incorrect, what happened. We were at Greenfield, New Mexico, which was around Dexter, and my dad had a

Hispanic man who got sunstroke and died working on a tie gang. So when all was said and done, that crew—which was predominantly from up around Anton Chico, Ribera, that area, almost all those guys were from that place—they were gone. And come Monday morning, he had 60 Navajos. It was very interesting, us adapting to them, and them adapting to us.

There was quite a large number of these bunk cars for 60 people. I'm going to guess there were probably eight men in each car. The foreman had his own car, the assistant foreman had his own car, and I believe the timekeeper had his own car. Then we had a cook car and a dining car, and I believe the cooks had their own car. We would have several tank cars of water. At this time, all these cars were old wooden boxcars. Well, it was quite a number of cars.

We also had a commissary car, which was neat, because you could buy a candy bar there. They sold—they sold snacks, work clothing, and toiletries. They would keep track of all that, and sometimes it took two timekeepers, because all of these things were deducted

FIG 6.19
Train headed through Abo Canyon
Train in 1946 headed east over Bridge 873.8 toward
the crusher at Sais (Courtesy of Randy Dunson).

*from these guys' wages. At the time, we thought that
these people were pretty crude and that their hygiene
was not good, but that was before today when we
know about saunas (steam baths). We had a shower
car, and it was steel and connected to the old tank car
for water. There was a hand pump, and you could pump
water up into this elevated tank across the top. Gravity
would let you take a shower, but it never got used. The
Navajos would go out and dig a big hole, and we had all
those crossties, so they lined it with crossties, covered
it with dirt, and got their hot rocks and got in there, and
did their thing, but they never took a regular shower.*

*Generally when they moved the gang, they would
move it on the weekends. We had rail passenger service at that time, and a lot of these guys would go back
to Gallup for the weekend. And it was real interesting,
they were real good about if they didn't come back, they
would send somebody in their place. So Monday morning generally my dad would still have 60 Navajos, but it
might not be the same 60.*

*He had a very hard time figuring out how to work
with them at first. My dad was the kind of guy that liked
to work real hard, and then lay back. He found out they
had one pace, but it was a good pace. He got more
production than he had ever got before, but he couldn't
hurry them up, he couldn't slow them down. And he
found that it seemed like there'd be one or two guys that
were natural leaders, and he'd put this guy in charge. Of
course there was a language problem—real or whether
they were just putting on, who knows? He found pretty
much that he didn't have a whole lot to do, once he got
the system figured out, and got them figured out.*

Sais Crusher and its closure

Another important component of the local economy along
the Belen Cutoff was railroad-related services, such as the
Sais Crusher. The crusher was a source of employment for
many local families well into the 1950s. AT&SF's operations
required large amounts of rock ballast, which was provided by
the Sais Crusher.

FIG 6.20
Running the crane at Sais Crusher
Crane at Sais Crusher sometime around 1945 to 1958
(Courtesy of Albert McNiel).

The everyday operation of the rock crusher involved the frequent use of heavy and dangerous equipment. Juan Sanchez worked there on two separate occasions in different positions. As a teenager during World War II he worked as a mechanic's assistant, or "grease monkey." Often his job required climbing up the crane on the drop hammer or shovel to service and grease the pulleys. After being in the armed services, Sanchez (2008) came back and worked as a truck operator for Sharp and Fellows.

We used to load what they called riprap for floods. They'd bring those dump cars, and we'd fill them up with riprap when I was driving. That's when they bought them Ukes (a type of truck), shortly before they closed, a year maybe.... [We would] drive up on top of the hill and start dumping off.... And we'd keep making that mountain bigger and bigger and bigger.

Another railroad and Sais Crusher employee, Billy Bob Williams, also has a long family history of living in the area. Williams grew up on his grandparents' homestead at Dripping Springs, where they operated "The Millers' Store." The store

was situated only a short distance from both Abo Canyon and Scholle, which made it and important source for local supplies. In later years, tourists along Highway 60 frequented the store and gas pumps. Throughout the 1950s, Billy Bob Williams (2007) worked during summer vacation, typically for the railroad, but one summer he was employed by the crusher instead. He recounts what it was like to work there and discusses some of the unexpected by-products of the industry that were used by locals such as his grandparents.

While I was in college, the summer of 1955, I worked on the extra gang for the AT&SF as a brakeman, and going back and forth to Vaughn, I was working a good portion of that summer on what they called the local; it was still running steam, a smaller steam engine that pulled usually about five or six cars, and we kind of acted like UPS does now.

You hauled things from various places where you could stop along the track at the passing tracks and in the sidings, and we would deliver stuff and pick up stuff and make stops various places. One of the stops that we made was into the Sais Crusher and we would push

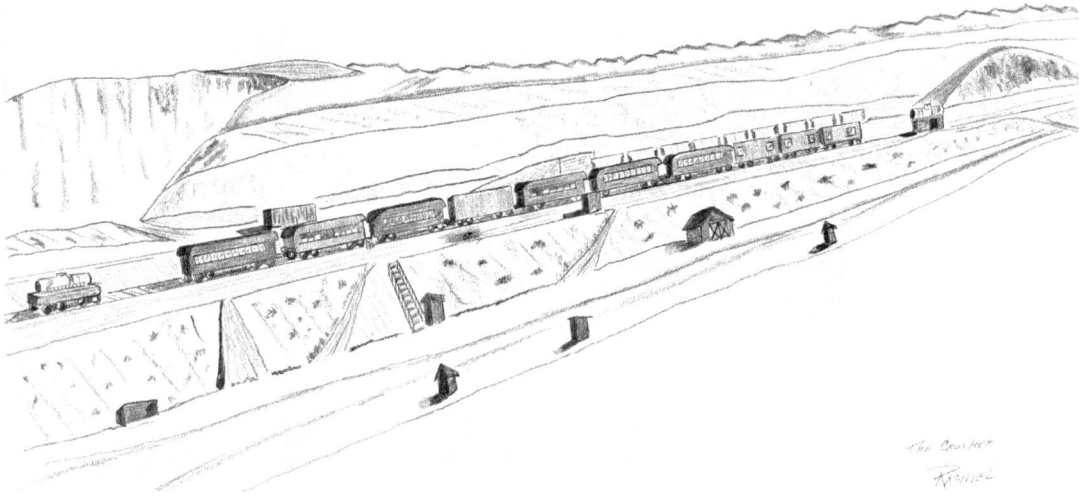

FIG 6.21
Sais Crusher
Drawing of the Sais Crusher by Robert or Roger McNeil, showing
the line of boxcars used as housing (Courtesy of Albert McNeil).

*two or three cars, up there, and you had a series of
tracks there where you get the cars up in front of the
engine and and push them into one track. The loaded
cars would come out of the crusher, and we would pick
those up and take them wherever. They had rock on
them. They were loaded with riprap, and riprap is the
rock that you see along the railroad track. And that was
always kind of fun because the crusher people would
feed us lunch or dinner or whatever time of day it was.*

*Then the summer after I graduated in 1957, I was
waiting to go into the Marine Corps, and I worked at
the Sais Crusher and was a truck driver and kind of an
errand boy. I'd go in to Albuquerque to pick up parts
and things like that. I spent a lot of time in the canyon
and in the crusher. The crusher was very much a part of
the early days there because, for one thing, there was
employment there and there were a lot of by-products
in there, I guess you would call them that. My grandfather used a lot of the boxes that the dynamite came
in. The dynamite came in very, very well-made wooden
boxes, and if you carefully took those boxes apart, you*

*had good pieces of wood that were like 2½ feet long
and maybe…18 inches and about three-eighths to a half
inch thick, but it was good building material to use in
various things. He had built a lot of the Dripping Springs
homesite and he used that wood and I remember it
was mostly from Hercules Powder Company, but it was
dynamite. And they used, of course, huge amounts of it
there at the Sais Crusher.*

By the late 1950s operations at the Sais Crusher started to
wind down. Albert McNiel's father, Louie, was the superin-
tendent of operations for Sharp and Fellows. His family lived
on-site at the crusher for a number of years during the mid-
1940s until the crusher closed. McNeil (2008) remembers helping dismantle and ship off the last of the crusher:

*They scrapped all those cars they had: that locomotive
that was down at the end of those tracks up there,
they cut it up with a torch, loaded it in railroad cars, and
hauled it off. They burned the cars [we lived in]. And then
cut up the iron and shipped it off. I don't know whether
they could have moved them or not. That car we lived in*

FIG 6.22
Transom window glass
Transom-window glass pane from the Tonopah and Tidewater
Railroad car used by Albert McNeil's family at the Sais Crusher

FIG 6.23
Crusher mills at Sais
Crusher mills and rail cars being loaded at Sais in
1946 (Courtesy of Randy Dunson).

was supposedly the president's car of the Tonopah and Tidewater Railroad in California. It was nice. It was all mahogany, brass doorknobs and all kinds of stuff.

That was in 1959 when they shipped the last [car].... I helped them load the last stuff. I was right out of high school, I guess—or about out of high school—and I helped the last guy that loaded that stuff up. I don't know that I helped him load it on the cars, but we were tying it down with cables and chains like that, with come-alongs and everything. That was the last load that went out of there, and that was probably in the spring of 1959.

The transition from steam to diesel

As discussed earlier, the steam locomotive required a robust infrastructure to maintain the engines and tracks and needed reliable access to water. Railroad companies created a complex economy to service these needs, resulting in the settlement of rural areas. In turn, rural settlements were ensured consistent access to employment, transportation, shipping infrastructure, and significant economic opportunities resulting from railroad-related services.

W. F. Cottrell (1951:360) eloquently describes the differences between the engine types.

In its demands for service the diesel engine differs almost completely from a steam locomotive. It requires infrequent, highly skilled service, carried on within very close limits, in contrast to the frequent, crude adjustments required by the steam locomotion. Diesels operate at abut 35 percent efficiency, in contrast to the approximately 4 percent efficiency of the steam locomotives in use after World War II. Hence diesels require much less frequent stops for fuel and water.

Although many communities understood their existence was based on the rail industry, few realized how much of that was based on an engine technology that would soon be replaced. The rapid pace at which the diesel train engine replaced steam locomotion was also unexpected. The accelerated production in the U.S. industrial sector, fueled by World War II, subsidized the costly and expedient transition to diesel engines.

FIG 6.24
Steam helper engine headed up Abo Pass toward Mountainair
Steam helper engine (5027) pulling an east-bound diesel freight train at Dead
Man's Cut on May 26, 1956, in between Scholle and Abo. US Highway 60 is
in the foreground. Photograph by John Schilling (Courtesy of Robert Eveleth).

Along the Belen Cutoff, many small communities suffered as a result of shifting engine technology and the changing dynamics of railroad operations. Almost overnight, section communities would lose several jobs and some of their town buildings, such as the depots. Bill Pohl (2009) talks about how the railroad disbanded the Scholle section gang, leaving many people without employment.

> It goes back to the railroad, because the railroad was the father of all this. So that's what created the town of Scholle, and that's what held it together. As soon as they had no more use for a local section gang, the town dissipated. And so that's the short and sweet of the whole thing: the railroad made it, and the railroad destroyed it. Common everyday improvement and a new way of doing has killed all these little towns, and consequently set those people out on the street looking for a job. The progress of our country today has actually been the father of our unemployment, there's no other way about it.

Although many towns begrudgingly accepted these painful changes, some local citizens took legal action against railroad companies in an effort to save their communities. For example, in 1958 citizens of Encino protested the closing of their station and requested a public hearing with AT&SF. About 35 residents appeared, and 10 testified in opposition. A rancher named Dillon who came to Encino in 1908 described his regret and almost gave a eulogy for the station about to close and towns and villages beginning to dissolve.

> I came here in 1908 and have been here ever since.... Well, we have gone on all these years and have been pretty good friends and have loaded thousands and thousands of sheep and millions of pounds of wool and everything else and so on. And then all at once came the panic in '29. That hit all the stocks and everything since. And you have had your drouths and everything since. Of course the revenue wasn't coming in to the railroad because the people were hard up. And then the railroad curtailed the passenger and freight service. We weren't at fault for it. They felt that. And then there was nothing

FIG 6.25
Scholle section gang at Scholle siding
Scholle section gang at Scholle siding in 1949, from left to right: Acacio Trujillo, Loreto Molina, Hermenes Sisneros, unidentified man, José Sisneros, Canuto Sisneros, and Luis Ortiz (Courtesy of Polly Sisneros).

for the people to do but go by buses and trucks. Now they haven't got either. I hope they don't take up the rails. We need the railroad (New Mexico Corporate Commission, New Mexico State Records Center and Archives, April 23, 1958).

The actual changes in technology for those who worked for the railroad were both exciting and unsettling. Diesel engines phased out the steam locomotive and came at a time when there was a major shift to a new and mechanized railroad focused on efficiency. Jack Hewett worked as a brakeman and was later promoted to a conductor, where he would pilot the helper train for AT&SF. Hewett (2008), who worked during the steam to diesel transition, talks about some of the changes and his work.

We had steam engines when I went to work at the railroad. Exclusively they were oil-fired. I never worked with a coal-fired steam engine when I went to work for the railroad. I worked oil-fired steam engines, and then in the early '50s, I guess—I don't know exactly when I caught my first diesel, but it was a treat. Those old steam engines were cold, and they just had canvas over

the windows (although some had sliding glass windows). And the diesel had glass and a heater.

Well, that was the heaviest equipment in the world, I guess—that railroad. Of course as a brakeman I had to work with all kinds…. We'd have a hot box, I'd have to fix that, or set the car out on a siding or something and go on. A lot of times we had to drop cars into a spur. We were going one direction and had to put the car in a spur or something, we'd have to rev it up and drop it in, to have a guy throw the switch, and drop that car into the siding. After the engine passed, we'd throw the switch, and the car would go, and you would have to stop it with a hand brake. That was quite an experience.

And if we had to talk to the dispatcher, we had to walk maybe a quarter of a mile to a telephone. They didn't have radios then, of course, until they brought in the diesels. But still, we had to talk to the dispatcher by phone—as long as I worked for them anyway.

Charlie Patterson was another interviewee who worked for the railroad during the steam to diesel shift. He was a career

FIG 6.26
Jack Hewett
Jack Hewett in 2008 with his 1926 Model T Ford
(Photograph by Shawn Kelley).

FIG 6.27
Steam Engine
Steam engine at the service crane in the Vaughn yards
around 1950 to1953 (Courtesy of Charlie Patterson).

railroader. His father before him worked at the Vaughn yards and in the power works. Below, Patterson (2008) discusses some of his roles working for the railroad, starting with his early jobs as a car tote moving rail cars and the transition from steam to diesel locomotion.

I was a car tote [in Vaughn] at the time, working out in the yards, and then running trains. And then when a passenger would come up or something, we had to quit what we were doing, get our grease guns all ready to grease a passenger train these steam engines. And you had a great big ol' grease gun, and you had to hook it up to air and all that stuff and get it all ready for the passenger trains to come in. Oh boy, that ol' grease would just sling everywhere, pretty near—you know, power. It was an air power outfit, and whenever you got enough grease on that one, you'd go back to the other driver. It had those big wheels, them driver there. There's two car tows, and the other guy, he was greasing the other side of the engine. I was greasing my side, and they had laborers to go up and put sand, oil, and water. So every time a

passenger would come in, that's what we'd have to do.

There at Vaughn, in later years, they put oil in those engines in those days. They had them coal burners [too], but that was way back. But this was in the late '40s and the '50s, when they had these [oil steam engines and]...put that diesel oil in the engines. That's where they really checked it out between Clovis and Belen, where they'd stop at Vaughn and put oil and stuff in their engines, see what it needed. One thing about those, they had water there, but they had big barrels, and they would put a big gallon of water softener in the water to soften the water, where it would make more steam. The water wouldn't be hard water, it would make good steam. You know, it took the hardening out of the water, where it would make more steam. They had that compound they'd put in there before they left, and there'd be engineers every once in a while that'd go get an extra gallon of it so he could put that in that water and make it even better, where he could get more steam. But that was the last of them [steam engines], and they finally run both steam and diesels, and then diesels, and

FIG 6.28
Vaughn yard crew
Vaughn Yard crew in 1957. Top row from left to right: Herald Thompson, Ardith Craft, Malcolm Simpson, Mr. Burwinkel, Lupe Storey, and Anestacio Rael; second row from left to right: Bill Patterson, Eddie McDowell, Lewis Roberson. Photograph by Charlie Patterson (Courtesy of Charlie Patterson).

then every once and a while steam. And then all of a sudden there wasn't anymore steam. They got them all out. But this was Vaughn, boy, and I'm telling you, I really enjoyed working on them old steam engines and everything. There was a lot of work to them, but I don't know, there was something about them I just liked. And then them diesels come in. Man, I didn't have nothing to do. They come in there, and they were just there. And they had plenty of diesel fuel in them.

The shift from diesel to steam was complete along the Belen Cutoff by the 1960s. However, many of the railroad employees from the steam era were unlike younger generations. Randy Dunson, a third-generation railroader, recalls some of his most memorable experiences on the Belen Cutoff and the dynamic of working with the old-time railroaders.

I think one of the most memorable trips was in 1974 [when] we left Belen going east. I was a fireman, I was running the engine. And we got up there, right at Billy the Kid Hole, stalled out. We had three engines, two of them had died. So this old engineer said, "Well, I'll take

over, you go back to see if you can get these engines going." That wasn't a very big deal, except the rear brakeman hollers on the radio, "Hey! I think the conductor's having a heart attack!" I mean, we're dead in the water. I finally was able to get one of those engines started so the two of them would pull the train, and we finally wiggled up into the siding—it was before the double track—the siding at Scholle. And there was a train behind us, and they came along and swapped engines with us. They had a little ol' bitty train. At that time, you couldn't talk to the dispatcher on the radio, you could just talk to other trains. So they had wayside phones, so we called the dispatcher and told him what the deal was. And I'd been out there, I knew that there was an ambulance in Mountainair, and he would not listen to me. "No, we'll call an ambulance from Albuquerque." So anyhow, a couple hours later, we finally got rid of our conductor. It turns out he just had a heatstroke. But then, we were going across the river bridge at Fort Sumner, this same rear brakeman hollers on the radio, "Hey! Somebody's shooting at me!" And somebody

FIG 6.29
Randy Dunson
BNSF railroad engineer and historian Randy Dunson in front
of his caboose in 2009 (Photograph by Shawn Kelley).

*shot the windows out of the cupola of the caboose
while we were going across there. So that was one of
the more memorable trips.*

*And then we had an 80-mile-an-hour train. It was
a pretty hot train, and it was pretty dangerous because
everybody was out to outdo the last guy on how fast you
could get from Clovis to Belen on that thing. You have four
or five engines and four or five cars and a caboose, so you
didn't have any braking power. I remember we're coming
off Culebra going down into Lucy, we were running 80
miles an hour, we got a yellow block, (warning signal) and
the thing was red down there at Lucy, and here comes
a train, and man, I'm upset, and I'm wanting to put the
train into emergency, and that ol' engineer, he was a hot
rodder, he said, "Oh, kid, don't do that. That signal will
turn green before we get to it." About two cars before we
got it, it turned green. Here we go by. And then he looked
at me and said, "We couldn't have stopped anyhow." And
now, looking back, we couldn't have stopped. There's no
way we could have stopped. You would have had to brake
some of those four cars and that caboose.*

*And he knew what he was doing. But that guy was
a whiz on the air brakes and stuff. He very seldom made
a trip without having to put the train into emergency.…
Those old guys, you'd think, "Man, this old man is harm-
less and stuff," but they get behind that throttle, and
man, it's just like they grew fangs! And there was some
of them—I mean, if it had a rocket motor on it, it wasn't
going fast enough to suit them.*

*It was the guys that had learned on a steam engine.
And those steam engines would run. Man, they would
run. And the guys that they worked with, when they
were firemen, some of them. Man, when they hired us,
some of them just hated our guts, because they would
remember. They went through periods where maybe if
you were on the tail end of a hiring cycle, it took you
forever to get promoted. That engineer I was with when
the train stalled out in the canyon, I was pretty new. I
thought, "Man, this old boy don't seem to be real on
the ball about running this engine." But anyhow, I got
to visiting with him, and he had been working 34 years.
He'd only been able to hold an engineer's job out of*

How "D" Handyman restores embankment shoulders, speeds maintenance for A. T. & S. F.

Cleaning drainage ditches is one of the many uses put to A.T. & S.F.'s D Tournapulls. This is an ideal project for "D's" rapid speed and mobility.

The Atchison Topeka & Santa Fe uses 3 off-track rubber-tired D Tournapulls to handle scattered maintenance along its right-of-way.

For example, on the Pecos Division, 5 miles east of Willard, New Mexico, the A.T. & S.F. restored embankment shoulders.

At one location the rubber-tired 138 hp D Tournapull hauled material from cuts at each end of fill. The material was a mixture of clay, sand and caliche. Tournapull self-loaded an average of 5 yards at each pass and spread its load along the fill in thin lifts. Travel back and forth on "D's" big low-pressure tires provided firm compaction.

FIG 6.30
"D" Handyman
Advertisement from *Railway Tracks and Structures* (May 1956) for the D Tournapull to handle scattered maintenance on the AT&SF right-of-way more efficiently (Courtesy of William Penner).

Clovis for the last three years. Took him 30 years! So some of those guys, when they hired us, [management] said, "Hey, we're going to have a big business boom, and we're going need these boys, and you let them run that engine, because we're going promote them in six months," they looked at us, and there wasn't nothing we could do that was right. They'd just eat on you. Man! And looking back, I can't blame them.

Automating the system

AT&SF's post-war technological changes were not limited to the shift from steam to diesel. They also included an increasing reliance on mechanized equipment and electronic traffic systems such as the Centralized Traffic Control (CTC). Newer machines were used for a range of tasks from dirt work to installing tracks—and resulted in the need for fewer employees. The job formerly held by a section gang could now be done by one person.

The core purpose of CTC was to allocate train traffic more efficiently and make the best use of the rail line. Dispatchers achieved this through electronic switching and remote control.

They could always know where the trains were at any time and move them to sidings or onto segments of double track to keep things moving. AT&SF's transcontinental line from Belen to Vaughn got this technology in the 1940s, the first section in the entire system to do so. CTC produced great results for AT&SF but continued the trend of removing track workers with increased efficiencies.

At the outbreak of the war, immediate attention was directed to the Pecos Division. With its single track, mountain grades, and limited water sources it stood out as the connecting link between two heavy converging lines to the East and the double track lines to the West.

It was certain to be called on to handle the heaviest traffic in history, and it could become a major bottleneck in system-wide operations. Company officials knew that capacity of the line must be increased. Since the line did not lend itself to double-track construction because of Abo Canyon, it was decided to install a modern CTC system...and produce the greatest capacity possible on a single track line (Santa Fe Magazine, January 1946).

7 | Conclusion

The social dynamics and realities of the Belen Cutoff today have been shaped by various regional and national trends. In some places so much has changed that entire communities that were once home to dozens of families have all but vanished, while others have found new vitality. Between AT&SF's division points in the cities of Belen and Clovis, vast stretches of open plains with isolated ranches remain the dominant landscape in east-central New Mexico. The railroad that began as the ERNM has evolved in its role but the importance of transcontinental freight traffic continues.

Consolidation, ranchettes, and subdivisions: social dynamics of the Belen Cutoff today

To me they're a different kind of people, they don't understand the area.... Ranches subdividing, people coming in that are not country people.... [They] don't care nothing about things that I care about—Juan J. Sanchez (2007)

One hundred years ago most people in the counties along the ERNM were dispersed almost evenly, living on homesteads and in small towns and villages (Figure 7.4). By 1960, demographics had shifted and younger generations emigrated to urban areas in search of employment opportunities. The cities of Belen and Clovis grew, smaller communities such as Willard and Fort Sumner began to diminish, and many section towns effectively ceased to exist. Today the same pattern continues and over 80 percent of individuals in the counties along the Cutoff live in cities and villages with greatly changed economies. Most of the residents of Valencia, Socorro, and Torrance Counties live in towns such as Los Lunas, Belen, and Estancia, and many commute to Albuquerque for work. At the other end of the Cutoff, Cannon Air Force Base and Eastern New Mexico University provide the major sources of employment for people in Clovis and Portales, with groundwater-supplemented agriculture still remaining an important component of the economy. BNSF's rail system still plays a critical role in local economies, particularly Clovis and Belen, and in 2010 the BNSF employed nearly 1,200 people in New Mexico (BNSF 2011). Increased efficiencies in technology and changes in operations such as running double-stacked trains nearly 2-miles long, however, have changed labor needs.

The social dynamics of the Belen Cutoff today reflect regional and national trends such as increased urbanization and greater mobility due to the ease of car travel. Communities that were once home to dozens of people now only include a small number of the Hispano and Anglo families that first settled in the region generations ago. With the exception of Belen, Clovis, and smaller towns such as Mountainair or Fort Sumner, the dominant landscape in east-central New Mexico is now given to vast stretches of open plains with isolated ranches. Randy Dunson (2009) gives valuable insight into the

	Valencia	Socorro	Torrance	Guadalupe	De Baca	Roosevelt	Curry
Population in 2010	76,569	17,866	16,383	4,687	2,022	19,846	48,376
Population in 1960	39,085	10,168	8,497	5,630	2,991	16,198	32,692
Population in 1910	13,320	14,761	10,119	10,927	N/A	12,064	11,443

FIG7.1

Populations changes in counties on the Belen Cutoff from 1910 to 2010
Data compiled from decennial census reports from the USCB 2012; 1963; 1913a.

relationship between homesteading and the railroad as well as the changes that occurred in the communities along the Cutoff in the latter half of the twentieth century.

The homesteaders were a commodity. As I've told schoolkids, the railroad made this country, eastern New Mexico; whether people want to admit it or not, [it] did. And one of the reasons that the railroad didn't come here to start with is they're in the business of hauling stuff. And there was nobody and nothing here to haul. So that's one reason they went to Raton Pass. With the acquisition of the Pecos Valley Northeastern [Railroad], they were looking at this again and homesteading start[ed] to be in the works.... I've got figures about how many immigrant cars came out in like 1908, 1909—I think somewhere around 1,800.

So that was something. Not only are you going to bring the family out here, but then that family's going to stay here and produce stuff, and there are no roads, and there are no cars to speak of. The only way in and out is on that railroad. So everything they produce and everything they buy is going to come on the railroad. One of the funny things one of the old-timers was telling me about, that those immigrant cars—if you had any livestock, they were divided into two parts. One person got to ride free to take care of the livestock. People are not dumb. He said there was not one family, if nothing else, did not at least have one chicken so somebody could ride free.

But that made the country, and in a lot of ways it sustained the country. Like my granddad's [place] and other places along the way, you noticed that the homesteading quickly disappeared away from the track. Closer to the track, where these guys got jobs on these section gangs, maybe as a telegraph operator or whatever, survived much longer, until the diesel engine came. And that was the deathblow, because that diesel engine required very little maintenance. [The steam engine] was rough on the track and the diesel was easy on the track, so they could almost immediately cut off half the section crews.

FIG 7.2
Woody Southard and George Dunson
Woody Southard and George Dunson, Randy Dunson's father, somewhere on the Belen Cutoff in the 1950s (Courtesy of Randy Dunson).

Homesteading was good for one and maybe two generations. Just the economics of things—what happened with World War II and farm prices and technology.... [The homesteading community] was very close-knit. I think they relied on each other for all kinds of support and shared activities and shared possessions, shared [taking care of] kids. I mean, the men would all get together. They'd go to what they called The Breaks up around Taiban and cut wood and fence posts. And all the women would stay together. You know, they would neighbor each other's sickness and having babies and whatever might come along. My grandmother would tell stories about what they did.

Melrose had quite a bit, even in my time. In my day Melrose had a movie theater, a hardware store, a big dry-goods store, three grocery stores, a bank, a post office, pool hall, filling stations. It started changing probably about the time I started school, along in there. I started school in 1955, and all that was still there. And I would say by the time I graduated from high school in

1967, I don't remember if any of those grocery stores.... Yeah, two of the three grocery stores were still open. The movie theater was closed. The dry-goods store was closed. The hardware store I believe might still have been open. And that little five-and-dime store that my great-uncle had was still open—The What Not Shop. When I was a kid in 1955, we'd go to town on Saturday. Everybody went to town on Saturday, and you couldn't find a parking place on Main Street in Melrose. And it was a neat thing, because everybody was there. What was funny to me [was that my parents and I] shopped at one grocery store, my Carter grandparents shopped at a different one, and my Dunson grandparents shopped at the third one. But where my grandparents shopped, there was a nice corner with some gliders and benches and stuff inside, and all the ladies would sit there and visit. I mean, they were there to buy groceries, but they were there to visit.

Out on the side of the building was this big long bench that kind of leaned up against the side of the

FIG 7.3
The Arrow Filling Station and Campground
This was the first gas station in Mountainair and it was built
some time in 1920s (Courtesy of Jack Hewett).

building. There was a little bit of a vacant lot there, and it would be in the sun and whatever, and all the men, the old men, were out there visiting. And I've always been a strange kid; I didn't want to go play with the [other] kids. I wanted to go with my granddad, and these were the original homesteaders, and they were telling stories, and I wanted to listen to the stories.

And then people started getting better cars, getting better roads, don't think anything about running to Clovis. And that generation of homesteaders dies off. The next generation doesn't have that close tie. They didn't develop those tight bonds. They developed friendships, but I don't think they developed the survival tie of that first generation—I mean, they had to have neighbors, and they had to be a neighbor, and rely on their neighbors to survive. The next generation didn't have to do that. And my generation thinks nothing at all about driving to Lubbock!

So the little stores, they start dying off. The little farms, I don't know that you couldn't make it, but

people are not satisfied with subsistence living. So all of these things changed. You just have to get bigger and bigger and bigger if you're going survive in agriculture. And now, you're going have to inherit it. There's no way you're going buy a farm and ever make it pay for itself legally.... It's changed. And Melrose, anymore, is a school and a truck stop and an Allsup's store and a grain elevator. That's what's there. I think that's what tied those people (the original homesteaders) so close to each other, and so close to the land. They were poor people [and] for many of [them] this piece of land was the first piece of land they'd ever owned.

The individuals who stayed on in the towns and villages often had connections to other multigenerational families and formed a small core that still holds a number of settlements together today. Over time, however, the difficult rural life that facilitated community interdependence was eroded by modern conveniences and affordable travel. The community experience lived by earlier generations of homesteaders through

FIG 7.4
Martina Brazil Franklin and Polly Sisneros
Martina Brazil Franklin and Polly Sisneros visiting their former
homes in Scholle in 2008 (Photograph by Shawn Kelley).

the tough times of the Great Depression and World War II was transformed. Jerry Shaw (2008) commented on this:

It used to be an all-day trip to go to Albuquerque. Now you can make two and three trips in one day to Albuquerque if you need something. And in fact, when I was a kid, if we were going to Albuquerque, we got up [in] early, early daylight and we went to [town]…and it would be late that night when we got home.

In recent years, some towns have experienced revitalization as new people moved to the area. The modern "homesteader" has different priorities than some of the long-standing residents. For example, large ranches in the Mountainair area are being subdivided into ranchettes or smaller lots for people interested in rural living but not large-scale ranching or farming. In some areas, art colonies have formed, and in others there are now vacation homes. The renewed interest in east-central New Mexico has multiple impacts on the community dynamics, most notably a shift in outlook and values. New residents bring their vision of rural life, which does not always combine with multigenerational residents' lifetimes of knowledge about the area.

The rise and fall of homesteading and boosterism in the wake of the ERNM is a story echoed elsewhere in the West. Arid and tenuous conditions on the high plains make for poor farming and rain does not follow the plow. The opportunity to make your own fortune on the Belen Cutoff, or at least the appearance of an opportunity, must have been wonderful while it lasted. This possibility for a new life was made easier for the short period in the first half of the twentieth century when AT&SF required section towns and large amounts of manual labor to maintain their lines and equipment. Drought, technological changes, and the migration to cities helped shatter the dream. The individuals and settlements that still remain along the Cutoff are a testament to an important history of railroading, ranching, farming, and the value of community.

Epilogue

Double-stack freight train in Abo Canyon
Photograph of double-stack intermodal freight trains eastbound
through Abo Canyon in 2008. Photograph by Moira Ellis.

Our efforts to tell the story of the Belen Cutoff in this book are a result of mitigation required for BNSF's Abo Canyon Second Track Project. BNSF knew it would be difficult to build a second track through Abo Canyon but realized its necessity given increases in transcontinental freight traffic and the bottleneck at the canyon that stopped trains for hours, sometimes backing up traffic into Arizona and Texas. Challenges included topography, permitting, and the economic recession of 2008, which required construction to stop for a brief time on the new track and echoed when work halted for a year on the Cutoff in 1903. As part of mitigation, we hoped to study the significance of the ERNM and illuminate a portion of AT&SF's system that had gone largely unnoticed. Further, we tried to target our efforts to speak to the communities and individuals who were affected by the Cutoff. It seems appropriate that the most rigorous accounting of the Belen Cutoff would come out of a project being built through its most difficult terrain.

The Belen Cutoff irrevocably transformed east-central New Mexico, and we hope this work helps serve as a catalyst for the towns and people along the line to renew their relationships and shared histories. Watching old friends from Scholle and elsewhere meet again when they had not seen one another in over 50 years was a rewarding experience. We are grateful for the opportunity to have introduced the reader to the Cutoff and its people and hope they are well met.

References cited

Abert, James W.
1847 *Abert's New Mexico Report.* Senate Executive Document No. 23 (30th Congress, 1st Session, Serial 506), Washington, DC. Reprinted 1962, Horn & Wallace, Albuquerque.

Atchison, Topeka, and Santa Fe
1978 *Santa Fe: The Chief Way Reference Series, System Standards*, Volume 2. Kachina Press, Dallas.

Autrey, James
2008 Formal interview conducted with Shawn Kelley for the Abo Canyon Second Track Project. Transcript on file at Parametrix, Albuquerque.

BNSF Railway (BNSF)
2011 *New Mexico: Delivering the World to the Enchanted State.* BNSF informational brochure distributed as part of the BNSF Railway Abo Canyon Site Tour, 2011. Manuscript on file at BNSF Public Relations, Fort Worth.

Brazil Franklin, Martina
2008 Formal interview conducted with Shawn Kelley for the Abo Canyon Second Track Project. Transcript on file at Parametrix, Albuquerque.

Brooks, James F.
2002 *Captives and Cousins: Slavery, Kinship, and Community in the Southwest Borderlands.* University of North Carolina Press, Chapel Hill.

Bryant, Keith L.
1974 History of the Atchison, Topeka and Santa Fe Railway. Macmillan, New York.

Bureau of Land Management
2010 *Bureau of Land Management General Land Office Records.* Electronic document, http://www.glorecords.blm.gov/, accessed May 1, 2010.

Campbell, Hardy Webster
1905 *Soil Culture Manual.* H. W. Campbell, Lincoln, Nebraska.

Cole, Dorothy
2008 Formal interview conducted with Shawn Kelley for the Abo Canyon Second Track Project. Transcript on file at Parametrix, Albuquerque.

Cottrell, W. F.
1951 Death by Dieselization: A Case Study in the Reaction to Technological Change. *American Sociological Review* 16(3):258–365.

Culbert, James I.
1941 Pinto Beans in the Estancia Valley of New Mexico. *Economic Geography* 17(1):50–60.

Ducker, James H.
1983 *Men of the Steel Rails.* University of Nebraska Press, Lincoln and London.

Dunson, Clifford (Randy)
2009 Formal interview conducted with Shawn Kelley for the Abo Canyon Second Track Project. Transcript on file at Parametrix, Albuquerque.

Foote, Cheryl J.
1989 *The Hispanic Reoccupation of Abo and Quarai, 1800–1940.* Unpublished manuscript on file, Salinas Pueblo Missions National Monument, Mountainair, New Mexico.

Forrest, Suzanne
1998 *The Preservation of the Village: New Mexico's Hispanics and the New Deal.* University of New Mexico Press, Albuquerque.

Gould, Joseph Edward
1961 *The Chautauqua Movement: An Episode in the Continuing American Revolution.* Quinn and Boden, Rahway, New Jersey.

Hall, G. Emlen
1991 San Miguel del Bado and the Loss of the Common Lands of New Mexico Community Land Grants. *New Mexico Historical Review* 66(4):413–432.

Hargreaves, Mary W. M.
1958 Hardy Webster Campbell (1850–1937). *Agricultural History* 32(1):62–65.

1948 Dry Farming, Alias Scientific Farming. *Agricultural History* 22(1):39–56.

Hertzog, Peter
1964 *The Gringo and the Greaser: Charles L. Kusz.* Press of the Territorian, Santa Fe.

Hewett, Jack
2008 Formal interview conducted with Shawn Kelley for the Abo Canyon Second Track Project. Transcript on file at Parametrix, Albuquerque.

Hodges, Carrie
1936 Letter report dated July 24, 1936. Vaughn Clip Folder. New Mexico History Library, Santa Fe.

Huckabay, Bill
2008 Formal interview conducted with Shawn Kelley for the Abo Canyon Second Track Project. Transcript on file at Parametrix, Albuquerque.

Hurt, Wesley
1941 *Manzano: A Study of Community Disorganization.* Master's thesis on file at the University of New Mexico, Albuquerque. Reprinted and revised 1989, AMS Press, New York.

Jefferson, Thomas
1819 Letter from Thomas Jefferson to Nathaniel Macon. In *The Writings of Thomas Jefferson*, edited by Andrew Lipscomb and Albert Ellergy Bergh. Memorial Edition, 1903. Thomas Jefferson Memorial Association, Washington, DC.

Julyan, R.
1996 *The Place Names of New Mexico.* University of New Mexico Press, Albuquerque.

Kayser, George
2007 Formal interview conducted with Shawn Kelley for the Abo Canyon Second Track Project. Transcript on file at Parametrix, Albuquerque.

Kayser, Paul
2007 Formal interview conducted with Shawn Kelley for the Abo Canyon Second Track Project. Transcript on file at Parametrix, Albuquerque.

Kelley, Shawn, and Kristen Reynolds
2010 *Route 66 and Native Americans in New Mexico.* Report by Parametrix for the New Mexico Department of Transportation, Santa Fe.

Kutzleb, Charles R.
1971 Can Forests Bring Rain to the Plains? *Forest History* 15(3):14–21.

Link, Eugene P., and Beulah Link
1999 *The Tale of Three Cities: Gran Quivira in the Southwest New Mexico, 1100 B.C. to A.D. 1963.* Vintage, New York.

McAlavy, Don
1976 *Clovis Remembered: Moments from the Past.* Clovis Clip Folder. New Mexico State University Special Collections, Las Cruces.

McDonald, Margaret Espinosa
1997 *"Vamos todos a Belen": Cultural Transformations of the Hispanic Community in the Rio Abajo Community of Belen, New Mexico, from 1850–1950*. Ph.D. dissertation on file at the University of New Mexico, Albuquerque.

McKinley, Weldon
2008 Formal interview conducted with Shawn Kelley for the Abo Canyon Second Track Project. Transcript on file at Parametrix, Albuquerque.

McMath, Gorden
2008 Formal interview conducted with Shawn Kelley for the Abo Canyon Second Track Project. Emma Lou (Biddie) McMath was also present for and participated in the interview. Transcript on file at Parametrix, Albuquerque.

1999 The Valley Is Still There. In *The Tale of Three Cities: Gran Quivira in Southwest New Mexico, 1100 B.C. to A.D. 1963* (Eugene Link and Beulah Link) Vintage, New York.

McNeil, Albert
2008 Formal interview conducted with Shawn Kelley for the Abo Canyon Second Track Project. Transcript on file at Parametrix, Albuquerque.

Myrick, David F.
2003 *New Mexico's Railroads: A Historical Survey*. Revised ed. University of New Mexico Press, Albuquerque.

New Mexico Bureau of Immigration
1907 *Ho! To the Land of Sunshine*. Santa Fe: The Bureau, 5th revised edition.

Padilla, Aurelio (Al), and Joe Padilla
2008 Formal interview conducted with Shawn Kelley for the Abo Canyon Second Track Project. Transcript on file at Parametrix, Albuquerque.

Padilla, Fidel
2007 Formal interview conducted with Shawn Kelley for the Abo Canyon Second Track Project. Transcript on file at Parametrix, Albuquerque.

2006 Formal interview conducted with William Penner for the Abo Canyon Second Track Project. Transcript on file at Parametrix, Albuquerque.

Patterson, Charles
2008 Formal interview conducted with Shawn Kelley for the Abo Canyon Second Track Project. Transcript on file at Parametrix, Albuquerque.

Peters, Kurt
1994 *Watering the Flower: Laguna Pueblo and the Atchison, Topeka, and Santa Fe Railroad, 1880–1980*. Ph.D. dissertation, University of California, Berkeley.

1998 Continuing Identity: Laguna Pueblo Railroaders. *Richmond, California.:American Indian Culture and Resource Journal* 22(4):187–199.

Pohl, Clarence (Bill)
2009 Formal interview conducted with Shawn Kelley for the Abo Canyon Second Track Project. Transcript on file at Parametrix, Albuquerque.

Sánchez, Javier E.
2009 Al Pie de la Sierra: La Historia del Pueblo de Manzano y sus alrededores, visto por la historia de sus habitantes. Self-published manuscript, Corrales, New Mexico.

Sanchez, Juan
2008 Formal interview conducted with Shawn Kelley for the Abo Canyon Second Track Project. Transcript on file at Parametrix, Albuquerque.

2007 Formal interview conducted with Shawn Kelley for the Abo Canyon Second Track Project. Transcript on file at Parametrix, Albuquerque.

Seery, Tom
1983 Interview conducted with Randy Dunson. Original tape in possession of Randy Dunson, Portales, New Mexico. Transcript on file at Parametrix, Albuquerque.

Shaw, Jerry
2007 Formal interview conducted with Shawn Kelley for the Abo Canyon Second Track Project. Transcript on file at Parametrix, Albuquerque.

Sisneros, Eliseo R.
2008 Formal interview conducted with Shawn Kelley for the Abo Canyon Second Track Project. Transcript on file at Parametrix, Albuquerque.

2007 Formal interview conducted with Shawn Kelley for the Abo Canyon Second Track Project. Transcript on file at Parametrix, Albuquerque.

Sisneros, Francisco
2008 Formal interview conducted with Shawn Kelley for the Abo Canyon Second Track Project. Transcript on file at Parametrix, Albuquerque.

2008 *The Chapel and Cemetery of San Lorenzo de Abo: Centennial, 1908–2008*. Self-published manuscript, Casa Colorada, New Mexico.

1996 *Sisneros: A New Mexico Family History*. Unpublished manuscript on file. Salinas Pueblo Missions National Monument, Mountainair, New Mexico.

1988 Interview with Cheryl J. Foote conducted for *The Hispanic Reoccupation of Abo and Quarai, 1800–1940*. Unpublished manuscript on file at the Salinas Pueblo Missions National Monument, Mountainair.

n.d. *Nineteenth Century Pueblo de Abo Settlers*. Unpublished manuscript on file. Salinas Pueblo Missions National Monument, Mountainair, New Mexico.

Sisneros, Paublita (Polly)
2008 Formal interview conducted with Shawn Kelley for the Abo Canyon Second Track Project. Transcript on file at Parametrix, Albuquerque.

Sisneros, Sylvestre
2008 Formal interview conducted with Shawn Kelley for the Abo Canyon Second Track Project. Francisco Sisneros was also present for and participated in the interview. Transcript on file at Parametrix, Albuquerque.

Sisneros, Sylvestre, and Francisco Sisneros
2008 Field interview conducted in Abo Canyon with Shawn Kelley and William Penner for the Abo Canyon Second Track Project. Transcript on file at Parametrix, Albuquerque.

Spencer, Richard
2008 Formal interview conducted with Shawn Kelley for the Abo Canyon Second Track Project. Transcript on file at Parametrix, Albuquerque.

Tainter, Joseph A., and Frances Levine
1987 Cultural Resources Overview Central New Mexico. USDA Forest Service Southwest Region and USDI Bureau of Land Management. Albuquerque and Santa Fe.

Thompson, Gerald E.
1972 "To the People of New Mexico": Gen. Carleton Defends the Bosque Redondo. *Arizona and the West* 14(4):347–366.

United States Census Bureau

2012 *U.S. Census Bureau, 2010 Census of Population and Housing, Summary Population and Housing Characteristics*, CPH-1-33, New Mexico U.S. Government Printing Office, Washington, DC. Electronic document, http://www.census.gov/prod/cen2010/, accessed January 12, 2013.

2002 *New Mexico: 2000, Summary Population and Housing Characteristics.* Electronic document, http://www.census.gov/prod/cen2000/phc-1-33.pdf, accessed April 23, 2010.

1973 *1970 Census of Population, Volume I, Characteristics of the Population, Part 33, New Mexico.* Electronic document, http://www2.census.gov/prod2/decennial/documents/37745099v1p33.pdf, accessed April 23, 2010.

1963 *The Eighteenth Decennial Census of the United States, Census of Population: 1960, Volume I, Characteristics of the Population, Part 33, New Mexico.* Electronic document, http://www2.census.gov/prod2/decennial/documents/1970a_nm-01.pdf, accessed April 23, 2010.

1960 *United States Census of Agriculture, 1959, Final Report, Volume 5.* Government Printing Office, Washington, DC.

1952a *A Report of the Seventeenth Decennial Census of the United States, Census of Population: 1950, Volume I, Number of Inhabitants.* Electronic document, http://www2.census.gov/prod2/decennial/documents/23761117v1.pdf, accessed April 23, 2010.

1952b *United States Census of Agriculture: 1950, Volume I, Part 30, Counties and State Economic Areas, New Mexico and Arizona.* Electronic document, http://www.agcensus.usda.gov/Publications/Historical_Publications/1950/vol1%20New%20Mexico%20Arizona/34059637v1p30.pdf, accessed April 23, 2010.

1942a *Sixteenth Census of the United States: 1940, Population, Volume I, Number of Inhabitants.* Electronic document, http://www2.census.gov/prod2/decennial/documents/33973538v1.pdf, accessed April 23, 2010.

1942b *Sixteenth Census of the United States: 1940, Agriculture, Volume I, Part 6, Statistics for Counties, Mountain Division.* Electronic document, http://www.agcensus.usda.gov/Publications/Historical_Publications/1940/Farms%20and%20Farm%20Property_New%20England/00179375v1p1.pdf, accessed April 23, 2010.

1932a *Fifteenth Census of the United States: 1930, Population, Volume III, Part 2, Reports by States, Montana-Wyoming.* Electronic document, http://www2.census.gov/prod2/decennial/documents/10612982v3p2.pdf, accessed April 22, 2010.

1932b *Fifteenth Census of the United States: 1930, Agriculture, Volume II, Part 3—The Western States.* Electronic document, http://www.agcensus.usda.gov/Publications/Historical_Publications/1930/Reports_by_State_Western/03337983v2p3.pdf, accessed April 22, 2010.

1921 *Fourteenth Census of the United States Taken in the Year 1920, Volume III: Population, Composition and Characteristics of the Population by States.* Electronic document, http://www2.census.gov/prod2/decennial/documents/41084484v3.pdf, accessed April 22, 2010.

1922a Fourteenth Census of the United States Taken in the Year 1920, Volume V: Agriculture, General Report and Analytical Tables. Electronic document, http://www2.census.gov/prod2/decennial/documents/06229676v5.pdf, accessed April 22, 2010.

1922b *Fourteenth Census of the United States Taken in the Year 1920, Volume VI, Part 3: Agriculture, the Western States and Outlying Possessions.* Government Printing Office, Washington, DC.

1913a Thirteenth Census of the United States Taken in the Year 1910, Volume III: Population, Reports by States, Nebraska-Wyoming. Electronic document, http://www2.census.gov/prod2/decennial/documents/36894832v3.pdf, accessed April 22, 2010.

1913b *Thirteenth Census of the United States Taken in the Year 1910, Volume VII: Agriculture, Reports by States, Nebraska-Wyoming.* Electronic document, http://www2.census.gov/prod2/decennial/documents/41033898v7.pdf, accessed April 22, 2010.

1901 *Census Reports Volume I, Twelfth Census of the United States Taken in the Year 1900: Population.* Electronic document, http://www2.census.gov/prod2/decennial/documents/33405927v1ch04.pdf, accessed April 22, 2010.

1902a *Census Reports Volume V, Twelfth Census of the United States Taken in the Year 1900: Agriculture Part I, Farms Livestock, and Animal Products.* Electronic document, http://www2.census.gov/prod2/decennial/documents/33398096v5.pdf, accessed April 22, 2010.

1902b *Census Reports Volume VI, Twelfth Census of the United States Taken in the Year 1900: Agriculture Part II, Crops and Irrigation.* Electronic document, http://www2.census.gov/prod2/decennial/documents/33398096v6p2.pdf, accessed April 22, 2010.

1895a *Report on the Population of the United States at the Eleventh Census: 1890 (Volume 1).* Electronic document, http://www2.census.gov/prod2/decennial/documents/1890a_v1-01.pdf, accessed April 21, 2010.

1895b *Report on the Statistics of Agriculture in the United States at the Eleventh Census: 1890 (Volume 5).* Electronic document, http://www2.census.gov/prod2/decennial/documents/1890a_v5-01.pdf, accessed April 21, 2010.

1882a *Statistics of the Population of the United States at the Tenth Census: 1880 (Volume 1).* Electronic document, http://www2.census.gov/prod2/decennial/documents/1880a_v1-01.pdf, accessed April 21, 2010.

1882b *Report on the Productions of Agriculture as Returned at the Tenth Census: 1880 (Volume 3).* Electronic document, http://www2.census.gov/prod2/decennial/documents/1880a_v3-01.pdf, accessed April 21, 2010.

1872 *Ninth Census-Volume I: 1870, The Statistics of the Population of the United States.* Electronic document, http://www2.census.gov/prod2/decennial/documents/1870a-01.pdf, accessed April 21, 2010.

White, Richard
1993 *It's Your Misfortune and None of My Own: A New History of the American West.* University of Oklahoma Press, Norman.

Wilson, John P.
2001 *When the Texans Came: Missing Records from the Civil War in the Southwest 1861–1862.* University of New Mexico Press, Albuquerque.

Wimberley, Frank
2009 Informal interview conducted with Shawn Kelley for the Abo Canyon Second Track Project. Transcript on file at Parametrix, Albuquerque.

Zierer, Clifford
1952 Tourism and Recreation in the West, *Geographical Review* 42(3):462–481.

List of Figures

3.14   Photograph of a mule teamster in Abo Canyon sometime from 1903 to 1906. AT&SF Coll., Series 5-2.08, DaRT ID 23901, Kansas State Historical Society.

3.15   Photograph titled *7th Xing Abo River, N.M.* View to the east of the bridge at milepost 871.4 in Abo Canyon with several piers on the under construction using cranes and cement mixers, sometime from 1905 to 1906. AT&SF Coll., Series 5-2.40, DaRT ID 23834, Kansas State Historical Society.

3.16   Photograph of a blasting episode with fly-rock right next to the "Big Cut" between the bridges at mileposts 871.4 and 871.5 in Abo Canyon, sometime in 1905 or 1906 (view to the west-southwest). AT&SF Coll., Series 5-2.70, DaRT ID 23929, Kansas State Historical Society.

3.17   Plans titled *The A.T. & S.F. Ry. System, Standard Concrete Piers, General Plans for Various Plans*, Topeka, July 1910. Originally published in Santa Fe System Standards Vol. 3 (1978). Kachina Press, Dallas.

3.18   Photograph titled *6th Xing Abo. Swinging Last Girder into Place.* View to the northwest of the final girder being placed on the bridge at milepost 871.5 in Abo Canyon, sometime in 1906. AT&SF Coll., Series 5-2.38, DaRT ID 23832, Kansas State Historical Society.

3.19   Photograph titled *Placing 100' Girder 5th Span.* View to west-southwest of girders being placed using gallows frames on the bridge over the Pecos River (with a flanking shoo-fly track) near Fort Sumner, sometime in 1906. MS24 Box 19/25, Lee C. Myers Coll., MS00240029, New Mexico State University Library, Archives and Special Collections.

3.20   Photograph titled *L-S Con. Co's Com No 12 Abo Canyon.* View to the east-southeast toward the "Big Cut" in the background and a Lantry-Sharp construction camp (LA 146942) in the foreground, sometime in 1905 or 1906. AT&SF Coll., Series 5-2.27, DaRT ID 23914, Kansas State Historical Society.

3.21   Photograph titled *Construction Pier 10 Pecos R.* Image shows a construction crew (with a steam boiler, cement mixer, and shoo-fly track) building Pier 10 on the Pecos River Bridge., sometime in 1906. MS24 Box 19/25, Lee C. Myers Coll., MS00240010, New Mexico State University Library, Archives and Special Collections.

3.22   Photograph of workers using mule teams to loading fill from a cut in Abo Canyon, sometime in 1903, 1905, or 1906. AT&SF Coll., Series 5-2.24, DaRT ID 23911, Kansas State Historical Society.

3.23   Photograph titled *L-S Con. Co's Corrall, Cam 2.* View to the northeast of the mule corral at the main Lantry-Sharp construction camp (LA 146933) in Abo Canyon at milepost 872.9, sometime in 1905 or 1906. AT&SF Coll., Series 5-2.19, DaRT ID 23907, Kansas State Historical Society.

3.24   Photograph of a dog on its hind legs surveying with a transit on a tripod near Sunnyside sometime in 1905 or early 1906. The dog belonged to Bert Day, instrument man for AT&SF engineer F. T. Tulley who helped build the Belen Cutoff. G. W. Harris, Chief Engineer for AT&SF, used to have the photo hanging over his desk in Chicago for many years. MS24 Box 19/25, Lee C. Myers Coll., MS00240002, New Mexico State University Library, Archives and Special Collections.

3.25   Photograph of William R. Lovelace standing in front of his AT&SF doctor's office in Sunnyside sometime in 1906. Originally appeared in a biography of William R. Lovelace in the Lovelace Clinical Review sent to Lee Myers by Dr. Lovelace. MS24 Box 6/25, Lee C. Myers Coll., New Mexico State University Library, Archives and Special Collections.

3.26   Photograph of AT&SF engineers relaxing in front of their bunkhouses in Sunnyside sometime in 1905 or 1906. AT&SF Coll., Series 5-2.22, DaRT ID 23909, Kansas State Historical Society.

3.27   Photograph of a blast somewhere along the Belen Cutoff during 1905 to 1907. MS24 Box 19/25, Lee C. Myers Coll., MS00240042, New Mexico State University Library, Archives and Special Collections.

3.28   Photograph of pouring concrete for the fifth pier on the Pecos River Bridge on the Belen Cutoff, sometime from 1905 to 1906. MS24 Box 19/25, Lee C. Myers Coll., MS00240051, New Mexico State University Library, Archives and Special Collections.

3.29   Photograph titled *Pile Driver June 13th 07.* Image of a pile driver being used to establish false work for a bridge somewhere near Ricardo. MS24 Box 19/25, Lee C. Myers Coll., MS0024000, New Mexico State University Library, Archives and Special Collections.

3.30   Photograph of a mule team under a culvert somewhere on the Belen Cutoff, sometime from 1903 to 1908. AT&SF Coll., Series 5-2.25, DaRT ID 23912, Kansas State Historical Society.

3.31   Poster titled *Westward the Star of Empire Takes Its Way.* The poster depicts Uncle Sam riding a chariot pulled by nine U.S. government mules and driven by a Greek goddess, sometime from 1870 to 1890. Used to promote travel on AT&SF lines in the western United States between Kansas City and San Francisco. K Port Scrapbook 385 Folder 2, DaRT ID 212275, Kansas State Historical Society.

Ch.4   Advertisement for Mountainair's 4th of July celebration that appeared in the July 8, 1920 edition of the Mountainair *Independent*. AN2 M232a, Center for Southwest Research, University Libraries, University of New Mexico.

4.1   Table showing populations in New Mexico and counties along the Belen Cutoff from 1870 to 1930. Data compiled from *Census of Population and Housing Decennial Censuses (1790-2000)*. Electronic document, http://www.census.gov/prod/www/abs/decennial/, accessed April 22, 2010.

4.2   Photograph of the Paul Fredrick August Kayser VI homestead near Eastview in 1921. Personal collection of Frank Wimberly.

4.3   Advertisement for AT&SF colonist excursions that appeared in the Socorro *Chieftain* on April 20, 1907. Microfilm roll AN2 S61, January 7, 1905 to December 26, 1908, Zimmerman Library, University Libraries, University of New Mexico.

4.4   Handbill advertising AT&SF excursions to New Mexico, ca. early 1880s. Broadsides and Ephemera, NM & Mexico AC 024-P, New Mexico History Library.

4.5   North Main Street in Clovis. Postcard of North Main Street in Clovis sometime from 1905 to 1910. Personal collection of William Penner.

4.6   Advertisement for AT&SF Homeseekers' Excursions that appeared in the Santa Fe *New Mexican* on August 28, 1903. Microfilm roll AN2 N39 72, April 1, 1903 to November 19, 1903, Zimmerman Library, University Libraries, University of New Mexico.

4.7   Advertisement for Mountainair Realty Company's relinquished lands that appeared in the Mountainair *Messenger* on October 29, 1909. Microfilm, New Mexico History Library.

4.8   Map showing the homestead applications in the Abo Pass area (1879 to 1945). Map developed by William Penner using homestead patent information from the General Land Office website (http://www.glorecords.blm.gov/).

4.9 Advertisement for Willard (The Gateway) that appeared in the September 8, 1905 edition of the Santa Fe *New Mexican*. Microfilm roll AN2 N89, August 17, 1905 to January 2, 1906, Zimmerman Library, University Libraries, University of New Mexico.

4.10 Advertisement showing a map for Willard (A Natural Commercial Center) that appeared in the February 9, 1907 edition of the Santa Fe *New Mexican*. The rail line shown heading roughly due south of Willard was never built (and was never really feasible based on the topography). Microfilm roll AN2 N89, October 6 to March 19, 1907, Zimmerman Library, University Libraries, University of New Mexico.

4.11 Advertisement for auction of town lots in Gran Quivira that appeared in the August 12, 1920 edition of the Mountainair *Messenger*. AN2 N89, Center for Southwest Research, University Libraries, University of New Mexico.

4.12 Photograph of the Belen Roundhouse around 1908. Personal collection of Randy Dunson.

4.13 Photograph of the AT&SF storehouse at Clovis in 1909. Personal collection of Randy Dunson.

4.14 Photograph of Clovis roundhouse employees around 1915. Personal collection of Randy Dunson.

4.15 Masthead of the December 26, 1912 edition of The Clovis *Journal*. Microfilm roll AN2 N39, August 17, 1908 to February 22, 1923, Zimmerman Library, University Libraries, University of New Mexico.

4.16 Advertisement explaining why Belen will grow that appeared in the May 19, 1914 edition of The Belen *News*. Microfilm roll AN2 B4, January 2, 1913 to December 28, 1916, Zimmerman Library, University Libraries, University of New Mexico.

4.17 Photograph titled *"Chautauqua Party," Including the President, Mr. Corbett, Gov. Curry, Hilton Trio, ect. (sic) Mountainair, N.M. "Dale Photo".* Image shows Mountainair Chautauqua Party in 1909 that includes Mountainair founder John Corbett and New Mexico Governor Curry. Personal collection of Jack Hewett.

4.18 Photograph titled *Willard, New Mexico, 1920, David Pascal Childers and his nine (9) men*. Personal collection of William Penner.

4.19 Advertisement in Spanish for the Mountainair Cash Store that appeared in Mountainair's *El Independiente* on July 19, 1924. AN2 M423a, Center for Southwest Research, University Libraries, University of New Mexico.

4.20 Figure appeared on page 13 of Campbell's 1905 edition of *The Soil Culture Manual*. SB110 .C2 1905 FT MEADE, The Library of Congress. Electronic document http://www.archive.org/stream/campbells1905soi00camp#page/n1/mode/2up.

4.21 Photograph of a two-mule team plowing new ground near Broncho right next to the Belen Cutoff sometime in the early 1900s. Personal collection of Dorothy Cole.

4.22 Advertisement in Spanish for the AT&SF special educational train for agriculture (headed by J D. Tinsley), which appeared in the February 9, 1924 edition of Mountainair's *El Independiente*. AN2 M423a, Center for Southwest Research, University Libraries, University of New Mexico.

4.23 Table showing bean production in New Mexico and Torrance County from 1900 to 1960. Data compiled from the *Census of Agriculture: Historical Census Publications*. Electronic document, http://www.agcensus.usda.gov/Publications/

Historical_Publications/index.asp, accessed April 22, 2010.

4.24 Advertisement for Mountainair's Bean Day that appeared in the October 23, 1919 edition of the Mountainair *Independent*. AN2 M232a, Center for Southwest Research, University Libraries, University of New Mexico.

4.25 Advertisement for the New Mexico Bean Grower's Association that appeared in the February 19, 1920 edition of the Mountainair *Independent*. AN2 M232a, Center for Southwest Research, University Libraries, University of New Mexico.

4.26 Photograph of the Trinidad bean elevator in Mountainair that was constructed sometime after 1918. Personal collection of Dorothy Cole.

4.27 Hauling beans to the thresher in Mountainair, date unknown. Personal collection of Dorothy Cole.

4.28 Syndicated column Rags-Ol' Iron written by Frank Bowden that appeared in the Belen *News* on January 1, 1925. Microfilm roll AN2 B4, January 3, 1924 to December 31, 1925, Zimmerman Library, University Libraries, University of New Mexico.

4.29 Cartoon depicting irrationally high commodity prices appeared in the May 18, 1922 edition of the Mountainair *Independent*. AN2 M423a, Center for Southwest Research, University Libraries, University of New Mexico.

Ch.5 Photograph of employees of the AT&SF roundhouse in Clovis sometime in the 1920s. The pictured Japanese workers were brought in 1922 as replacements during a strike. Personal collection of Randy Dunson.

5.1 Advertisement for B. B. Spencer's sawmill operation that appeared in the July 8, 1910 of the Mountainair *Messenger*. Microfilm roll, New Mexico History Library.

5.2 Advertisement for 4th of July celebration that appeared in the June 26, 1924 edition of the Mountainair *Independent*.

5.3 Map showing the homestead patents in the Scholle area (1879 to 1945). Map developed by William Penner using homestead patent information from the General Land Office website (http://www.glorecords.blm.gov/) Patent dates are shown rather than application dates. Prior to 1912 it took five years to prove up on a homestead and after 1912 it only took three years.

5.4 Drawing of Scholle around 1935 as remembered and drawn by Joe J. Brazil. Personal collection of Martina Brazil Franklin.

5.5 Photograph of Mrs. Marie E. Brazil and her pupils in front of the schoolhouse in Scholle (built by local residents using Works Progress Administration funding) sometime in 1938 or 1939. Personal collection of Frank Wimberly.

5.6 Photograph of Paublina (Polly) Sisneros in 2008 at her family's home in Scholle. The home was occupied mostly in the 1930s. Photographed by Shawn Kelley, Parametrix, 2008.

5.7 Photograph of Bill Pohl in 2008 visiting an abandoned homestead in Scholle just north of the juncture of US 60 and the Belen Cutoff. Photograph by Shawn Kelley.

5.8 Photograph of August Kayser, long-time Scholle section foreman, in front of a boxcar converted to a residence with his grand-children Frank Wimberly and Deborah Kayser sometime in the 1930s. Personal collection of Frank Wimberly.

5.9 Photograph of AT&SF engine in the Vaughn yards sometime from 1920 to 1940. Personal collection of Steve Haines.

5.10 Advertisement for D. H. Womack's summer dry goods sales that appeared in the September 8, 1923 edition of the Mountainair *Independent*. AN2 M423a,

Center for Southwest Research, University Libraries, University of New Mexico.

5.11 Photograph of employees of the AT&SF roundhouse in Clovis sometime in the 1920s. The pictured Japanese workers were brought in 1922 as replacements during a strike. Personal collection of Randy Dunson.

5.12 Photograph of the Scholle section gang in 1949 working near milepost 872.0. From left to right: Canuto Sisneros, Acacio Trujillo, Luis Ortiz, Loreto Molina, Fidel Padilla, Hermenes Sisneros and José Sisneros. Personal collection of Paublina (Polly) Sisneros.

5.13 Photograph of Fidel Padilla in 2008 at Culvert 874.5 in Abo Canyon. Photographed by William Penner, Parametrix, 2008.

5.14 Photograph of work crew at the Sais Crusher in the late 1920s or early 1930s. Loreto Molina is shown at center with the cigar. Personal collection of Julia Molina.

5.15 Photograph of lumber truck in the Manzano Mountains sometime between 1920 and 1940. Personal collection of Dorothy Cole.

5.16 Advertisement for the Kayser Brothers lumber business that appeared in the February 16, 1922 edition of the Mountainair *Independent*. AN2 M423a, Center for Southwest Research, University Libraries, University of New Mexico.

5.17 Photograph of Bill Pohl in 2008 at a well-hidden still in a tributary of Priest Canyon. The former occupants had blasted a reservoir in the bedrock to capture the spring water in sufficient quantity to make moonshine. The still's location in a box canyon was not visible from more than 50 feet away. Photograph by Shawn Kelley.

5.18 Photograph of a pinto bean farm in east-central New Mexico sometime in the 1930s or 1940s. RG-84-114 Box 5/7 AT&SF Agricultural Coll., RG84-114-965, New Mexico State University Library, Archives and Special Collections.

5.19 Photograph of the Williams family threshing pinto beans near Mountainair during the 1929 harvest. Personal collection of Gorden and Biddie McMath.

5.20 Photograph of farmer in Mountainair area sometime in the 1920s or 1930s. Personal collection of Dorothy Cole.

5.21 Map of land utilization near the Manzano Mountains ca. 1941. Originally appeared in James I Culbert's article titled Pinto Beans in the Estancia Valley of New Mexico. *Economic Geography*, Vol. 17, No. 1 (Jan. 1941), pp. 50-60.

5.22 Photograph of children outside shack near Mountainair sometime in the 1920s or 1930s. Personal collection of Dorothy Cole.

5.23 Photograph of Juan J. Sanchez in 2008 on his ranch that was homesteaded in the late 1800s by his grandfather Elias Sanchez. Photograph by Shawn Kelley.

5.24 Postcard titled *H-2056 Mexican Water Carrier on the Belen Cut-off, N. M.* Postcard was published by the Fred Harvey Company (date unknown) and depicts a two-horse team somewhere in a small Hispano community somewhere along the Belen Cutoff, most likely in the Manzano Mountains. Personal collection of William Penner.

5.25 Photograph of Joe and Al Padilla at the camp next to Sais crusher (LA 146950) in 2008 with Bridge 874.8 in the background. Photograph by Shawn Kelley.

5.26 Advertisement showing cattle brands from Fort Sumner that appeared in the March 31, 1917 edition of the Fort Sumner Review. Microfilm roll AN2 F65,

July 17, 1909 to February 11, 1909, Zimmerman Library, University Libraries, University of New Mexico.

5.27 Photograph of men appraising sheep in northeast New Mexico. RG-84-114, Box 5/7 AT&SF Agricultural Coll., RG84-114-832, New Mexico State University Library, Archives and Special Collections.

5.28 Photograph of the east side of the Manzano Mountains sometime in the 1930s or 1940s. Personal collection of Dorothy Cole.

5.29 Photograph of Hispano sheep shearers somewhere in eastern New Mexico, date unknown. RG-84-114, Box 5/7 AT&SF Agricultural Coll., RG84-114-833, New Mexico State University Library, Archives and Special Collections.

5.30 Postcard titled H-2061 A New Mexico sheep ranch on the Belen Cut-off, published by the Fred Harvey Company. Personal collection of William Penner.

5.31 Photograph of the excavation crew that assisted Joseph H. Toulouse in his excavations of the Mission of San Gregorio de Abo during 1938 or 1939. The Works Progress Administration funded the work and the group was composed almost entirely of local residents from the greater Scholle, Abo, and Mountainair area. Personal collection of George Lopez.

5.32 Photograph of the McMath family in 1936 during their bean harvest. Personal collection of Gorden and Biddy McMath.

5.33 Photograph of a square dance in Mountainair, date unknown. Personal collection of Dorothy Cole.

5.34 Photograph of the Kayser and Tarin children at the section foreman's house in Scholle sometime in the 1930s. Personal collection of Frank Wimberly.

5.35 Photograph of a parade on Main Street in Mountainair in 1937. Personal collection of Jack Hewett.

5.36 Advertisement for farm implements appeared in the May 6, 1920 edition of the Mountainair *Independent*. AN2 M232a, Center for Southwest Research, University Libraries, University of New Mexico.

5.37 Table showing average farm and ranch sizes in New Mexico and along the Belen Cutoff from 1900 to 1960. Data compiled from the Census of Agriculture: Historical Census Publications. Electronic document, http://www.agcensus.usda.gov/Publications/Historical_Publications/index.asp, accessed April 22, 2010.

5.38 Advertisement for the AT&SF showing Vegetables of War and the railroad's contribution to agriculture during the war effort. The advertisement appeared in 1945 in an unknown publication. Personal collection of William Penner.

5.39 Photograph of Mountainair's Main Street sometime in the 1940s. Personal collection of Jack Hewett.

Ch.6 Photograph of Juan J. Sanchez in 2008 at Culvert 871.2 in Abo Canyon. The culvert includes many early twentieth-century inscriptions from local residents and those who worked for the railroad in Abo Canyon. Photograph by Shawn Kelley.

6.1 Photograph of Williams family harvesting beans sometime around 1912 to 1915, from left to right: John Williams, Durey (Dude) Boyd, Lester Williams, and an unidentified neighbor. Personal collection of Gorden and Biddie McMath.

6.2 Photograph of steam engine pulling refrigerator cars in Abo Canyon at milepost 872.9 sometime from 1940 to 1949. AT&SF Coll., Series 1#52-13, Image 1756, DaRT ID 61728, Kansas State Historical Society.

6.3   Photograph of driving cattle near Mountainair sometime in the 1950s. Personal collection of Dorothy Cole.

6.4   Photograph of McMath family using tractors to thresh beans in 1954. Individuals pictured from left to right: Gorden, Robert, and W. P. McMath. Personal collection of Gorden and Biddie McMath.

6.5   Photograph of Gorden McMath in 2008 with his some of his metal folk-art sculptures. Photograph by Shawn Kelley.

6.6   Photograph of pinto bean plants in a field in northeastern New Mexico. RG-84-114, Box 5/7 AT&SF Agricultural Coll., RG84-114-830, New Mexico State University Library, Archives and Special Collections.

6.7   Photograph of construction of the masonry schoolhouse in Scholle that was funded by the Works Progress Administration, sometime around 1937. Personal collection of Paublina (Polly) Sisneros.

6.8   Photograph of a drill at the Sais crusher sometime in the 1940s or 1950s. Personal collection of Albert McNeil.

6.9   Photograph of an unknown individual on the left and Margaret Spencer on the right posing in front of the Scholle siding in Scholle in 1949. Personal collection of Frank Wimberly.

6.10   Photograph of Sylvestre (Sy) Sisneros and his nephew Francisco Sisneros in 2008 in Veguita, New Mexico. Photograph by Shawn Kelley.

6.11   Advertisement for an auto-tour loop encompassing the Mountainair region that was published in an unknown periodical circa 1950. Ward Hicks Advertising Printing Samples Coll., MSS 411 BC, Center for Southwest Research, University Libraries, University of New Mexico.

6.12   Advertisement for Mountainair Community Chamber of Commerce circa 1950. Ward Hicks Advertising Printing Samples Coll., MSS 411 BC, Center for Southwest Research, University Libraries, University of New Mexico.

6.13   Image touting the benefits of travelling at the "scenic level" on AT&SF in 1965. Originally included in AT&SF's Travel Agent's Sales Guide of Santa Fe Rail Travel from 1965. Personal collection of William Penner.

6.14   Photograph of the San Francisco Chief headed east over Bridge 874.2 near the mouth of Abo Canyon in April 9, 1969. This train operated in the last years of passenger service on the line. Personal collection of Randy Dunson.

6.15   Photograph of Fidel Padilla and Eliseo R. Sisneros in Abo Canyon in 2008. Photograph by Shawn Kelley.

6.16   Photograph of inscription at Culvert 871.2 in Abo Canyon. Eliseo R. Sisneros wrote his name on the culvert in the 1960s as did many other railroad workers in the early- and mid-twentieth-century. Photograph by Shawn Kelley.

6.17   Photograph of a Navajo extra gang, date unknown. Photographed by Jack Delano. Farm Security Administration - Office of War Information Photograph Collection, LC-USW3- 021222-E, Library of Congress Prints and Photographs Division (http://hdl.loc.gov/loc.pnp/pp.print).

6.18   Photograph of Hazel Carter Dunson with her son Randy in their converted boxcar living somewhere on the Belen Cutoff in 1950. Personal collection of Randy Dunson.

6.19   Photograph of an eastbound train headed through Abo Canyon over Bridge 873.8 toward the Sais Crusher in 1946. Personal collection of Randy Dunson.

6.20   Photograph of crane at Sais crusher sometime around 1945 to 1958. Personal collection of Albert McNiel.

6.21   Drawing of the Sais Crusher showing the line of box cars used as housing, water tank, along with the rail line where box cars were filled with ballast as remembered and drawn by Robert McNiel. Personal collection of Albert McNiel.

6.22   Photograph of transom-window glasspane from the Tonopah and Tidewater Railroad car used by Albert McNeil's family at the Sais crusher. Photograph by William Penner. Personal collection of Randy Dunson.

6.23   Photograph of crusher mills and rail cars being loaded at Sais in 1946. Personal collection of Albert McNeil.

6.24   Photograph of steam helper-engine (5027) pulling an east-bound diesel freight train at Dead Man's Cut on May 26, 1956 in between Scholle and Abo. US Highway 60 is in the foreground. Photograph by John Schilling. Personal collection of Robert Eveleth.

6.25   Photograph of Scholle section gang at Scholle siding in 1949. Individuals from left to right: Acacio Trujillo, Loreto Molina, Hermenes Sisneros, unidentified man, José Sisneros, Canuto Sisneros and Luis Ortiz. Personal collection of Paublina (Polly) Sisneros.

6.26   Photograph of Jack Hewett in 2008 with his 1926 Model T Ford. Photographed by Shawn Kelley.

6.27   Photograph of a steam engine at the service crane in the Vaughn yards sometime around 1950 to 1953. Personal collection of Charlie Patterson.

6.28   Photograph of Vaughn Yard crew in 1957. Individuals from left to right are: (back row) Herald Thompson, Ardith Craft, Malcolm Simpson, Mr. Burwinkel, Lupe Storey, and Anestacio Rael; (front row) Bill Patterson, Eddie McDowell, Lewis Roberson. Photograph by Charlie Patterson. Personal collection of Charlie Patterson.

6.29   Photograph of BNSF Railway engineer and historian Randy Dunson in front of his caboose at home in Portales in 2009. Photograph by Shawn Kelley.

6.30   Advertisement for the D Tournapull to handle scattered maintenance on the AT&SF right-of-way more efficiently, which appeared in *Railway Tracks and Structures* in May 1956. Personal collection of William Penner.

Ch.7   Photograph of a ruined building in 2008 in the former community of La Cienega located northwest of Mountainair. Photograph by Shawn Kelley.

7.1   Table showing populations in counties along the Belen Cutoff from 1910 to 2010. Data compiled from decennial reports from the United States Census Bureau (USCB) 2012; 1953; 1913a.

7.2   Photograph of Woody Southard and George Washington Dunson, Randy Dunson's father, somewhere on the Belen Cutoff in the 1950s. Personal collection of Randy Dunson.

7.3   Photograph of the Arrow Filling Station and Campground—the first gas station in Mountainair, built in the 1920s. Personal collection of Jack Hewett.

7.4   Photograph of Martina Brazil Franklin and Paublita (Polly) Sisneros visiting their former homes in Scholle in 2008. Photograph by Shawn Kelley.

Epi.   Photograph of double-stack intermodal freight trains eastbound through Abo Canyon in 2008. Photograph by Moira Ellis.

Bibliography

Collections

Brigham Young University
William Henry Jackson Collection.

Kansas State Historical Society
Atchison, Topeka, and Santa Fe Railway (AT&SF) Collection.
AT&SF Corporate Records.
AT&SF Photo Collection.

Library of Congress
Farm Security Administration - Office of War Information Collection, Prints and Photographs Division.

Museum of New Mexico, Palace of the Governors
Fray Angélico Chavez History Library.
Palace of the Governors Photo Archives.

New Mexico State Archives
Governor Merritt C. Mechem Papers.
Guadalupe County, New Mexico Records (1893-1942).
James Lowery Photograph Collection.
Lucien A. File Research Files.
New Mexico Secretary of State Records (1851-present).
New Mexico State Corporation Commission Records (1870-1994).
United States Territorial and New Mexico District Courts for Torrance County Records (1904-1942).

New Mexico State University Library, Archives and Special Collections
AT&SF Agricultural Collection.
John Becker Collection.
Lee C. Myers Collection.

Northern Arizona University Library Special Collections
Colorado Plateau Digital Archives.

University of Arizona Library Special Collections
Fred Harvey Collection.
Pamphlet and Printed Ephemera Collection.

Center for Southwest Research, University of New Mexico
Alice Bullock Pictorial Collection.
AT&SF Stockyard Records (1916-1928).
Bainbridge Bunting Papers (1849-1981).
E. P. Davies Papers (1909-1921).
Felipe Chavez Family Papers.
George McCrosen Collection.
George Pritchard Family Papers (1894-1940).
Gross, Kelly and Company Collection.
John Gaw Meem Collection: Non-job Specific Photos (1859-1980).
Laird Family Correspondence (1903-1938).
Pioneers Foundation Collection.
Rio Grande Historical Collections, Southwest Photograph Collection (1860-1900).
Ward Hicks Advertising Printing Samples (1933-1972).
William Jackson Parish Papers.
Works Progress Administration New Mexico Collection (1936-1940).

Newspapers and magazines

Kansas State Historical Society
Santa Fe Magazine. May 1907; January 1918; September 1909; March 1934; June 1934; January 1946; July 1948.

Museum of New Mexico, Fray Angélico Chavez History Library
Clovis *News Journal.* June 1935.
Mountainair *Messenger.* March 1909 to February 1912.

New Mexico State Archives
Curry County *Times.* December 1969.
El Paso *Times.* January 1966.
Estancia Valley *Citizen.* October 1964.
Torrance County *Citizen.* June 1967.

New Mexico State Library
Willard *Record.* July 1917 to October 1921.

Center for Southwest Research. University of New Mexico
Mountainair *Independent.* September 1919 to June 1925; March 1952

Zimmerman Library, University of New Mexico
Albuquerque *Daily Citizen.* January to December 1902.
Belen *News* and *Hispano Americano.* May 1914 to January 1925.
Belen *Tribune.* January to August 1909; January to March 1912.
Clovis *Journal.* February 1912 to December 1916; January 1921 to March 1929.
Fort Sumner *Leader.* January 1913 to August 1916.
Fort Sumner *Review.* April 1911; March 1917 to 1918.
The Gringo and the Greaser. August 1883 to February 1884.
Roy *Spanish American.* February 1905 to December 1907.
Santa Fe *New Mexican.* August 1901 to July 1910.
Socorro *Chieftain.* January 1905 to December 1908.

Oral Histories

New Mexico Farm and Ranch Heritage Museum
Prisoners of War in New Mexico Agriculture Oral History Collection.
Rural Lifeways Oral History Collection.

New Mexico State Archives
Fort Sumner Oral History Collection.

Randy Dunson personal collection
Clay, L. P., interviewed by Randy Dunson in 1983.
Seery, Tom, interviewed by Randy Dunson in 1984.

University of California at Berkeley, Bancroft Library
American Homefront Oral History Collection.

Published Sources

Abert, James W.

1847 *Abert's New Mexico Report*. Senate Executive Document No. 23 (30th Congress, 1st Session, Serial 506), Washington, D.C. Reprinted 1962, Horn & Wallace Publishers, Albuquerque.

Atchison, Topeka and Santa Fe Railway

1978 *Santa Fe, The Chief Way Reference Series, System Standards*, Volume Two. Kachina Press, Dallas, Texas.

1978 *Santa Fe, The Chief Way Reference Series, System Standards*, Volume Three. Kachina Press, Dallas, Texas.

1964 *Quick, Easy-to-Use Travel Agent's Sales Guide of Santa Fe Rail Travel Information*. Prepared for use by Travel Agents and their staffs by Santa Fe Railway, Chicago.

1948 *Agriculture in the Santa Fe Southwest*. Chicago.

Berkman, Pamela

1988 *The History of the Atchison, Topeka & Santa Fe*. Bonanza Books, Greenwich, Connecticut.

Best, Thomas Doniphan

1959 *The role of the Atchison, Topeka, and Santa Fe railway system in the economic development of Southwestern United States, 1859-1954*. Masters thesis on file at Northwestern University, Chicago.

Campbell, Hardy Webster

1905 *Soil Culture Manual*. H. W. Campbell Publisher, Lincoln, Nebraska.

Carleton, James Henry

1854 Diary of an excursion to the ruins of Abo, Quarra, and Gran Quivira, in New Mexico. In *Smithsonian Institution Ninth Annual Report*, Washington D.C.

Daniel, Karen Stein and Elizabeth Louise Albright

2005 *Naturalization Records by New Mexico Courts: Volume I: Loose Documents (1852-Forward)*. New Mexico Genealogical Society, Albuquerque.

Ervin, Morton L., Doris Ann Ervin, and Barbara Duckworth

1998 *A Genealogical Index of Early Torrance County, New Mexico Deeds, 1903-1920*. Ervin Publishing, Albuquerque.

Hodges, Carrie

1936 Letter report dated July 24, 1936. Vaughn Clip Folder. New Mexico History Library, Santa Fe.

Lang, Charles H. and Carroll L. Riley, editors.

1970 *The Southwestern Journals of Adolph F. Bandelier 1883-1884*. University of New Mexico Press, Albuquerque.

1966 *The Southwestern Journals of Adolph F. Bandelier, 1880-1882*. University of New Mexico Press, Albuquerque.

Morris, Charles

1919 New Mexico Map. In *Winston's Cumulative Encyclopedia Volume 7.* Private collection of Roy Winkelman. The John C. Winston Company, Philadelphia.

New Mexico Bureau of Immigration

1907 *Ho! To the Land of Sunshine*. Santa Fe: The Bureau, 5th revised edition.

United States Census Bureau

2012 *U.S. Census Bureau, 2010 Census of Population and Housing, Summary Population and Housing Characteristics*, CPH-1-33, New Mexico U.S. Government Printing Office, Washington, DC. Electronic document, http://www.census.gov/prod/cen2010/, accessed January 12, 2013.

2002 *New Mexico: 2000, Summary Population and Housing Characteristics*. Electronic document, http://www.census.gov/prod/cen2000/phc-1-33.pdf, accessed April 23, 2010.

1973 *1970 Census of Population, Volume I, Characteristics of the Population, Part 33, New Mexico*. Electronic document, http://www2.census.gov/prod2/decennial/documents/37745099v1p33.pdf, accessed April 23, 2010.

1963 *The Eighteenth Decennial Census of the United States, Census of Population: 1960, Volume I, Characteristics of the Population, Part 33, New Mexico*. Electronic document, http://www2.census.gov/prod2/decennial/documents/1970a_nm-01.pdf, accessed April 23, 2010.

1952a *A Report of the Seventeenth Decennial Census of the United States, Census of Population: 1950, Volume I, Number of Inhabitants*. Electronic document, http://www2.census.gov/prod2/decennial/documents/23761117v1.pdf, accessed April 23, 2010.

1952b *United States Census of Agriculture: 1950, Volume I, Part 30, Counties and State Economic Areas, New Mexico and Arizona*. Electronic document, http://www.agcensus.usda.gov/Publications/Historical_Publications/1950/vol1%20New%20Mexico%20Arizona/34059637v1p30.pdf, accessed April 23, 2010.

1942a *Sixteenth Census of the United States: 1940, Population, Volume I, Number of Inhabitants*. Electronic document, http://www2.census.gov/prod2/decennial/documents/33973538v1.pdf, accessed April 23, 2010.

1942b *Sixteenth Census of the United States: 1940, Agriculture, Volume I, Part 6, Statistics for Counties, Mountain Division*. Electronic document, http://www.agcensus.usda.gov/Publications/Historical_Publications/1940/Farms%20and%20Farm%20Property_New%20England/00179375v1p1.pdf, accessed April 23 2010.

1932a *Fifteenth Census of the United States: 1930, Population, Volume III, Part 2, Reports by States, Montana-Wyoming*. Electronic document, http://www2.census.gov/prod2/decennial/documents/ 10612982v3p2.pdf, accessed April 22 2010.

1932b *Fifteenth Census of the United States: 1930, Agriculture, Volume II, Part 3—The Western States*. Electronic document, http://www.agcensus.usda.gov/Publications/Historical_Publications/1930/Reports_by_State_Western/03337983v2p3.pdf, accessed April 22 2010.

1921 *Fourteenth Census of the United States Taken in the Year 1920, Volume III: Population, Composition and Characteristics of the Population by States*. Electronic document, http://www2.census.gov/pwrod2/decennial/documents/41084484v3.pdf, accessed April 22, 2010.

1922a Fourteenth Census of the United States Taken in the Year 1920, Volume V: Agriculture, General Report and Analytical Tables. Electronic document, http://www2.census.gov/prod2/decennial/documents/06229676v5.pdf, accessed April 22, 2010.

1922b *Fourteenth Census of the United States Taken in the Year 1920, Volume VI, Part 3: Agriculture, The Western States and Outlying Possessions.* Government Printing Office, Washington D.C.

1913a *Thirteenth Census of the United States Taken in the Year 1910, Volume III: Population, Reports by States, Nebraska-Wyoming.* Electronic document, http://www2.census.gov/prod2/decennial/documents/36894832v3.pdf, accessed April 22, 2010.

1913b *Thirteenth Census of the United States Taken in the Year 1910, Volume VII: Agriculture, Reports by States, Nebraska-Wyoming.* Electronic document, http://www2.census.gov/prod2/decennial/documents/ 41033898v7.pdf, accessed April 22, 2010.

1901 *Census Reports Volume I, Twelfth Census of the United States Taken in the Year 1900: Population.* Electronic document, http://www2.census.gov/prod2/decennial/documents/33405927v1ch04.pdf, accessed April 22, 2010.

1902a *Census Reports Volume V, Twelfth Census of the United States Taken in the Year 1900: Agriculture Part I, Farms Livestock, and Animal Products.* Electronic document, http://www2.census.gov/prod2/decennial/documents/33398096v5.pdf, accessed April 22, 2010.

1902b *Census Reports Volume VI, Twelfth Census of the United States Taken in the Year 1900: Agriculture Part II, Crops and Irrigation.* Electronic document, http://www2.census.gov/prod2/decennial/documents/ 33398096v6p2.pdf, accessed April 22, 2010.

1895a *Report on the Population of the United States at the Eleventh Census: 1890 (Volume 1).* Electronic document, http://www2.census.gov/prod2/decennial/documents/1890a_v1-01.pdf, accessed April 21, 2010.

1895b *Report on the Statistics of Agriculture in the United States at the Eleventh Census: 1890 (Volume 5).* Electronic document, http://www2.census.gov/prod2/decennial/documents/1890a_v5-01.pdf, accessed April 21, 2010.

1882a *Statistics of the Population of the United States at the Tenth Census: 1880 (Volume 1).* Electronic document, http://www2.census.gov/prod2/decennial/documents/1880a_v1-01.pdf, accessed April 21, 2010.

1882b *Report on the Productions of Agriculture as Returned at the Tenth Census: 1880 (Volume 3).* Electronic document, http://www2.census.gov/prod2/decennial/documents/1880a_v3-01.pdf, accessed April 21, 2010.

1872 *Ninth Census-Volume I: 1870, The Statistics of the Population of the United States.* Electronic document, http://www2.census.gov/prod2/decennial/documents/1870a-01.pdf, accessed April 21, 2010.

Wheat, Carl I.
1957 *Mapping the Trans-Mississippi West, 1540-1861, Volume I.* Institute of Historical Cartography, San Francisco.

Secondary sources

Athearn, Robert
1977 *The Denver and Rio Grande Western Railroad.* Reprinted. Bison Books, University of Nebraska Press, Lincoln. Originally published in 1967 under the title *Rebel of the Rockies: A History of the Denver and Rio Grande Western Railroad,* Yale University Press, New Haven.

Berman, M. J.
1979 *Cultural Resources Overview of Socorro Area, New Mexico.* USDA Forest Service, Southwestern Region and Bureau of Land Management New Mexico State Office. Washington, D.C.

BNSF Railway (BNSF)
2011 *New Mexico: Delivering the World to the Enchanted State.* BNSF informational brochure distributed as part of the BNSF Railway Abo Canyon Site Tour, 2011. Manuscript on file at BNSF Public Relations, Fort Worth.

Bogener, Stephen Dean
1997 *Ditches Across the Desert: A Story of Irrigation Along New Mexico's Pecos River.* Ph.D. dissertation, Texas Tech University. University Microfilms, Ann Arbor.

Boyle, Dixie
2010 *Highway 60 and the Belen Cutoff: A Brief History.* Outskirts Press, Denver.

Boyle, Susan Calafate
1997 *Los Capitalistas: Hispano Merchants and the Santa Fe Trade.* University of New Mexico Press, Albuquerque.

Briegel, Kaye Lynn
1974 *Alianza Hispano-Americana, 1894-1965: A Mexican American Fraternal Insurance Society.* Ph.D. dissertation, University of Southern California. University Microfilms, Ann Arbor.

Briggs, Alton King
1974 *The Archaeology of 1882 Labor Camps on the Southern Pacific Railroad, Val Verde County, Texas.* Unpublished Master's thesis, Department of Anthropology, University of Texas, Austin.

Bryant, Keith L.
1974 *History of the Atchison, Topeka and Santa Fe Railway.* Macmillan Publishing, New York.

Brooks, James F.
2002 *Captives and Cousins: Slavery, Kinship, and Community in the Southwest Borderlands.* University of North Carolina Press, Chapel Hill.

Carroll, Ray L.
1965 *Gross, Blackwell & Company Mercantile Capitalists in the Southwest 1867-1902.* Unpublished Master's thesis, Department of Business Administration, University of New Mexico, Albuquerque.

Cole, Dorothy
2001 *Diamonds in the Field: A Musical History of Life on the Bean Fields, Mountainair, New Mexico.* The Mountainair Heritage Foundation, Mountainair, New Mexico.

Culbert, James I.
1941 Pinto Beans in the Estancia Valley of New Mexico. *Economic Geography,* Vol. 17, No. 1 (Jan. 1941), pp. 50-60.

Cumiford, William L.
1978 *Fort Sumner Railroad Bridge National Register of Historic Places Nomination Form.* National Register 551, listed March 21, 1979. Manuscript on file at the New Mexico Historic Preservation Division, Santa Fe.

Daniels, Rudolph
2000 *Trains Across the Continent North American Railroad History.* 2nd ed. Indiana University Press, Bloomington and Indianapolis.

deBuys, William
1988 *Enchantment and Exploitation: The Life and Hard Times of a New Mexico Mountain Range.* University of New Mexico Press, Albuquerque.

Ducker, James H.
1983 *Men of the Steel Rails.* University of Nebraska Press, Lincoln and London, Nebraska.

Dunson, Randy
n. d.   The Abo Pass Gang. *The Pecos Handbill,* Portales, New Mexico.

n. d.   Dead Man's Curve. *The Pecos Handbill,* Portales.

2004   History of the AT&SF Railway in eastern New Mexico. In *Burlington Northern Santa Fe Railroad, Clovis Employee Directory.* Clovis News Journal Publications, Clovis.

1996   Early Days on the Belen Cut-off. *The Pecos Handbill,* Vol. III, Issue IV, Portales.

1996   Building the Belen Cut-off Part Four-The Finale. *The Pecos Handbill,* Vol. III, Issue III, Portales.

1996   Building the Belen Cut-off Part Three. *The Pecos Handbill,* Vol. III, Issue II, Portales.

1996   Building the Belen Cut-off 1902 Part Two. *The Pecos Handbill,* Vol. III, Issue I, Portales.

1995   Building the Belen Cut-off 1902. *The Pecos Handbill,* Vol. II, Issue II, Portales.

Dye, Victoria E.
2005 *All Aboard for Santa Fe: Railway Promotion of the Southwest, 1890s to 1930s.* University of New Mexico Press, Albuquerque.

2001 *The making of a mecca: the promotion of Santa Fe by the Atchison, Topeka and Santa Fe Railway system.* Thesis, D99548, 2001, Masters thesis on file at California State University, Sacramento.

Eliot, Jane
1995 *The History of the Western railroads.* Crescent Books, New York.

Espinosa, Gilberto and Tibo J. Chavez
n.d. *El Rio Abajo.* Bishop Publishing, Portales, New Mexico.

Foote, Cheryl J.
1989 *The Hispanic Reoccupation of Abo and Quarai, 1800-1940.* Unpublished manuscript on file, Salinas Pueblo Missions National Monument, Mountainair, New Mexico.

Forrest, Suzanne
1998 *The Preservation of the Village: New Mexico's Hispanics and the New Deal.* University of New Mexico Press, Albuquerque.

Foster, Barbara Spencer
2001 *Girl of the Manzanos.* Sunstone Press, Santa Fe.

Glischinski, Steve
2008 *Santa Fe Railway.* Voyageur Press, Minneapolis.

Gould, Joseph Edward
1961 *The Chautauqua Movement: An Episode in the Continuing American Revolution.* Quinn and Boden Company, Rahway, New Jersey.

Greever, William
1954 *Arid Domain: The Santa Fe Railway and its Western Land Grant.* Stanford University Press, Stanford.

Hall, G. Emlen
1991   San Miguel del Bado and the Loss of the Common Lands of New Mexico Community Land Grants. *New Mexico Historical Review* 66:4:413-432.

Hargreaves, Mary W. M.
1958   Hardy Webster Campbell (1850-1937). *Agricultural History,* Vol. 32, No. 1 (Jan. 1958), pp. 62-65.

1948   Dry Farming, Alias Scientific Farming. *Agricultural History,* Vol. 22, No. 1 (Jan. 1948), pp. 39-56.

Harmon, Don
2006 *Postcard History of the Early Santa Fe Railway.* Harmon Publishing Company, Shawnee Mission, Kansas.

Henricks, Rick
2008 *New Mexico in 1801: The Priests' Report.* Rio Grande Books, Los Ranchos de Albuquerque.

Herrman, Bert
2003 *Mountainair, N.M. Centennial History 1903-2003.* Mountainair Public Schools, Mountainair, New Mexico.

Hertzog, Peter
1964 *The Gringo and the Greaser: Charles L. Kusz.* The Press of the Territorian, Santa Fe.

Huebner, Donald James
2002 *From the foothills to the crest: Landscape history of the southern Manzano Mountains, central New Mexico, USA, since 1800.* Unpublished Ph.D. dissertation on file at the Department of Geography, University of Texas at Austin, Austin.

Hurt, Wesley
1941 *Manzano: A Study of Community Disorganization.* Masters thesis on file at the University of New Mexico, Albuquerque. Reprinted and revised 1989, AMS Press, New York.

Ivey, James
1988 *In the Midst of a Loneliness.* Southwest Cultural Resources Center Professional Papers No.15. Santa Fe.

Jackson, Donald C.
1988 *Great American Bridges and Dams.* John Wiley & Sons, Inc., New York.

Jefferson, Thomas
1819   Letter from Thomas Jefferson to Nathaniel Macon. In *The Writings of Thomas Jefferson* (Memorial Edition) 1903. Editors Andrew Lipscomb and Albert Ellergy Bergh. Thomas Jefferson Memorial Association, Washington D. C.

Jenkins, M. E., and A. H. Schroeder
1974   *A Brief History of New Mexico*. University of New Mexico Press, Albuquerque.

Julyan, R.
1996   *The Place Names of New Mexico*. University of New Mexico Press, Albuquerque.

Kelley, Shawn and William Penner
2007   *Results of Interviews with Local Residents in the Vicinity of Abo Canyon, Valencia and Socorro Counties, New Mexico*. Parametrix, Albuquerque.

Kelley, Shawn, and Kristen Reynolds
2010   *Route 66 and Native Americans in New Mexico*. Forthcoming report by Parametrix for the New Mexico Department of Transportation, Santa Fe.

Kutzleb, Charles R.
1971   Can Forests Bring Rain to the Plains? *Forest History*, Vol. 15, No. 3 (Oct. 1971), pp. 14-21.

Link, Eugene P. and Beulah M. Link
1999   *The Tale of Three Cities: Gran Quivira in the Southwest New Mexico, 1100 B.C. to A.D. 1963*. Vantage Press, New York.

Lomeli, Francisco A., Victor A. Sorell, and Genaro M. Padilla
2002   *Nuevomexicano Cultural Legacy Forms, Agencies, and Discourse*. University of New Mexico Press, Albuquerque.

Marshall, James
1945   *Santa Fe, the Railroad that Built an Empire*. Random House, New York.

Martin, Patricia P.
2004   *Beloved Land: An Oral History of Mexican Americans in Southern Arizona*. The University of Arizona Press, Tucson.

McAlavy, Don
1976   *Clovis Remembered: Moments From the Past*. Clovis Clip Folder. New Mexico State University Special Collections, Las Cruces.

McDonald, Margaret Espinosa
1997   *"Vamos todos a Belen": Cultural Transformations of the Hispanic Community in the Rio Abajo Community of Belen, New Mexico from 1850-1950*. Ph.D. dissertation on file at the University of New Mexico, Albuquerque.

McDonald, Margaret Espinosa and Richard Melzer
2002   *Valencia County, New Mexico: History through the Photographer's Lens*. The Donning Company Publishers, Virginia Beach.

McMath, Emma Lou Williams
2004   *Some History of Mountainair*. Electronic document, http://www.usgen-net.org/usa/nm/county/torrance/mtnrhstry.htm, accessed December 7, 2004.

McMath, Gorden
1999   The Valley is Still There. In *The Tale of Three Cities: Gran Quivira in the Southwest New Mexico, 1100 B.C. to A.D. 1963* (Eugene Link and Beulah Link) Vantage Press, New York.

Melzer, Richard
2008   *Fred Harvey Houses of the Southwest*. Arcadia Publishing, Mount Pleasant, South Carolina.

2003   *When we Were Young in the West: True Stories of Childhood*. Sunstone Press, Santa Fe.

1994   Chautauquas: Caravans of Culture. *New Mexico Magazine*, Vol. 72, Sept. 1994, pp 56-63.

Middleton, William D.
1999   *Landmarks on the Iron Road Two Centuries of North American Engineering*. Indiana University Press, Bloomington and Indianapolis.

Morrissey, Charles T.
1993   More that Embers of Sentiment: Railroad Nostalgia and Oral History Memories of the 1920s and 1930s. *The Public Historian*, Vol.15, No.3, Summer 1993), pp 29-35.

Mosk, Sanford A.
1944   *Land Tenure Problems in the Santa Fe Railroad Grant Area*. Reprinted 1981. Arno Press, New York. Originally published, Publications of the Bureau of Business and Economic Research University of California, University of California Press, Berkeley and Los Angeles.

Myers, Lee
1964   Building the Belen Cut-off. *New Mexico Magazine* 42(4):2-5.

Myrick, David F.
2003   *New Mexico's Railroads: A Historical Survey*. Revised edition. University of New Mexico Press, Albuquerque.

Nickens, Paul, and Kathleen Nickens
2009   *Touring the West with the Fred Harvey Co. & the Santa Fe Railway*. Schiffer Publishing, Atglen, Pennsylvania.

Noble, David (editor)
1982   *Salinas: archaeology, history, prehistory*. School of American Research, Santa Fe.

Nostrand, Richard L.
1987   The Century of Hispano Expansion. *New Mexico Historical Review* 62:4:361-386.

Penner, William
2008   *Abo Canyon Second Track Project—Interim Data Recovery and Mitigation Report*. Parametrix, Albuquerque.

2005   *An Addendum to A Cultural Resource Survey of Abo Canyon, Socorro and Valencia Counties, New Mexico*. Taschek Environmental Consulting Report No. 600-248, Albuquerque.

Penner, William, Danny Gregory, Berenika Byszewski, Hollis Lawrence, Chris Parrish, Teresa Hurt, and Kimberly Parker
2005   *Abo Canyon Cultural Resource Survey, Valencia and Socorro Counties, New Mexico*. Taschek Environmental Consultants Report 600-229, Albuquerque.

Penner, William, and Teresa Hurt
2005   *A Plan For Archaeological Testing At Thirteen Sites Located Along The Proposed New BNSF Railroad Alignment In Abo Canyon, Socorro And Valencia Counties, New Mexico*. Taschek Environmental Consultants Report 600-244, Albuquerque.

Penner, William, Danny Gregory, Teresa Hurt, Chris Parrish, Nicholas Parker, Berenika Byszewski, Hollis Lawrence, Kimberley Parker, and Gerry Raymond

2006 *The Abo Canyon Double Track Project: Cultural and Historical Investigations in Abo Canyon, Valencia and Socorro Counties, New Mexico.* Taschek Environmental Consulting Report No. TEC 2006-4, Albuquerque.

Penner, William and Nicholas Parker

2008 *The Abo Canyon Second Track Project: A Plan for Mitigation of Adverse Effects, Valencia and Socorro Counties, New Mexico.* Taschek Environmental Consulting Report No. 2008-1, Albuquerque.

Peters, Kurt

1994 *Watering the Flower: Laguna Pueblo and the Atchison, Topeka, and Santa Fe Railroad, 1880-1980.* PhD, Dissertation. University of California, Berkeley.

1998 Continuing identity: Laguna Pueblo railroaders, Richmond, California. *American Indian Culture and Resource Journal.* 1998, Vol. 22 Issue 4, pp 187-199.

Riskin, Marci L.

2005 *The Train Stops Here: New Mexico's Railway Legacy.* University of New Mexico Press, Albuquerque.

Sais, Valentin

n.d. *Mi Familia: The History of the Sais y Chavez Familia.* Unpublished manuscript on file with author.

Szasz, Ferenc M.

2006 *Larger Than Life: New Mexico in the Twentieth Century.* University of New Mexico Press, Albuquerque.

Sánchez, Joseph P.

1996 *The Rio Abajo Frontier: 1540-1692.* The Albuquerque Museum, Albuquerque.

Sánchez, Javier E.

2009 *Al Pie de la Sierra: La Historia del Pueblo de Manzano y sus alrededores, visto por la historia de sus habitantes.* Self-published manuscript, Corrales, New Mexico.

Sisneros, Francisco

2008 *The Chapel and Cemetery of San Lorenzo de Abo: Centennial, 1908-2008.* Self-published manuscript, Casa Colorada, New Mexico.

1997 *Genealogy of Eulalio Padilla.* Unpublished manuscript on file with author, Casa Colorada, New Mexico.

1996 *Sisneros: A New Mexico Family History.* Unpublished manuscript on file. Salinas Pueblo Missions National Monument, Mountainair, New Mexico.

n.d. *Nineteenth Century Pueblo de Abo Settlers.* Unpublished manuscript on file. Salinas Pueblo Missions National Monument, Mountainair, New Mexico.

Sisneros, Pauline S.

2007 *Mail Call at: Canuto Sisneros "Ranchito," Scholle, Socorro County, New Mexico.* Unpublished manuscript on file with author, Albuquerque, New Mexico.

1993 *El Veterano y Yo.* Unpublished manuscript on file with author, Albuquerque, New Mexico.

Stanley, Francis

1969 *The La Lande, New Mexico Story.* Self-published manuscript, Pep, Texas.

1969 *The Taiban, New Mexico Story.* Self-published manuscript, Pep, Texas.

1969 *The Yeso, New Mexico Story.* Self-published manuscript, Pep, Texas.

1967 *The Tolar, New Mexico Story.* Self-published manuscript, Pep, Texas.

1966 *The Abo, New Mexico Story.* Self-published manuscript, Pep, Texas.

1966 *The Clovis, New Mexico Story.* Self-published manuscript, Pampa, Texas.

1966 *The Texico, New Mexico Story.* Self-published manuscript, Pep, Texas.

1965 *The Melrose, New Mexico Story.* Self-published manuscript, Pantex, Texas.

1962 *The Manzano, New Mexico story.* Self-published manuscript, Pantex, Texas.

Sterner, Matthew A. (editor)

2004 *Ranching, Rails, and Clay The Development and Demise of the Town of Rincon/Prado Archaeological Data Recovery at CA-RIV-1039H and CA-RIV-1044H, Riverside County, California.* Technical Series 83, Statistical Research, Inc., Tucson, Arizona.

Tainter, Joseph A., and Frances Levine

1987 *Cultural Resources Overview Central New Mexico.* USDA Forest Service Southwest Region and USDI Bureau of Land Management. Albuquerque and Santa Fe.

Thompson, Gerald E.

1972 "To the People of New Mexico": Gen. Carleton Defends the Bosque Redondo. *Arizona and the West*, Vol. 14, No. 4, pp. 347-366.

Tice, Henry Allen

1965 *Early Railroad Days in New Mexico.* Stagecoach Press, Santa Fe.

Torrance County Historical Society

1976 *History of Torrance County.* Torrance County Historical Society, Estancia.

Twitchell, Ralph Emerson

1911 *The Leading Facts of New Mexico History.* Torch Press, Cedar Rapids, Iowa.

Valencia County Historical Society

1976 *Rio Abajo Heritage: A History of Valencia County.* Valencia County Historical Society, Belen.

Waters, L. L.

1950 *Steel Trails to Santa Fe.* University of Kansas Press, Lawrence, Kansas.

Weigle, Marta

1990 Southwest Lures: Innocents Detours, Incensed Determined. *Journal of the Southwest* 32:4:499-540.

Weigle, Marta, and Barbara Babcock, eds.

1996 *The Great Southwest of the Fred Harvey Company and the Santa Fe Railroad.* The Heard Museum, Phoenix.

Weigle, Marta, and Peter White

1988 *The Lore of New Mexico.* University of New Mexico Press, Albuquerque.

Westphall, Victor

1958a The Public Domain in New Mexico 1854-1891. *New Mexico Historical Review* 33:1:24-52.

1958b The Public Domain in New Mexico 1854-1891. *New Mexico Historical Review* 33:2:128-143.

White, Richard

1993 *It's Your Misfortune and None of My Own: A New History of the American West*. University of Oklahoma Press, Norman, Oklahoma.

Wilson, John P.

2001 *When the Texans Came: Missing Records from the Civil War in the Southwest 1861–1862*. University of New Mexico Press, Albuquerque.

Worley, Dale E.

1965 *Iron Horses of the Santa Fe Trail: A definitive history, in fact and photographs, of the motive power of one of America's great railroads*. Southwest Railroad Historical Society, Dallas.

List of Interviewees

Aker, Georgia, formal interview, December 30, 2008

Autrey, James, formal interview, August 26, 2008

Baca, Benjamin (Benji), formal interview, August 13, 2008

Baca, Juan, formal interview, March 20, 2007

Baca, Catalina, formal interview, June 24, 2008

Baca, Ruperto, formal interview, September 5, 2008

Bibiano, Manuel Jr., formal interview, September 25, 2008

Bilbrey, Robert, formal interview, March 16, 2007

Brazil, Greg, formal interview, March 21, 2007

Carrejo, Roy, formal interview, August 11, 2008

Chilton, Randy, formal interview, March 22, 2007

Cole, Dorothy, formal interview, August 14, 2008

Dunson, Randy, formal interview, June 2, 2009

Dunson, Randy, informal interview, June 2, 2009

Foster (nee Spencer), Barbara, formal interview, June 30, 2009

Franklin (nee Brazil), Martina, formal interview, April 24, 2008

Franklin (nee Brazil), Martina, field interview in Scholle, August 5, 2008

Gabaldon, Felix, formal interview, August 18, 2008

Garcia, Cris, formal interview, March 19, 2008

Garcia, Cris, field interview in Abo Canyon and La Cienega, April 2, 2008

Grider (nee McKinley), Welda, formal interview, March 15, 2007

Hewett, Jack, formal interview, June 25, 2008

Hewett, Jack, field interview in Abo Canyon and Eastview, July 28, 2008

Hewett, Jack, Follow-up interview, August 7, 2008

Hill, Frank, formal interview, March 12, 2007

Hill, Frank, field interview in Abo Canyon and Dripping Springs, February 28, 2008

Hill, Henry, formal interview, March 30, 2007

Huckabay, Bill, formal interview, March 3, 2008

Huckabay, Bill, field interview in Abo Canyon, May 3, 2008

Kayser, George, formal interview, March 22, 2007

Kayser, George, field interview in Abo Canyon and Eastview, July 28, 2008

Kayser, Paul, formal interview, March 22, 2007

Lopez, George, formal interview, September 15, 2008

Lovato, Bartizar, formal interview, August 8, 2008

Maes, Frank, formal interview, August 7, 2008

McDonald, Margaret, informal interview, June 27, 2008

McDonald, Margaret, formal interview, September 3, 2008

McKinley, Margaret, formal interview, March 12, 2008

McKinley, Weldon, formal interview, March 12, 2008

McMath (nee Williams), Emma Lou (Biddie), formal interview, May 22, 2008

McMath (nee Williams), Emma Lou (Biddie), field interview in Abo Canyon, Ewing and bean fields around Mountainair, June 14, 2008

McMath, Gorden, formal interview, May 22, 2008

McMath, Gorden, field interview in Abo Canyon and bean fields around Mountainair, June 14, 2008

McNeil, Albert, formal interview, March 7, 2008

McNeil, Albert, field Interview in Abo Canyon, May 3, 2008

Miranda, Audi, formal interview, September 26, 2008

Molina, Julia, formal interview, January 28, 2009

Padilla, Aurelio (Al), formal interview, April 30, 2008

Padilla, Aurelio (Al), field interview in Abo Canyon, May 28, 2008

Padilla, Eulalio (E. H.), formal interview, March 19, 2007

Padilla, Fidel, formal interview, February 2, 2006

Padilla, Fidel, formal interview, March 6, 2007

Padilla, Fidel, informal interview, February 20, 2008

Padilla, Fidel, field interview in Abo Canyon, March 4, 2008

Padilla, Joe, formal interview, April 30, 2008

Padilla, Joe, field interview in Abo Canyon, May 28, 2008

Parker (nee Hill), Mildred (Millie), formal interview, May 5, 2008

Patterson, Charlie, formal interview, July 15, 2008

Patterson, Charlie, Follow-up interview, August 29, 2008

Pineda, Victor, field interview at LA 146940, February 13, 2008

Pineda, Victor, field interview in Abo Canyon, February 20, 2008

Pineda, Victor, formal interview, March 5, 2008

Pineda, Victor, Follow-interview at Pineda Homestead, March 5, 2008

Pohl, Clarence (Bill), formal interview, March 13, 2007

Pohl, Clarence (Bill), field interview in Abo Canyon, February 26, 2008

Pohl, Clarence (Bill), field interview in Messenger and Priest Canyons, April 9, 2008

Pohl, Clarence (Bill), field interview at Scholle, May 15, 2008

Pohl, Clarence (Bill), field interview at LA146940 and in the Scholle area, August 22, 2008

Pohl, Clarence (Bill), formal interview, January 27, 2009

Sanchez, Apolonio, formal interview, April 15, 2008

Sanchez, Apolonio, field Interview in Priest Canyon, April 15, 2008

Sanchez, Apolonio, field interview in Abo Canyon, May 13, 2008

Sanchez, Juan A., formal interview, April 4, 2008

Sanchez, Juan A., field interview at Padilla Ranch and Priest Canyon, May 9, 2008

Sanchez, Juan J., formal interview, March 15, 2007

Sanchez, Juan J., field interview in Abo Canyon, April 10, 2008

Sanchez, Juan J., field interview in the Scholle and Dripping Springs area, May 7, 2008

Sanchez, Juan J., formal interview, October 28, 2008

Sanchez, Juan J., Follow-up interview, February 28, 2010

Shaw, Jerry, formal interview, March 21, 2007

Shaw, Jerry, field interview in Abo Canyon, May 3, 2008

Shaw, Jerry, formal interview, September 18, 2008

Sisneros, Eliseo, formal interview, May 9, 2008

Sisneros, Eliseo R., formal interview, March 20, 2007

Sisneros, Eliseo R., informal interview, February 27, 2008

Sisneros, Eliseo R., field interview in Abo Canyon, March 4, 2008

Sisneros, Ernestine, formal interview, May 9, 2008

Sisneros, Francisco, formal interview, March 23, 2007

Sisneros, Francisco, field interview in Abo Canyon, March 20, 2008

Sisneros, Francisco, field interview at homesteads south of Scholle near Tenabo, May 29, 2008

Sisneros, Francisco, field interview in Abo and La Joya, July 30, 2008

Sisneros, Francisco, formal interview, September 17, 2008

Sisneros, Martin, formal interview, March 20, 2007

Sisneros, Martin, field interview in Abo Canyon, April 5, 2008

Sisneros, Martin, field interview at homesteads south of Scholle near Tenabo, May 29, 2008

Sisneros, Paublita (Polly), informal interview, July 15, 2008

Sisneros, Paublita (Polly), formal interview, July 24, 2008

Sisneros, Paublita (Polly), field interview in Scholle, August 5, 2008

Sisneros, Paublita (Polly), Follow-up interview, August 28, 2009

Sisneros, Sylvestre, formal interview, March 21, 2007

Sisneros, Sylvestre, field interview in Abo Canyon, March 20, 2008

Sisneros, Sylvestre, formal interview, September 17, 2008

Spencer, Richard, formal interview, August 24, 2008

Spencer, Richard, Follow-up interview, February 28, 2010

Tafoya, Abenecio, informal interview, July 30, 2008

Thompson, Robert (Bob), formal interview, March 12, 2007

Thompson, Robert (Bob), field interview in Abo Canyon, March 10, 2008

Torres, Beatrice, formal interview, August 6, 2008

Trujillo (nee Contreras), Ramona (Ramoncita), formal interview, May 19, 2008

Ulibarri, Esequiel, formal interview, August 6, 2008

Valencia, Napoleon, formal interview, April 4, 2008

Vigil, Larry, formal interview, August 11, 2008

Williams, Billy Bob, formal interview, March 30, 2007

Williams, Billy Bob, field interview in Abo Canyon and Scholle, June 18, 2008

Wilson, Buck, formal interview, June 22, 2009

Wimberly, Frank, informal interview, March 28, 2010

P3 / PLANNING

6100 4th Street NW no. 442
Albuquerque, New Mexico 87107

Developed in concert with

Parametrix   HDR   BNSF RAILWAY

Designed by Masumi Shibata
ISBN: 978–0–578–13409–3